George Alfred Henty

Through Russian Snows

A Story of Napoleon's Retreat from Moscow

George Alfred Henty

Through Russian Snows
A Story of Napoleon's Retreat from Moscow

ISBN/EAN: 9783337258467

Printed in Europe, USA, Canada, Australia, Japan

Cover: Foto ©ninafisch / pixelio.de

More available books at **www.hansebooks.com**

THROUGH RUSSIAN SNOWS

"I GIVE YOU THE POST OF HONOUR, COMRADES"

THROUGH RUSSIAN SNOWS

A Story of Napoleon's Retreat
from Moscow

BY

G. A. HENTY

Author of "Beric the Briton" "One of the 28th"
"In the Reign of Terror" &c.

Illustrated

BLACKIE AND SON LIMITED
LONDON GLASGOW AND BOMBAY

*Printed in Great Britain by
Blackie & Son, Limited, Glasgow*

PREFACE.

There are few campaigns that, either in point of the immense scale upon which it was undertaken, the completeness of its failure, or the enormous loss of life entailed, appeal to the imagination in so great a degree as that of Napoleon against Russia. Fortunately, we have in the narratives of Sir Robert Wilson, British commissioner with the Russian army, and of Count Segur, who was upon Napoleon's staff, minute descriptions of the events as seen by eye-witnesses, and besides these the campaign has been treated fully by various military writers. I have as usual avoided going into details of horrors and of acts of cruelty and ferocity on both sides, surpassing anything in modern warfare, and have given a mere outline of the operations, with a full account of the stern fight at Smolensk and the terrible struggle at Borodino. I would warn those of my readers who may turn to any of the military works for a further history of the campaign, that the spelling of Russian places and names varies so greatly in the accounts of different writers, that sometimes it is difficult to believe that the same person or town is meant, and even in the narratives by Sir Robert Wilson, and by Lord Cathcart, our ambassador at St. Petersburg, who was in constant communication with him, scarcely a name will be found similarly spelt. I mention this, as otherwise much confusion might be caused by those who may compare my story with some of these recognized authorities, or follow the incidents of the campaign upon maps of Russia.

G. A. HENTY.

CONTENTS.

CHAP.		Page
I.	Two Brothers,	11
II.	Before the Justices,	31
III.	In a Fresh Scrape,	49
IV.	The Smuggler's Cave,	68
V.	Following a Trail,	86
VI.	A Commission,	106
VII.	A French Prison,	126
VIII.	Pistol Practice,	143
IX.	A Duel,	163
X.	Smolensk,	182
XI.	With the Russian Army,	201
XII.	Borodino,	220
XIII.	With the Rear-guard,	250
XIV.	Ney's Retreat,	272
XV.	In Comfortable Quarters,	302
XVI.	An Unexpected Meeting,	320

ILLUSTRATIONS.

Facing Page

"I GIVE YOU THE POST OF HONOUR, COMRADES" . *Frontis.*

JULIAN FINDS HIMSELF A PRISONER AMONG THE SMUGGLERS   64

ON THE MARCH LITTLE STEPHANIE OFTEN CHOSE TO BE CARRIED ON JULIAN'S SHOULDER 272

"I AM THE COUNTESS STEPHANIE WORONSKI. I AM GLAD TO SEE YOU" 288

THE LAST OF A VETERAN OF NAPOLEON'S *GRANDE ARMÉE* 320

THROUGH RUSSIAN SNOWS

CHAPTER I

TWO BROTHERS

WHEN Colonel Wyatt died, all Weymouth agreed that it was a most unfortunate thing for his sons Julian and Frank. The loss of a father is always a misfortune to lads, but it was more than usually so in this case. They had lost their mother years before, and Colonel Wyatt's sister had since kept house for him. As a housekeeper she was an efficient substitute, as a mother to the boys she was a complete failure. How she ever came to be Colonel Wyatt's sister was a puzzle to all their acquaintances. The Colonel was quick and alert, sharp and decisive in speech, strong in his opinions, peremptory in his manner, kindly at heart, but irascible in temper. Mrs. Troutbeck was gentle and almost timid in manner; report said that she had had a hard time of it in her married life, and that Troutbeck had frightened out of her any vestige of spirit that she had ever possessed. Mrs. Troutbeck never argued, and was always in perfect agreement with any opinion expressed, a habit that was constantly exciting the wrath and indignation of her brother.

The idea of controlling the boys never once entered her mind. So long as the Colonel was alive there was no occasion for such control, and in this respect she did not attempt after his death to fill his place. It seemed, indeed, that she simply transferred her allegiance from the Colonel to them. Whatever they did was right in her eyes, and they were allowed to do practically whatever they pleased. There was a difference in age of three years and a half between the brothers; Julian at the time of his father's death being sixteen, while Frank was still a few months short of thirteen. Casual acquaintances often remarked that there was a great likeness between them; and, indeed, both were pleasant-looking lads with somewhat fair complexions, their brown hair having a tendency to stand up in a tuft on the forehead, while both had grey eyes, and square foreheads. Mrs. Troutbeck was always ready to assent to the remark as to their likeness, but would gently qualify it by saying that it did not strike her so much as it did other people.

"Their dispositions are quite different," she said, "and knowing them as I do, I see the same differences in their faces."

Any close observer would, indeed, have recognized it at once. Both faces were pleasant, but while Julian's wore an expression of easy good temper, and a willingness to please and to be pleased, there was a lack of power and will in the lower part of the face; there was neither firmness in the mouth nor determination in the chin. Upon the other hand, except when smiling or talking, Frank's lips were closely pressed together, and his square chin and jaw clearly indicated firmness of will and tenacity of purpose. Julian was his aunt's favourite, and was one of the most popular boys at his school. He liked being popular, and as long as it did not put him to any great personal trouble was always ready to fall in with any proposal, to take part in every prank, to lend or give money if he had it in his pocket, to sympathize with any one in trouble.

"He has the most generous disposition of any boy I ever saw!" his aunt would frequently declare. "He's always ready to oblige. No matter what he is doing, he will throw it aside in a moment if I want anything done, or ask him to go on an errand into the town. Frank is very nice, he is very kind and all that sort of thing, but he goes his own way more, and I don't find him quite so willing to oblige as Julian; but then, of course, he is much younger, and one can't expect a boy of twelve to be as thoughtful to an old woman as a young fellow of nearly seventeen."

As time went on, the difference in their characters became still more marked. Julian had left school a year after his father's death, and had since been doing nothing in particular. He had talked vaguely of going into the army, and his father's long services would have given him a claim for a commission had he decided upon writing to ask for one, but Julian could never bring himself to decide upon anything. Had there been an old friend of his father's at hand ready to settle the matter for him he would have made no opposition whatever, but his aunt was altogether opposed to the idea, and so far from urging him to move in the matter she was always ready to say, whenever it happened to be mentioned, "There is no hurry, my dear Julian. We hear terrible stories of the hardships that the soldiers suffer in Spain; and although, if you decide upon going, of course I can't say no, still there can be no hurry about it."

This was quite Julian's own opinion. He was very comfortable where he was. He was his own master, and could do as he liked. He was amply supplied with pocket-money by his aunt; he was fond of sailing, fishing, and shooting; and as he was a general favourite among the boatmen and fishermen he was able to indulge in his fondness for the sea to as large an extent as he pleased, though it was but seldom that he had a chance of a day's shooting. Julian had other tastes of a less healthy character; he was fond of billiards and of society, he had a fine voice and a taste for music, and the society he chose was not that most calculated to do him good. He spent less and less of his time at home, and rarely returned of an evening until the other members of the household were in bed. Whatever his aunt thought of the matter she never remonstrated with him, and was always ready to make the excuse to herself, "I can't expect a fine young fellow like that to be tied to an old woman's apron-strings. Young men will be young men, and it is only natural that he should find it dull at home."

When Julian arrived at the age of nineteen it was tacitly understood that the idea of his going into the army had been altogether dropped, and that when a commission was asked for, it would be for Frank. Although Julian was still her favourite, Mrs. Troutbeck was more favourably disposed towards Frank than of old. She knew from her friends that he was quite as popular among his school-mates as his brother had been, although in a different way. He was a hard and steady worker, but he played as hard as he worked, and was a leader in every game. He, however, could say "no" with a decision that was at once recognized as being final, and was never to be persuaded into joining in any forbidden amusement or to take share in any mischievous adventure. When his own work was done he was always willing to give a quarter of an hour to assist any younger lad who found his lessons too hard for him, and though he was the last boy to whom any one would think of applying for a loan of money, he would give to the extent of his power in any case where a subscription was raised for a really meritorious purpose.

Thus when the school contributed a handsome sum towards a fund that was being raised for the relief of the families of the fishermen who had been lost, when four of their boats were wrecked in a storm, no one except the boys who got up the collection knew that nearly half the amount for which the school gained credit came from the pocket of Frank Wyatt.

The brothers, though differing so widely in disposition, were very fond of each other. In his younger years Frank had looked up to his big brother as a sort of hero, and Julian's good-nature and easy-going temper led him to be always kind to his young brother, and to give him what he valued most—assistance at his lessons and a patient attention to all his difficulties. As the years went on, Frank came to perceive clearly enough the weak points in his brother's character, and with his usual outspokenness sometimes remonstrated with him strongly.

"It is horrible to see a fellow like you wasting your life as you do, Julian. If you don't care for the army, why don't you do something else? I should not care what it was, so that it but gave you something to occupy yourself, and if it took you out of here, all the better. You know that you are not doing yourself any good."

"I am not doing myself any harm, you young beggar," Julian replied good-temperedly.

"I don't know, Julian," the boy said sturdily; "you are not looking half as well as you used to do. I am sure late hours don't suit you, and there is no good to be got out of billiards. I know the sort of fellows you meet there are not the kind to do you any good, or that father would have liked to see you associate with if he had been alive. Just ask yourself honestly if you think he would. If you can say 'yes', I will shut up and say no more about it; but can you say 'yes'?"

Julian was silent. "I don't know that I can," he said after a pause. "There is no harm in any of them that I know of, but I suppose that in the way you put it, they are not the set father would have fancied, with his strict notions. I have thought of giving it up a good many times, but it is an awkward thing, when you are mixed up with a lot of fellows, to drop them without any reason."

"You have only got to say that you find late hours don't agree with you, and that you have made up your mind to cut it altogether."

"That is all very well for you, Frank, and I will do you justice to say that if you determined to do a thing, you would do it without minding what any one said."

"Without minding what any one I did not care for, said," Frank interrupted. "Certainly; why should I heed a bit what people I do not care for say, so long as I feel that I am doing what is right."

"I wish I were as strong-willed as you are, Frank," Julian said rather ruefully, "then I should not have to put up with being bullied by a young brother."

"You are too good-tempered, Julian," Frank said, almost angrily. "Here are you, six feet high and as strong as a horse, and with plenty of brain for anything, just wasting your life. Look at the position father held here, and ask yourself how many of his old friends do you know. Why, rather than go on as you are doing, I would enlist and go out to the Peninsula and fight the French. That would put an end to all this sort of thing, and you could come back again and start afresh. You will have money enough for anything you like. You come into half father's £16,000 when you come of age, and I have no doubt that you will have Aunt's money."

"Why should I?" Julian asked in a more aggrieved tone than he had hitherto used.

"Because you are her favourite, Julian, and quite right that you should be. You have always been awfully good to her, and that is one reason why I hate you to be out of an evening; for although she never says a word against you, and certainly would not hear any one else do so, I tell you it gives me the blues to see her face as she sits there listening for your footsteps."

"It is a beastly shame, and I will give it up, Frank; honour bright, I will."

"That is right, old fellow; I knew you would if you could only once peep in through the window of an evening and see her face."

"As for her money," Julian went on, "if she does not divide it equally between us, I shall, you may be sure."

"I sha'n't want it," Frank said decidedly. "You know I mean to go into the army, and with the interest of my own money I shall have as much as I shall possibly want, and if I had more it would only bother me, and do me harm in my profession. With you it is just the other way. You are the head of the family, and as Father's son ought to take a good place. You could buy an estate and settle down on it, and what with its management, and with horses and hunting and shooting, you would be just in your element."

"Well, we will see about it when the time comes. I am sure I hope the old lady will be with us for a long time yet. She is as kind-hearted a soul as ever lived, though it would have been better for me, no doubt, if she held the reins a little tighter. Well, anyhow, Frank, I will cut the billiards altogether."

They exchanged a silent grip of the hand on the promise, and Julian, looking more serious than usual, put on his hat and went out. There was a curious reversal of the usual relations between the brothers. Julian, although he always laughed at his young brother's assumption of the part of mentor, really leant upon his stronger will, and as often as not, even if unconsciously, yielded to his influence, while Frank's admiration for his brother was heightened by the unfailing good temper with which the latter received his remonstrances and advice. "He is an awfully good fellow," he said to himself when Julian left the room. "Anyone else would have got into a rage at my interference; but he has only one fault; he can't say no, and that is at the root of everything. I can't understand myself why a fellow finds it more difficult to say no than to say yes. If it is right to do a thing one does it, if it is not right one leaves it alone, and the worst one has to stand, if you don't do what other fellows want, is a certain amount of chaff, and that hurts no one."

Frank, indeed, was just as good-tempered as Julian, although in an entirely different way. He had never been known to be in a passion, but put remonstrance and chaff aside quietly, and went his own way without being in the slightest degree affected by them.

Julian kept his promise, and was seen no more in the billiard saloon. Fortunately for him the young fellows with whom he was in the habit of playing were all townsmen, clerks, the sons of the richer tradesmen, or of men who owned fishing-boats or trading vessels, and others of that class—not, indeed, as Frank had said, the sort of men whom Colonel Wyatt would have cared for his son to have associated with—but harmless young fellows who frequented the billiard-rooms as a source of amusement and not of profit, and who therefore had no motive for urging Julian to play. To Mrs. Troutbeck's delight he now spent four or five evenings at home, only going out for an hour to smoke a pipe and to have a chat with the fishermen. Once or twice a week he would be absent all night, going out, as he told his aunt, for a night's fishing, and generally returning in the morning with half a dozen mackerel or other fish as his share of the night's work.

Sometimes he would ask Frank to accompany him, and the latter, when he had no particular work on hand, would do so, and thoroughly enjoyed the sport.

Smuggling was at the time carried on extensively, and nowhere more actively than between Weymouth and Exmouth on the one hand, and Swanage on the other. Consequently, in spite of the vigilance of the revenue men, cargoes were frequently run. The long projection of Chesil Beach and Portland afforded a great advantage to the smugglers; and Lieutenant Downes, who commanded the revenue cutter *Boxer*, had been heard to declare that he would gladly subscribe a year's pay if a channel could be cut through the beach. Even when he obtained information that a cargo was likely to be run to the west, unless the winds and tides were alike propitious, it took so long a time to get round Portland Bill that he was certain to arrive too late to interfere with the landing, while, at times, an adverse wind and the terrors of the "race" with its tremendous current and angry waves would keep the *Boxer* lying for days to the west of the Island, returning to Weymouth only to hear that during her absence a lugger had landed her cargo somewhere to the east.

"Job himself would have lost his temper if he had been a revenue officer at Weymouth," Lieutenant Downes would exclaim angrily. "Why, sir, I would rather lie for three months off the mouth of an African river looking for slavers, than be stationed at Weymouth in search of smuggling craft, for a month; it is enough to wear a man to a thread-paper. Half the coast population seem to me to be in alliance with these rascals, and I am so accustomed to false information now, that as a rule when one of my men gets a hint that a cargo is going to be run near Swanage I start at once for the west, knowing well enough that wherever the affair is to come off it certainly will not be within ten miles of the point named. Even in Weymouth itself the sympathy of the population lies rather with the smugglers than the revenue men."

The long war with France had rendered brandy, French wines, lace, and silks fabulously dear, and the heavy duties charged reduced to a minimum the legitimate traffic that might otherwise have been carried on; therefore, even well-to-do people favoured the men who brought these luxuries to their doors, at a mere fraction of the price that they would otherwise have had to pay for them. Then, too, there was an element of romance in the career of a smuggler who risked his life every day, and whose adventures, escapes, and fights with the revenue men were told round every fireside. The revenue officer was not far wrong when he said that the greater portion of the population round the coast, including all classes, were friendly to, if not in actual alliance with, the smugglers. Julian was well aware that many of the fishermen with whom he went out often lent a hand to the smugglers in landing their goods and taking them inland, or in hiding them in caves in the cliffs known only to the smugglers and themselves. He had heard many stories from them of adventures in which they had been engaged, and the manner in which, by showing signal lights from the sea, they had induced the revenue men to hurry to the spot at which they had seen a flash, and so to leave the coast clear for the landing of the goods.

"It must be great fun," he said one day. "I must say I should like to take part in running a cargo, for once."

"Well, Master Julian, there would not be much difficulty about that, if so be you really mean it. We can put you up to it easy enough, but you know, sir, it isn't all fun. Sometimes the revenue men come down upon us in spite of all the pains we take to throw them off the scent. Captain Downes is getting that artful that one is never sure whether he has been got safely away or not. A fortnight ago he pretty nigh came down on a lugger that was landing a cargo in Lulworth Cove. We thought that it had all been managed well. Word had gone round that the cargo was to be run there, and the morning before, a woman went on to the cliffs and got in talk with one of the revenue men. She let out, as how her husband had been beating her, and she had made up her mind to pay him out. There was going, she said, to be a cargo run that night at a point half-way between Weymouth and Lyme Regis.

"I know she did the part well, as she acted it on three or four of us afterwards, and the way she pretended to be in a passion and as spiteful as a cat, would have taken any fellow in. In course the revenue chap asked her what her name was and where she lived, and I expect they did not find her when they looked for her afterwards in the place she told him. He wanted her to go with him to the officer of the station, but she said that she would never do that, for if it got to be known that she had peached about it, it would be as much as her life was worth. Well, a boy who was watching saw the revenue chap go off, as soon as she was out of sight, straight to the coast-guard station, and ten minutes later the officer in charge there set off for Weymouth.

"The boy followed and he saw him go on board the *Boxer*. Directly afterwards Captain Downes came ashore with him and had a long talk with the chief of the coast-guard there; then he went on board again, and we all chuckled when we saw the *Boxer* get up her anchor, set all sail, make out to Portland, and go round the end of the rock. Two hours later a look-out on the hills saw her bearing out to sea to the south-west, meaning, in course, to run into the bay after it was dark. On shore the officer at Weymouth got a horse and rode along the cliffs to the eastward. He stopped at each coast-guard station, right on past Lulworth, and soon afterwards three parts of the men at each of them turned out and marched away west.

"We thought that we had fooled them nicely, and that evening half a dozen of our boats sailed into Lulworth harbour and anchored there quiet. One of them rowed ashore and landed two hands to look round. They brought back news as there were only two or three revenue men left at the station, and it would be easy enough to seize them and tie them up till it was all over. In course, everything worked for a bit just as we thought it would. The lugger we were expecting showed her light in the offing and was signalled that the coast was clear. It was a dark night, and the two revenue men on duty in the cove were seized and tied up by some of the shore band without a blow being struck. Two or three chaps were placed at the door of the station, so that if the two men left there turned out they would be gagged at once. Everything was ready, and a big lot of carts came down to the water's edge. The lugger anchored outside the cove; we got up our kedges and rowed out to her, and a dozen shore-boats did the same. As soon as we got alongside they began to bundle the kegs in, when not three hundred yards away came a hail, 'What craft is that?'

"It struck us all into a heap, and you could have heard a pin drop. Then came the hail again, 'If you don't answer I will sink you;' whereupon the skipper of the lugger shouted out, 'The *Jennie* of Portsmouth.' 'Lend a hand, lads, with the sails,' he whispered to us; 'slip the cable, Tom.' We ran up the sails in a jiffy, you may be sure, and all the sharper that, as they were half-way up, four guns flashed out. One hulled the lugger, the others flew overhead. Close as they were they could not have seen us, for we could scarce see them and we were under the shadow of the cliffs, but I suppose they fired at the voices. 'Sink the tubs, lads,' the skipper said as the lugger glided away from us. There was a nice little air blowing off shore, and she shot away into the darkness in no time. We all rowed into the mouth of the cove for shelter, and were only just in time, for a shower of grape splashed the water up a few yards behind us.

"We talked it over for a minute or two, and settled that the *Boxer* would be off after the lugger and would not pay any more attention to us. Some of them were in favour of taking the kegs that we had got ashore, but the most of us were agin that, and the captain himself had told us to sink them, so we rowed out of the cove again and tied sinkers to the kegs and lowered them down three or four hundred yards west of the mouth of the cove. We went on board our boats and the other chaps went on shore, and you may guess we were not long in getting up our sails and creeping out of the cove. It was half an hour after the first shots were fired before we heard the *Boxer* at it again. I reckon that in the darkness they could not make out whether the lugger had kept along east or west under the cliffs, and I expect they went the wrong way at first, and only found her at last with their night-glasses when she was running out to sea.

"Well, next morning we heard that the shore men had not landed five minutes when there was a rush of forty or fifty revenue men into the village. There ain't no doubt they had only gone west to throw us off our guard, and, as soon as it was dark, turned and went eastward. They could not have known that the job was to come off at Lulworth, but were on the look-out all along, and I reckon that it was the same with the *Boxer*. She must have beaten back as soon as it was dark enough for her not to be seen from the hills, and had been crawling along on the look-out close to the shore, when she may have caught sight of the lugger's signal. Indeed, we heard afterwards that it called back the coast-guard men, for they had passed Lulworth and were watching at a spot between that and St. Alban's Head, where a cargo had been run a month or two before, when they caught sight of the signal off Lulworth. Well, you may guess they did not get much for their pains The carts had all made off as soon as they heard the *Boxer's* guns, and knew that the game was up, for the night anyhow, and they found every light out in Lulworth, and everyone, as it seemed, fast asleep. I believe, from what I have heard, that there was a great row afterwards between Captain Downes and the revenue officer ashore. The chap ashore would have it that it was all the captain's fault for being in such a hurry, and that if he had waited an hour they would have got all the carts with the cargo, even if he had not caught the lugger.

"Well, that was true enough; but I don't see that Downes was to blame, for until he came along he could not be sure where the lugger was, and indeed she was so close in under the cliff that it is like enough he would have missed her altogether and have gone on another two or three miles, if it had not been that they caught the noise of the boats alongside her taking in the kegs. The lugger got away all right; she is a fast craft, and though the *Boxer* can walk along in a strong wind, in a light breeze the lugger had the legs of her altogether. That shows you, Mr. Julian, that Captain Downes has cut his eye-teeth, and that it is mighty hard to fool him. He was never nearer making a good capture than he was that night. The lugger ran her cargo two nights afterwards at the very spot where the woman had told the revenue man that she was going to do it.

There was a little bit of a fight, but the coast-guard were not strong enough to do any good, and had to make off, and before they could bring up anything like a strong force, every bale and keg had been carried inland, and before morning there was scarce a farmhouse within ten miles that had not got some of it stowed away in their snug hiding-places. Downes will be more vicious than ever after that job, and you see, master, you are like to run a goodish risk of getting your head broke and of being hauled off to jail. Still, if you would like to join some night in a run we can put you in the way."

"Yes, I should like it very much," Julian said. "There can't be much risk, for there has not been anything like a regular fight anywhere along this part of the coast for the last two years, and from what I have heard, there must have been twenty cargoes run in that time."

"All that, sir, all that; nigher thirty, I should say. There is three luggers at it reg'lar."

"Are they French or English?"

"Two of them is French and one English, but the crews are all mixed. They carry strong crews all of them, and a longish gun in their sterns, so that in case they are chased they may have a chance of knocking away a spar out of anything after them. They would not fight if a cutter came up alongside them—that might make a hanging matter of it, while if none of the revenue chaps are killed it is only a case of long imprisonment, though the English part of the crew generally have the offer of entering on a king's ship instead, and most of them take it. Life on board a man-of-war may not be a pleasant one, but after all it is better than being boxed up in a prison for years. Anyhow, that is the light in which I should look at it myself."

"I should think so," Julian agreed. "However, you see

there is no great risk in landing the kegs, for it is very seldom you get so nearly caught as you did at Lulworth. Let me know when the next affair is coming off, Bill, and if it is anywhere within a moderate distance of Weymouth I will go with you if you will take me. Anyhow, whether I go or not, you may be quite sure that I shall keep the matter to myself."

"The most active chap about here," Bill said after he had hauled his nets, and the boat was making her way back to Weymouth, "is that Faulkner. He is a bitter bad one, he is. Most of the magistrates about here don't trouble their heads about smuggling, and if they find a keg of first class brandy quite accidental any morning on their doorstep, they don't ask where it comes from, but just put it down into their cellars. Sometimes information gets sworn before them, and they has to let the revenue people know, but somehow or other, I can't say how it is," and the fisherman gave a portentous wink, "our fellows generally get some sort of an idea that things ain't right, and the landing don't come off as expected; queer, ain't it? But that fellow Faulkner, he ain't like that. He worries hisself about the smugglers just about as much as Captain Downes does. He is just as hard on smugglers as he is on poachers, and he is wonderful down on them, he is. Do you know him, sir?"

"I know him by sight. He is a big, pompous man; his place is about two miles up the valley, and there are some large woods round it."

"That is so, sir; and they say as they are choke-full of pheasants. He has a lot of keepers, and four years ago there was a desperate fight there. Two keepers and three poachers got shot, and two others were caught; they were tried at the 'sizes for murder, and hanged. He is a regular bully, he is, but he ain't no coward. If he was he would never stir out after sunset, but instead of that he is out night after night on the cliffs, when there is any talk of a cargo being run. He is known to carry pistols about with him, and so, though his life has been threatened many times, nothing has ever come of it. One thing is, he has got a big black horse, about the best horse there is in this part of the country, and he always rides mighty fast down into the town or up on to the cliffs, where he gets among the revenue men, and in course he is safe enough. He was down with that lot at Lulworth that night, and they say he cussed and swore loud enough to be heard all over the village, when they found that they had got there too late. He is a bitter, bad weed, is Faulkner."

"I know he is very unpopular even in the town," Julian said. "He is the hardest magistrate on the bench, and if it were not for the others not a man brought before him would ever get off. I have heard that he is very much disliked by the other magistrates, and that some time ago, when he wanted to join the club, they would not have him at any price. I can't make out why a fellow should go out of his way to make himself disliked. I can understand his being down on poachers; no one likes to be robbed, but the smuggling cannot make any difference to him one way or the other."

"No; that is what we says. It don't concern him, 'cept that magistrates are bound in a sort of way to see that the law is not broken. But why shouldn't he do like the others and go on his way quiet, onless he gets an information laid before him, or a warning from the revenue people as he is wanted. You mark my words, Master Julian, some night that chap will get a bullet or a charge of shot in his body."

After this Julian went on more than one occasion with Bill and other fishermen to look on at the landing of contraband cargoes. If the distance was within a walk they would start from Weymouth straight inland, and come down by the road along which the carts were to fetch the goods up, for it was only occasionally that the fishermen would take their boats. At Lulworth, of course, there had been no risk in their doing so, as boats, when fishing to the east, would often make their way into the cove and drop anchor there for a few hours. But when the run was to be made at lonely spots, the sight of fishing boats making in to anchor would have excited the suspicions of the coast-guard on the cliffs. The number of fishermen who took part in the smugglers' proceedings was but small. All of these had either brothers or other relations on board the luggers, or were connected with some of the smugglers' confederates on shore. They received a handsome sum for their night's work, which was at times very hard, as the kegs had often to be carried up steep and dangerous paths to the top of the cliffs, and then a considerable distance across the downs to the nearest point the carts could come to.

It was the excitement of the adventure, however, rather than the pay, and the satisfaction derived from outwitting the revenue men, that was the main attraction to the fishermen. Julian took no share in the work. He went dressed in the rough clothes he wore on the fishing excursions at night, and heartily enjoyed the animated bustle of the scene, as scores of men carrying kegs or bales on their backs, made their way up some narrow ravine, silently laid down their loads beside the carts and pack-horses, and then started back again for another trip. He occasionally lent a hand to lash the kegs on either side of the horses, or to lift a bale into the cart. No one ever asked any question; it was assumed that he was there with one of the carts, and he recognized the wisdom of Bill's advice the first time he went out.

"It is best not to speak till you are spoken to, Master

Julian; there is more chaps there besides yourself, as are thought to be sound asleep in their beds at Weymouth, and it is just as well to keep yourself to yourself. There is never no knowing when things may go wrong, and then it is as likely as not that some one may peach, and the fewer names as comes out the better. Now you mind, sir, if there is an alarm, and the revenue chaps come down on us, you just make a bolt at once. It ain't no business of yours, one way or the other. You ain't there to make money or to get hold of cheap brandy; you just go to look on and amuse yourself, and all you have got to do is to make off as hard as you can go directly there is an alarm. Everyone else does the same as gets a chance, I can tell you. The country people never fight; though the smugglers, if they are cornered and can't get back to the lugger without it, will use their weapons if they see a chance; but you have got nothing to do with that. Don't you wait a minute for me and my mates, for we shall bolt too. If we were on the shore when they came on us we should embark with the crew and get on board the lugger. In course, if just a few of the revenue men were fools enough to come on us, they would be tumbled over in double quick time, and tied up till the goods were all taken inland, and be left till some of their mates found them in the morning.

"That is how it is, you know, that we get most of our cargoes run. One of the chaps on the cliff may make us out, but you see it takes a long time to send along the line and get enough of them together to interfere with us. Unless they have got a pretty good strong force together, they ain't such fools as to risk their lives by meddling with a hundred men or more, with a lot of valuable goods to land, and the knowledge that if they are caught it is a long term in jail. The men know well enough that if there is anything on, there will be a watch kept over them, and that if they were to fire a pistol as a signal, there would be news of it sent to the smugglers in no time. Sometimes, too, the coast-guards nearest the point where the landing is to be, are pounced on suddenly and tied up. I reckon, too, that a good many of them keep an eye shut as long as they can, and then go off pretty leisurely to pass the word along that they have heard oars or have seen signals, especially if they have got a hot-headed boatswain in charge of their station, a sort of chap who would want to go down to meddle with a hundred men, with only five or six at his back. A man with a wife and some children, perhaps, don't relish the thought of going into a bad scrimmage like that if he can keep out of it; why should he? He gets a bit of money if they make a good seizure, but he knows well enough that he ain't going to make a seizure unless he has got a pretty strong party; and you take my word for it, four times out of five when we make a clear run, it is because the coast-guard keep an eye closed as long as they dare. They know well enough that it ain't such an uncommon thing for a man to be found at the bottom of the cliff, without anything to show how he got there, and the coroner's jury finds as it was a dark night and he tumbled over, and they brings in a verdict according. But it ain't every man as cares about taking the risk of accidents of that kind, and, somehow or other, they happens to just the chaps as is wonderful sharp and active. They have all been sailors, you know, and are ready enough for a fight when they are strong enough to have a chance, but that is a very different thing from walking backwards and forwards on a dark night close to the edge of a cliff, three or four hundred feet high, without a comrade within a quarter of a mile, and the idea that an accident of this kind might occur any time."

CHAPTER II.

BEFORE THE JUSTICES.

ONE morning when Frank was dressing, the servant came up and told him that a fisherman, who said his name was Bill Bostock, wanted to speak to him. As he had often been out with Julian in the man's boat, he put on his jacket and ran to the door.

"Good morning, Bill!" he said; "what is it?"

"I will talk with you outside, sir, if you don't mind."

A good deal surprised, Frank put on his cap and went out with him.

"There has been a bad business, Master Frank, a mighty bad job."

"What sort of a job, Bill?"

"A smuggling affair, Master Frank. There was a fight. I hears one of the revenue men was killed. I don't know as that is so, but some of them have been knocked about, and have got some pistol wounds, no doubt. But that ain't the worst part of the business. Mr. Julian is among those as has been caught."

"Julian!" Frank exclaimed in astonishment. "Why, what in the world had Julian got to do with it?"

"Well, sir," the sailor said apologetically, "you see it was like this. Mr. Julian is a young gentleman as loves a bit of a spree, and he has been out many a night with some of us to see a cargo run."

Frank uttered an exclamation of surprise and consternation.

"I thought perhaps as you knowed it, sir."

"I never dreamt of such a thing, Bill. How could Julian have been so mad as to mix himself up in such a business?

I suppose this is your doing; you must have led him into this mischief."

"No, sir," the sailor said in an aggrieved voice. "How was I to lead a young gentleman like your brother into a thing as he didn't choose to do? I don't say as I didn't mention to him, promiscuous like, that I lent a hand sometimes in running a cargo; but how was I to know as he would up and say, 'I will go with you some night, Bill'. Well, I argues with him, and I points out to him as he might get into a scrape; but, says he, 'I am not going to take no share in it, but just want to look on and see the fun', as he calls it. I points out to him as it was not always fun, but he puts that aside, and, says he, it would not be fun unless there was a little excitement about it. He promised me faithful that he would always cut and run as soon as he heard there was any talk of the revenue men a-coming, and what was I to do? I don't say, sir, as how if it had been you I would have taken you with me, 'cause you are young, you see, and I should have felt as I was 'sponsible for you. But Mr. Julian is a man now, and when he says, 'I mean to go with you anyhow, Bill', it was not for me to say, you sha'n't go. Mr. Julian, he is a sort of gent that gets over one somehow, and there ain't no saying 'no' to him."

"Well, it is of no use talking about that now," Frank said impatiently. "First tell me all about it, and then we will see what had best be done."

"Well, Master Frank, it was eight miles to the west. The chaps concerned in it thought they had managed to throw dust into the eyes of Captain Downes, and to get the *Boxer* away to Swanage, and how he got wind of the affair, and where it was to be, is more nor I can tell. Everything was going on smooth enough, and half the cargo was in the carts, when all of a sudden there was a shout 'Surrender, you scoundrels!' and that fellow Faulkner dashed up with a pistol in his hand, and behind him came a score of revenue men. I dodged under a cart and bolted. I heard some pistol shots fired, for just at that time a lot of the smugglers had come up to the carts with kegs. As if the firing on shore had been a signal, I heard directly after some guns down by the water, and knew that Downes and the *Boxer* had come on the lugger. I made straight back, but I could not sleep all night for wondering whether Mr. Julian had got off too, and I was up afore it was light, and went round to one or two of the other chaps as was there. One had not come back; the other had only been in half an hour. He had hid up, close to where we was surprised.

"After it was over the revenue chaps lit a lot of lanterns and then made a big fire, and by its light my mate could see pretty well what was going on. They had got about twenty prisoners. Most of the country people and carts had, luckily enough for them, gone off with their loads a few minutes afore the revenue men came up. A dozen pack-horses and three or four carts had been took, and, in course, all the loads the men were carrying up. Among those who was took was Mr. Julian. He was standing close to me when they came up, and I expect he was collared immediate. Faulkner, he sat down on a tub by the side of the fire and takes out a book, and the prisoners was brought up one by one and questions asked them. Mr. Julian was one of the last. Faulkner got up from his seat and rowed him tremendous. What he said my mate could not catch, but he could hear his voice, and he was going on at him cruel; then I suppose Mr. Julian lost his temper, and my mate says he could see that he was giving it him back hot. I expect it was something wonderful hard and nasty he said, for Faulkner jumped at him and hit him in the face. Then your brother threw himself on him. My mate says he would have thrown him backwards into the fire, if some of the revenue men had not seized him and dragged him off.

"After that there was a row between Faulkner and Captain Downes, who had come up just before with half a dozen sailors. I expect Downes was telling him that he ought to be ashamed of himself. Anyhow they got to high words, as was easy to be heard. Half an hour later most of them started with the prisoners, leaving half a dozen of the officers to look after the things they had taken. When they had gone, my mate went down close to the water, and was able to make out the cutter and the lugger anchored close together—so she has been caught. There was nothing else to wait for, so he tramped off home and had only been in a few minutes before I came to him."

"This is awful," Frank said, in dismay. "The only thing I see that can be done is for me to go and have a talk with Captain Downes. He was a friend of my father's; and I think he is a kind-hearted man, though, of course, he has to be sharp in carrying out his duty of trying to put down smuggling. Well, I will run in for breakfast now, or my aunt will wonder what has become of me; then I will go straight on board the *Boxer*."

"She is not in yet," Bill said. "She would not start until daylight; and I don't suppose she will be round for another two hours. You see she is not clear of Portland Bill yet."

"That is unfortunate. However, I hope I shall see him before the magistrates sit. What time do they meet?"

"They generally sit at eleven o'clock; but it ain't their day, and they will have to be summoned special. I should not wonder if they don't meet till two o'clock; because they could not be sure what time the *Boxer* will get round, and, as he will have taken some prisoners in the lugger, they would not begin until he arrived."

"Very well; I will go round to the court-house after breakfast, and inquire what time the sitting will be. Anyhow, I hope to be able to see the lieutenant before they meet. I don't know that any good can come of it; for, as he had nothing to do with Julian's capture, he certainly would not be able to save him from appearing, especially after that row with Faulkner."

"He's a bad un that, Master Frank, and I wish your brother had chucked him into that fire. A bit of burning might have done him good; and, if ever a chap deserved it, he did."

Frank went back into the house.

"My dear Frank," Mrs. Troutbeck exclaimed, "where have you been? I have never known you keep breakfast waiting before. Why, what is the matter, dear? Nothing about Julian, I hope; hasn't he come home yet?"

"No, Aunt; and I am sorry to say that he has got into an awkward scrape. It seems that he went out, for the fun of the thing, to see a cargo run. The revenue people came up, and he was one of those who were caught. Of course he had nothing to do with the smuggling part of the business, nor with a bit of a fight there was. Still, as he was there, I am afraid there is no doubt that he will have to appear before the magistrates with the others."

Mrs. Troutbeck sat in speechless consternation.

"Oh, dear! oh, dear!" she exclaimed at last. "How could he have been so silly? It is dreadful, my dear, and it will be such a disgrace. What shall we do?"

"There is nothing to do, Aunt, that I can see. As to the disgrace, that is nothing very dreadful. No end of people are mixed up in smuggling; and I have heard that many of the gentry wink at it, and are glad enough to buy a keg of brandy cheap without asking any questions where it comes from. So the mere fact that Julian went to have a look at a cargo being run is not anything very serious.

I suppose it was against the law even to be present, but there was nothing disgraceful about it. It is lucky my holidays began last week, and if there is anything to be done I can do it."

"Could not Mr. Downes get him off? He used often to be here in your father's time, though I have not seen much of him since; but I am sure he would do anything he could."

"I have been thinking of that, Aunt. The *Boxer* was there last night and captured the smuggler, but her crew had nothing to do with the fight on shore; and, therefore, I don't think there is any chance of his being able to interfere in the matter. Still, I will see him as soon as the cutter comes in."

On going down to the court-house, Frank found that the magistrates would meet at two o'clock. Then, as the *Boxer* had only just appeared round Portland, he went and saw the chief officer of the coast-guard, to endeavour to obtain permission to have an interview with Julian.

"I am sorry I can do nothing in the matter, lad," he replied. "It is out of my hands, owing to a magistrate being present at the capture. It was, indeed, his business more than ours; for it was he who obtained information of the affair, and called upon us to aid him in the capture of men engaged in unlawful practices. Therefore, you see, the prisoners are in the hands of the civil authorities. I hear he has given strict orders that no one is, on any pretence, to speak to the prisoners."

"I hear that he struck my brother."

"I don't know how you heard it, lad, but it is true. However, I do not feel at liberty to say anything about it. I am very sorry for your brother, who is a fine young fellow. However, I hope that as he was unarmed, and was not, I suppose, actually concerned in the smuggling business, the matter will be passed over lightly, even if he is not discharged at once. At any rate, we shall in no way press the case against him."

Frank, indeed, afterwards learned that the officer dropped a hint to the men to make as little as possible of Julian's capture, and of the vigorous resistance he had made when first seized.

The *Boxer* dropped anchor off the town at twelve o'clock, and the lieutenant landed at once. The officer of the coast-guard went down to meet him on the quay, and for half an hour they walked up and down the parade together, in earnest conversation. Frank remained on the opposite side of the road until they stopped, and the commander of the *Boxer* beckoned to him.

"Well, lad," he said, as Frank came up, "this is a nasty scrape that your brother has got into; but I don't think they can do anything to him. Mr. Moorsby has been telling me that you have been to him; but neither he nor I can do anything in the matter—it is in the civil hands. If it had been anyone else but Faulkner who had been in charge, I have no doubt it could have been managed. Of course, your brother ought not to have been there, but as he was only looking on, and taking no active part in the affair, he might have been released without any difficulty. However, I don't think you need worry yourself. Certainly, we shall not press the case against him. It is unfortunate that he used his tongue as sharply as he did to Mr. Faulkner, though I don't say but that he had great provocation, or that what he said was not perfectly true; still, it would have been much better left unsaid. However, I question if before the hearing is over Faulkner will not have cause to regret that he did not let your brother go home as soon as they got back here."

He nodded, and Frank understood that there was no more to say, and, thanking the officer, turned and walked off home. The fisherman met him on the way.

"You keep up your heart, Mr. Frank. Me and some of the others have been having a talk with the coast-guards, and they will be all right. Of course, there is not one of them that does not know Mr. Julian, so they won't say more than they can help against him; and every one of them is glad to hear that he gave it to that Faulkner hot. He ain't no more a favourite with them than he is with other people, and it was not by their own will that they ran in and pulled your brother off him. If they hadn't, he would not have been sitting on the bench to-day, nor for many a week, I reckon; for he would have been pretty badly burned if he had fallen across that fire. So you may be sure that they will make it easy for Mr. Julian, and I expect you will have him back home this evening. They would never have took him at all if they had known who he was; but, of course, being dark, and he in his fishing togs, they did not see it was him."

Frank returned home in much better spirits than he had left. His aunt was standing at the window, and hurried to the door to let him in.

"Well, Frank, have you got him out? I hoped you would have brought him home with you."

"There was no chance of that, Aunt. Of course, when anyone is taken and locked up, he cannot be discharged until the case has been gone into. But I have seen Mr. Moorsby, the coast-guard officer on shore, and Captain Downes, and they both say that the case will not be pressed against him, and that, as he was not taking any part in the affair, and merely looking on, they don't think anything will be done to him. The coast-guardsmen who will have to give evidence all know him, and will not say anything against him if they can help it. So I should not be at all surprised, Aunt, if we have him back here this afternoon."

"Oh, I do wish," Mrs. Troutbeck said tearfully, "that it

could have been managed so that he would not have been obliged to be placed in the dock with smugglers and all sorts of people."

"It would, no doubt, have been better if it could have been avoided, Aunt, but there is no helping it; and if he is discharged it won't go for much against him—certainly not here, where nobody regards smuggling as a crime."

At half-past one Frank went down to the court-house. It was already crowded, but Captain Downes, who came up at the same moment, took him in, and obtained a place for him at the solicitors' table. The seizure had created quite a sensation in Weymouth, not only because two or three Weymouth men were among the prisoners, but because, owing to the fight that had taken place, the matter was very much more serious than a mere capture of contraband goods. There was a general buzz of conversation until three magistrates came in and took their places, and there was a little murmur of satisfaction as Colonel Chambers, the chairman, took his seat; for, had he not been present, Mr. Faulkner, who was next in seniority, would have taken the chair. A minute later, twelve prisoners were brought in. Five Frenchmen and two English were a portion of the crew of the smuggler; two were farmers' men, the drivers of the carts; one was a local fisherman; the eleventh was one of the party that had gone from Weymouth; Julian Wyatt made up the number.

Two or three of the party had their heads bandaged up; one had his arm in a sling; several others had marks of hard knocks, and Julian a pair of black eyes. When the little murmur that followed the entry of the prisoners had subsided, and the crier had called out "Silence in court!" the inquiry began.

Mr. Moorsby was the first witness. He deposed that having received information that a landing of contraband goods was likely to take place, he, accompanied by Mr. Faulkner, who represented the civil authorities, went to the spot. They perceived that a landing of goods was taking place; but, as it had been arranged that his party should not show themselves until the revenue cutter came up and seized the lugger, they remained in hiding until they heard from a man placed down by the shore that the cutter was coming in. Then they rushed out and seized the parties engaged in the proceedings. Some of them resisted violently, and a serious fray took place. Three of his men were wounded with pistol shots, one of them very seriously. One of the smugglers had been killed, and three were so seriously injured that they could not at present be placed in the dock.

"Are any of the prisoners represented in court?" the chairman asked.

A solicitor sitting next to Frank rose. "I represent Mr. Julian Wyatt," he said. Frank looked up at him in surprise. The idea of obtaining legal assistance for Julian had not occurred to him, and he wondered how his brother had been able to communicate with a solicitor. "I would suggest, your honour," the latter went on, "that the evidence should be taken separately in the different charges, as there is a considerable difference in the position of prisoners."

Another solicitor rose. "I appear for John Turnbull and William Sims," he said, "and I would support the appeal of Mr. Probert. My clients, who are farming men, took no part whatever in the fray, which is the serious portion of the affair. While I am ready to admit that they were engaged in the illegal operation of aiding in the landing of contraband goods, I shall be able to prove that they are innocent of the more serious charge of resisting by force their capture by the revenue officers, and with using deadly weapons against the representatives of the law, and that their case stands in an altogether different category to that of the main body of the prisoners."

"You do not intend, I hope," Mr. Faulkner said, "to express a wish that we should have what would practically be twelve investigations instead of one, or that the witnesses should all be obliged to go that number of times into the box."

"By no means, your honour; I am only intimating my intention of cross-examining each witness as to the share my clients took in the affair, and pointing out beforehand that their case stands on an entirely different footing to that of the men who took part in the more serious charge of resisting the officers."

One after another of the coast-guard men gave their evidence, each identifying one or more of the prisoners in whose capture they had taken a personal part. None of the first five had anything to say regarding Julian. Then James Wingfield entered the box. After stating that he was the coxswain of the Weymouth coast-guard boat he proceeded:

"When Mr. Moorsby gave the order I ran forward. I saw a biggish man standing with his hands in the pockets of his pea-jacket. He seemed to be looking on, and was not at work; but, thinking that he might be a leader, me and Harry Wilkens ran at him and seized him. It was not until afterwards we knew that he was Mr. Julian Wyatt. After we had caught him I handed him over to Wilkens, and that is all I know about him."

He then proceeded to testify against several of the other prisoners in whose capture he had taken part. When he had finished his evidence, Julian's solicitor rose.

"You say that the prisoner you first took, Mr. Wyatt, was taking no active part in the affair?"

"No, sir, he was just standing there looking on."

"And did he resist the capture?"

"Not to say resist, sir. When we first clapped hands on

him he gave a start, for we had come upon him sudden, without noise. He just tried to shake us off, not knowing, I reckon, who we were; but as soon as I said, 'In the King's name, you are my prisoner', he was just as quiet as a lamb."

The solicitor sat down. Then the chairman asked the witness if any arms were found on the prisoner.

"No, sir."

"Not even a stick?"

"I won't say as he may not have had a bit of a stick, your honour, though I did not notice it, his hands being in his pockets; anyhow, he did not try to use it."

Wilkens was the next witness, and his evidence, as far as Julian was concerned, was precisely similar to that of the coxswain. Against the seven men of the lugger the evidence was conclusive. All had resisted desperately, and this had enabled several of their party to make their escape in the darkness. The Weymouth fisherman had been caught coming up from the beach with a keg on his shoulder, and had thrown it down and attempted to run away, but had made no resistance when he had been taken; the two farm men had been captured at their horses' heads, and had at once surrendered. When the evidence had been gone through, Mr. Probert addressed the court on behalf of Julian. He urged that there was no evidence whatever to show that he was concerned either in the smuggling operations or in the resistance to the revenue officers.

"I do not pretend," he said, "that he was there by accident; but I maintain that he was there simply in the capacity of a looker-on. He stands, in fact, precisely in the same position that any member of the general public might do, who had been present as a spectator at any sort of riot. It is unquestionably a very unwise action on the part of any individual to attend a meeting of any sort at which it is possible that riotous proceedings may take place, but

I maintain that, however imprudent and foolish, there is nothing criminal in his doing so, and I am sure that there is no case on record in which a man has been punished for his presence at a riot in which he did not participate. My client acted foolishly, but I ask the court to say that his foolishness was not criminal. He had accidentally learned that there was to be a landing of contraband goods, and, with the thoughtlessness of youth, he went to see what he considered the fun. Even if there had been a shadow of criminality in his being present, I should ask you to say that the unpleasant experience that he has undergone—his detention for twelve hours in a police cell, and his appearance here—is ample punishment for his boyish escapade, which might have been committed by any high-spirited young fellow of nineteen."

After the other solicitor had addressed the court on behalf of the two farmer's men, the magistrates consulted together. The spectators, watching them attentively, saw that for a time they seemed unanimous, then it was equally evident that there was a difference of opinion on some point or other, and they presently rose and left the court.

"It is Faulkner against the other two," Mr. Probert whispered to Frank. "Of course they were unanimous about the smugglers, but I expect they differed as to the others. It is lucky that the Colonel is in the chair. Harrington is a mild little fellow, and Faulkner would be able to twist him round his finger if there were only the two of them, but there is no fear of that with the Colonel there to keep him straight."

In ten minutes they returned, and by the flushed, angry face of Mr. Faulkner, Frank judged at once that he had been overruled. The chairman briefly announced the decision of the court, and committed the seven smugglers for trial on the whole of the charges. The Weymouth fisherman was also committed, but only on the charge of being engaged in the unlawful act of defrauding His Majesty's revenue, and was allowed out on bail. The two farm labourers were fined fifty pounds apiece, which their solicitor at once paid.

"The majority of the bench are in favour of your immediate discharge, Mr. Wyatt, being of opinion that the evidence has failed altogether to prove any of the charges against you, and, being of opinion that you have already paid dearly enough for your reckless folly in attending an unlawful operation of this kind, they trust that it will be a lesson to you for life. The other and more serious charge against you will now be taken."

Frank, who was in the act of rising from his seat in delight at Julian's acquittal, sank down again in dismay at the concluding words. He had no idea of any further charge.

"What is it?" he whispered to Mr. Probert.

"Faulkner has charged him with an attempt to murder him. Have you not heard of it? Don't be frightened. I have seen the witnesses, and have no doubt that this case will break down like the other."

After all the prisoners but Julian had been removed from the dock, Mr. Faulkner left the bench and took his seat in the body of the court. The charge was then read over by the clerk, and Mr. Faulkner's name was called; as he stepped into the witness-box, a low hiss ran through the fishermen who formed a large proportion of the spectators.

"Silence!" the chairman said angrily. "If I hear any repetition of this indecent demonstration, I will have the court cleared at once."

Mr. Faulkner then proceeded to give his evidence. "He had," he said, "spoken severely to the prisoner in his quality as a magistrate, upon his taking part in smuggling transactions. At this the prisoner became violently abusive and uttered such murderous threats that he thought he would have struck him, and in self-defence he (the witness) gave him a blow, whereupon the prisoner had sprung upon him like a tiger, had lifted him in his arms, and had carried him bodily towards the fire, and would assuredly have thrown him into it had he not been prevented from doing so by some of the coast-guardsmen."

Mr. Probert rose quietly. "You are a magistrate, Mr. Faulkner, I believe?" Mr. Faulkner gave no reply to the question, and after a little pause the solicitor went on: "Do you consider that, as a magistrate, Mr. Faulkner, it comes within your province to abuse a prisoner unconvicted of any crime?"

"I deny that I abused him," Mr. Faulkner said hotly.

"There is no occasion for heat, sir," Mr. Probert said quietly. "You are in the position of a witness at present and not of a magistrate, and must reply like any other witness. Well, you deny having abused him. Do you consider that calling a gentleman of good standing in this town, the son of a distinguished officer, a loafing young scoundrel, not abuse; or by telling him that six months in one of His Majesty's jails would do him a world of good?"

"I deny that I used those words."

"Well, sir, that is a question of pure credibility. It is possible that I may be in a position to prove to the satisfaction of the bench that you did use them, and many others of an equally offensive character. Mr. Wyatt naturally resented such language, which you had no more right to address to him than you would have to address to me. If a magistrate forgets his position, and abuses a prisoner in the language of a fish-fag, he must expect to be answered in the same way by anyone of spirit. You say that, thereupon, he became abusive and used murderous threats? Now we should like to hear a little more about this. First of all, let us hear the abuse, will you? Tell the court, if you please, Mr. Faulkner, what were the abusive expressions," he added.

"He said, sir, that I was a disgrace to the bench."

There was a general laugh in the court, which was instantly repressed. Mr. Faulkner's eyes ran furiously over the crowded benches.

"I must ask you to look at me, Mr. Faulkner," the solicitor said mildly. "Well, he said that you were a disgrace to the bench. That is scarcely, perhaps, as much a matter of abuse as one of private opinion. What did he say next?"

"He said I was a curse to the whole neighbourhood."

"Again a mere matter of opinion."

"And after that, that I was a sneaking, meddlesome, interfering old fox."

There was again a buzz of laughter, mingled with exclamations of "So you are," "He wasn't far wrong"; upon which Colonel Chalmers directed the constable to turn all the offending parties out of court. Some fishermen nearest to the door were hustled out.

"Well, I am afraid that I must admit," Mr. Probert said, "that to call you a meddlesome old fox was abusive, although nothing like so abusive as to call a man a loafing young scoundrel. Now as to the threats."

"He said that I would be brought home one of these days with a bullet in my body."

"That is purely a matter of prophecy, Mr. Faulkner, and not a threat, unless he intended you to understand that it was he who would fire the bullet. Do you mean to tell the court that you had any reason to suppose that this young gentleman, whose reputation is untarnished, and who has never had a charge brought against him except the ridiculous one that has just been dismissed, intended to imply by those words that he himself had any idea of taking your life?"

"It might bear that construction."

"It might bear any construction in the mind of a man determined to see everything in the worst possible light. It is a matter of public notoriety, Mr. Faulkner, that you have received several threatening letters, and that the active part you have taken against poachers and smugglers has caused some feeling against you. Do you not think it likely that when Mr. Wyatt used the words you have repeated he referred to this circumstance?"

"A magistrate who does his duty must necessarily be unpopular with the criminal classes."

"Possibly, Mr. Faulkner, though I have known many magistrates who did their duty and who were by no means unpopular; but you have not answered my question. Do you not think that in saying what he did Mr. Wyatt simply alluded to the fact of your well-known unpopularity, and to the threatening letters that you had received?"

"Possibly he did," Mr. Faulkner admitted reluctantly, "although that was not my impression at the time."

"Well, then, unless there were further threats, as you call them, I think we have disposed of the alleged abuse and the alleged murderous threats. Now we come to the other charge. You thought that he was about to strike you, and in self-defence gave him a blow. What made you think that he was going to strike you?"

"He made a step towards me with a threatening gesture."

"Oh! I dare say that he was angry, but a gentleman who has been called a loafing young scoundrel is somewhat apt to lose his temper. You might even do so yourself, Mr. Faulkner, if so addressed. Well, then, he made a step towards you; thereupon you struck him in the face, and judging from his appearance you struck him pretty hard, and then you say he caught you up and carried you along. It says a good deal for his strength that he was able to do so. Now you say he carried you towards the fire, and would have thrown you upon it had not some of the coast-guardsmen interfered in time. Now, how do you know that that was his intention?"

"I firmly believe that it was so."

"It is not a question of belief. You might believe that he was going to throw you up to the moon. You struggled, I suppose—you would scarcely submit to be carried like a baby—I imagine that is about the long and short of it. But even if he had intended to throw you on the fire, which certainly seems to be merely a matter of your imagination, you can hardly pretend that had he carried out this intention that it would have been murder. Surely with a score of your friends standing by, you would have been hauled out immediately, none the worse except for a few singes and a burn or two. This was not a burning fiery furnace, Mr. Faulkner, but merely a bit of a bonfire from a few sticks that had been set on fire in order to throw a little light on the proceedings."

"I might have been very seriously burnt."

"Well, even supposing that you had been, that is not a question of murder. I presume that you framed this indictment. You have charged the prisoner, not with an intention of committing grievous damage upon you, but with murder, and if you now admit that, under the circumstances, death could hardly have resulted by any possibility from this imaginary intention of throwing you on the fire being carried out, it is clear that the charge of murder must drop through. I have no further questions to ask you, though I may have some remarks to make after having heard your witnesses."

CHAPTER III.

IN A FRESH SCRAPE.

THE first witness called by Mr. Faulkner was Captain Downes.

"Will you tell us what you know about this affair?" the chairman said.

"After having captured the smuggler, I took six men and went up to see if I could be of any assistance to Mr. Moorsby, and also to hear whether he had been as successful with his capture as I had. I found that everything was over, and that a fire had been lighted. I was talking to Mr. Moorsby when my attention was excited by loud words between Mr. Faulkner and Mr. Wyatt, with whom I am acquainted. Mr. Faulkner struck him in the face, and there was a scuffle, the prisoner lifting the magistrate, although a much heavier man, completely off his feet. In the course of the scuffle they approached the fire, and being afraid that they might fall into it, I ran up with Mr. Moorsby and some of the men, and pulled them away."

"Did it seem to you, Captain Downes, that the prisoner was carrying Mr. Faulkner straight to the fire?"

"He was certainly going straight in that direction, but whether intentionally or not I am unable to say."

"Do you think that if you and your men had not interfered they would have fallen into the fire?"

"I think they certainly would have done so."

"Do you think that the prisoner intended to throw Mr. Faulkner into the fire?"

"That I cannot say."

"Have you any questions to ask the witness, Mr. Faulkner?" the chairman asked.

"You do not think it likely, I suppose, that the prisoner could have intended himself to tumble into the fire?"

"I should think it very unlikely."

Mr. Faulkner sat down, and Mr. Probert rose.

"You think it very unlikely, Captain Downes, that Mr. Wyatt would deliberately have walked into the fire, and I quite share your opinion; but it has not yet been proved that he was deliberately going towards the fire at all. You say he lifted Mr. Faulkner in his arms. Now it seems to me that, having done so, he would not be able to see at all which way he was going, as Mr. Wyatt's eyes would both be on a level with Mr. Faulkner's chest; moreover, it must be evident that, judging from his present appearance, he could scarcely have seen anything at all, after receiving such a blow. Does it not strike you as being still more likely that, partially blinded as he was, and being unwilling to strike the magistrate in return, however much the latter had forfeited all claim to respect, he closed with him, and in the heat of passion lifted him up and carried him along at random?"

"I think that very likely," the Captain replied.

"Had you yourself been struck as the prisoner was struck, Captain Downes, what course do you think it would have been proper for you to pursue?"

"I don't know what would have been proper, but I know what I should have done. Magistrate or no magistrate, I should have knocked my assailant down, or at any rate I should have tried to."

"As a naval man, Captain Downes, you have had some experience of the conduct gentlemen generally observe to their prisoners. I presume that it is not their custom to strike them, even if they did make a somewhat free use of their tongues?"

"Certainly not," Captain Downes said emphatically.

"Would you go so far as to say that you would consider it to be a disgraceful and cowardly act?"

"I should so consider it."

There was again a murmur of applause in court, which was instantly arrested when Mr. Probert held up his hand deprecatingly. "Thank you, Captain Downes," he went on. "Now we come to the question of the quarrel that gave rise to this affair. Mr. Faulkner has not thought fit to ask you any questions about it. Were you standing close enough to hear what passed?"

"I was standing close by, and both Mr. Faulkner and the prisoner spoke loudly enough to be heard at such a distance."

"The magistrate first began the conversation?"

"He did."

"He used very strong language, did he not?"

"Very strong."

"Did you think that he was justified in using such strong language?"

"Certainly not; I thought that it was most improper."

"And do you think that a gentleman accosted so improperly is to be greatly blamed if he uses strong language in return?"

"It would no doubt have been better if he had held his tongue at the time, and have called him to account afterwards."

"Still the provocation was very strong, Captain Downes, and you could not altogether blame him."

"I did not blame him at all," the witness said curtly.

"And what did you think when Mr. Faulkner suddenly struck his prisoner in the face?"

"Am I to answer that question?" the witness asked the bench.

"I do not think that it is an improper question," the chairman replied.

"Very well, sir. Then, if I must say it, I thought it was one of the most blackguardly and cowardly things I ever saw done."

"Thank you, Captain Downes. I do not think it necessary to ask you any further questions."

"Have you any more witnesses to call, Mr. Faulkner?" the chairman asked coldly.

Mr. Faulkner's face was white with rage. "I have a dozen other witnesses," he said hoarsely, "but I have no doubt they will all follow the lead their officer has set them. I shall therefore call no more."

"I do not think, your worships," Mr. Probert said, rising, "that it is necessary for me to address you. I would only submit to you that there is not a shadow of evidence to support the charge of an attempt to murder. As to the abusive language, I cannot say that my client's words were a retort courteous, but they were only a retort natural, and were simply the consequence of the extraordinary conduct of Mr. Faulkner, acting at the time in his capacity of magistrate. As to the charge of threatening language, it is altogether absurd. My client simply asserted what is true by common report—that Mr. Faulkner had been threatened, and that it was possible that those threats might some day or other be carried into effect. I have only, therefore, to leave the case in the hands of your worships."

The two magistrates put their heads together for a short time. Then the chairman said: "The bench is of opinion that the charge of attempted murder is altogether without foundation, and that of abusive language and the use of threats should never have been brought, seeing that they were the result of what we cannot but consider the very ill-judged and improper conduct of the plaintiff. You are therefore discharged, Mr. Wyatt; but my colleague and myself cannot but again express a hope that this and the preceding charge may prove a lesson to you to avoid taking part, even as a spectator, in such breaches of the law as those which led to this very regrettable occurrence."

As the magistrate concluded, a roar of applause rose in the court. In vain the constables shouted for silence. The chairman at once ordered the room to be cleared, and at the same time motioned to Julian not to leave the court, as he was preparing to do. When the court was cleared, he called Julian up to him.

"I think, Mr. Wyatt," he said, "it would be as well for you to remain here for a time, and then go out by the back way. It would be very unfortunate if any demonstration took place. Enough harm has been done already; do not let us make it any worse."

"Certainly not, sir. I am heartily sorry for what has occurred;" and beckoning to Frank, who was still seated at the solicitors' table, he retired with him to a waiting-room.

"Thank goodness, Julian, you have got out of that scrape!"

"Thank goodness, indeed, Frank! I behaved like an awful fool, but I never dreamt that anything like this would come of it. I have been to see cargoes run several times. It was very good fun. I never helped in any way, and had always made up my mind that I would make myself scarce if the revenue people should turn up, but it all happened so suddenly that I was a prisoner before I knew what was going on. As to the other affair, no doubt it would have been better for me to have said nothing, but of course I knew that he had no right to say what he did, and I had not the least idea that he would hit me; when he did, I went at him in a fury, and I don't mind acknowledging that I did intend to chuck him in the fire— not with any idea of killing him, you know, though I did think he would be burnt a bit."

"It was lucky you sent for Probert, Julian; I had never thought of it."

"No more did I, Frank. I was perfectly astonished when he got up and said that he appeared for me, but I supposed that Aunt or you had sent for him."

"I am sure Aunt didn't, or she would have told me."

"I should not be surprised, Frank, if it were Captain Downes. In the first place, he was a friend of Father's, and in the next place, because he is heartily sick of Faulkner's constant interference and the way he goes on. I expect that if Mr. Moorsby had got up he would have said just the same things."

"I will leave you here for a few minutes, Julian. I must run round and tell Aunt; she is in a fearful stew about you."

Frank ran out at the main entrance. A number of fishermen were hanging about outside. Bill came up to him:

"Isn't Mr. Julian coming out, Master Frank?"

"Not at present. The magistrates don't want any fuss in the streets, no more does my brother, and he will stay there till everyone has cleared off, so the best thing you can do, Bill, is to persuade the others to go off home. Julian knows well enough that you are all pleased that he has got off, but you see if there were a fuss got up about it in the streets it would do him harm and not good."

"All right, sir, I will get them off. They just wanted to give him a cheer."

"Well, they did that in Court, Bill, and you know that he appreciates their good intentions. Well, I must be off."

Mrs. Troutbeck was still on the watch. However, she did not come to the door. Frank opened it, and ran into the parlour. His Aunt had dropped into a chair, with her handkerchief to her eyes.

"So he has not come back with you, Frank. It is dreadful. What are they going to do with him?"

"They are not going to do anything, Aunt. He has been acquitted. Only he did not come home with me because there are a lot of sailors waiting outside to cheer him, and the magistrates did not want a row over him, nor did Julian either. I have just run home to tell you that it is all right, and now I am going back for him. I expect by the time I get there they will all have gone, and we may be home in a quarter of an hour, so I think, Aunt, the best thing you can do is to get tea ready, for I don't expect he has had much to eat there, or any appetite to eat it."

It was good advice, for Mrs. Troutbeck was on the point of going into hysterics from joy and relief. However, the thought of the necessity for getting a good meal to welcome Julian on his arrival turned her thoughts into another channel, and, wiping her eyes hastily, she rose and gave directions, while Frank started again for the court-house. The fishermen had left, but there were still a number of boys about the place. The private entrance was, however, free from observers, and the brothers started at once, keeping to the back streets until they neared the house.

"My dear Julian," Mrs. Troutbeck exclaimed as she threw her arms round his neck, "what a relief it is to have you back again! It has been terrible for you."

"It hasn't been very pleasant, Aunt," he replied cheerfully, "but it is all right now, and certainly I ought not to grumble. I have had better luck than I deserved. I was a fool to go there, but I did not think that there was any real chance of the revenue people coming down upon us. It was thought they had been thrown off the scent altogether."

"What a dreadful face you have got, Julian!"

"Oh, that is nothing, Aunt! it will go off in a few days, and until it has I must either stay indoors or keep out of the town altogether."

"I am afraid tea won't be ready for a few minutes, Julian. You see I have had such a very short notice."

"I can hold on comfortably, Aunt; besides, I have got to have a change and a wash. That is of more importance than tea just at present."

After the meal was over, Frank gave the details of the examination, the narrative being very frequently stopped by exclamations and questions on the part of Mrs. Troutbeck.

"I have never heard of such a wicked thing. The idea of that man charging you with attempting to murder him! Julian, he ought to be punished for it."

"I fancy he has been punished, Aunt. I don't see how he is to keep his commission as a justice after what was said in court. Still, it is a bad thing for me. I was discharged, but it will always be against me. If I ever get into any sort of trouble again, people will say: 'Ah! yes; he was charged with attempting murder when he was a young fellow, and although he was lucky enough to get off then, there must have been something in it. He is evidently a man of ungovernable temper.'"

"But, my dear Julian, everyone knows that you have a very sweet temper."

"I was not in a sweet temper then at any rate, Aunt."

"Of course not, Julian. I should not have been so myself if anyone had hit me such a terrible blow as that in the face."

Her nephews both laughed, for they had never seen her ruffled out of her usual serenity.

"Well, Aunt, don't let us talk any more about it," Julian said. "I would give a good deal if it hadn't happened. As it is, one must make the best of it, and I hope that it will be forgotten in time. I wish now that I had gone into the army, but it is too late for that. I shall think over what I had best take to. I should certainly like to get away from here until it has blown over altogether."

On the following morning Frank met Captain Downes, and learned that he was right in his conjecture, and that it was he who had retained Mr. Probert's services in Julian's behalf before the magistrates.

For the next few days Julian kept in the house, except that after nightfall he went out for a long walk. The report of the proceedings in the court had caused a great sensation in Weymouth, and the feeling was so strong against Mr. Faulkner that he was hooted in the streets when he rode into the town. The general expectation was that he would resign his position on the bench; and when at the end of a week he did not do so, a private meeting of the other magistrates was held, and it was whispered in the town that a report of the proceedings at the court had been sent to the Home Secretary, with an expression of opinion that Mr. Faulkner's brother magistrates felt that they could not sit again with him on the bench after what had taken place.

Ten days after the affair Julian started early one morning for a day's rabbit-shooting at the house of a friend who lived some six miles up the valley. Some snow fell in the course of the afternoon and put a stop to shooting, and he started to walk home. When he was within a few hundred yards of Mr. Faulkner's place he heard a horse coming along behind him. The snow that had fallen had deadened the sounds of the hoofs on the road, and, looking round, he saw Mr. Faulkner riding fast, at a distance of but fifty yards away. Had he caught sight of him sooner Julian would have left the road and entered the wood to avoid him, but it was too late now, and he hoped that at any rate the man would pass on without speaking. The horseman had apparently not recognized Julian until he came abreast of him, when, with a sudden exclamation, he reined in his horse.

"So it is you, Julian Wyatt?" he said, in a tone of suppressed fury.

"It is I, Mr. Faulkner," Julian replied quietly; "and as I don't want to have anything to say to you, I think that you had better go on your way without interfering with me."

"Mark my words, you young scoundrel, I will be even with you yet."

"The debt is not all on your side, Mr. Faulkner. I, too, have got a debt to pay; and perhaps some day we may square matters up, when you have not got a score of coast-guardsmen at your back. However, I am content to leave matters as they are so long as you do the same. As to your owing a debt to me, it is yourself you have to thank for the trouble you have got into; it was no doing of mine. However, I warn you that you had better abstain from insulting me again. I did not strike you back when you hit me last time, but if you call me scoundrel again you shall see that I can hit as hard as you can, and I will teach you to keep a civil tongue in your head."

"You mark my words," Mr. Faulkner repeated. "I will have you watched, and I will hunt you down, and if I am not mistaken I will put a rope round your neck one of these days." So saying, he struck spurs into his horse and galloped on.

Julian stood looking after him until he saw him turn in at his gate. The drive to the house led, as he knew, diagonally through the wood, and as he walked forward he heard the horse's galloping hoofs grow louder and louder. Suddenly there was the report of a gun some seventy or eighty yards away. It was mingled with that of a sudden cry, and Julian heard the horse galloping on even faster than before. With an exclamation of "Good heavens! something has happened!" he broke through the hedge and ran in the direction of the sound. As he approached it he thought that he caught sight of a man running through the trees, but he kept straight on until he came upon the drive. Twenty yards away Mr. Faulkner lay stretched on the ground. He went up to him, and stooped over him. His eyes were closed, and as he lay on his back Julian saw blood oozing through a bullet-hole in his coat high up on the left side of the chest.

Feeling sure that Mr. Faulkner was dead he started up, and without a moment's hesitation ran into the wood again, in the direction where he had thought that he had seen a figure. A minute later he came upon some footprints on a bare spot between the trees, where the snow had fallen lightly. Noting the direction they took, he followed at once. He saw no more signs of footprints, but followed the direction as nearly as he could until he came to the farthest side of the wood; then he leaped out into the field beyond, and followed the edge of the wood until he again reached the road. He then turned and went back again, and fifty yards from the point where he had first run out he came upon the footprints again.

"He was going to take to the hills," he muttered, as he set off along the track. He ran at a trot, and as he went, loaded both barrels of his gun. "Very likely the villain will show fight," he said to himself; "I must take him by surprise if I can."

After a quarter of a mile's run he reached the foot of the hill, and near its crest, three quarters of a mile away, caught sight of the figure of a man. A moment later he had passed over the crest. Julian started at full speed up the hill.

There was no need to follow the footprints now; indeed the strong wind that was blowing had swept the snow into the hollows, and the face of the hill was bare. When he reached the top of the hill he had decreased his distance considerably. He saw to his surprise that the man was bearing to the right, a course that would ere long bring him to the edge of the cliff. The run up the hill had left him breathless, and for some time the man, who was also running, fully maintained his lead. Then Julian began to gain upon him. The man had again changed his course, and was now going parallel with the line of cliffs. Three miles from the point where he had reached the top Julian was within a quarter of a mile of him. He would have caught him before this, had he not been obliged at times to make detours so as to avoid passing high ground, where the man, if he looked back, would have perceived him. By this time he was almost sure that the fugitive was a poacher, who had been recently released from a term of two years in prison for poaching in Mr. Faulkner's preserves. At last he saw him turn sharp to the right again. "Where on earth is he going?" Julian said to himself. "The cliffs are not many hundred yards away."

Hitherto he had supposed that the man was keeping away from the cliff to avoid meeting any of the coast-guards who would be on duty there, but this change of direction puzzled him completely. Keeping his eye on the poacher, he saw him enter a small clump of bushes, from which he did not emerge. Julian at once slackened his pace down to a walk. It was likely enough that the man had noticed that he was being pursued, and had determined to rid himself of the pursuer. It was not a pleasant idea, that the fellow might now be kneeling among the bushes with his gun at his shoulder.

"It could hardly be that either," he said to himself, "for

if he intended to shoot me he would have turned the other way; for the sound of his gun would be probably heard by some of the coast-guard, and they could not fail to see him running away. At any rate," he muttered, "I am not going to turn back after such a chase as I have had."

Standing still and looking at the spot, he saw that the clump of bushes grew in a slight hollow, and that by turning to the right he would be able to approach within twenty or thirty yards of it without exposing himself to view. This he did, and in a short time lost sight of the bushes. Moving with great caution, he made his way towards them, and when he approached the slope into the hollow, lay down and crawled along, keeping his gun in front of him. As he neared the spot he lay down on his stomach in the short turf and wound himself along until he could see down into the bushes. With his gun at his shoulder, and his finger on the trigger, he gazed down into the hollow. To his surprise he could see no signs of the fugitive. The leafless boughs afforded but slight shelter, and after gazing fixedly at them for two or three minutes, he became convinced that the man was no longer there. As soon as he came to this conclusion he stood up and looked over the surrounding country. It was bleak and bare, and entirely destitute of hedges or any other shelter.

It was but for five or six minutes at the utmost that he had lost sight of the bushes, and in that time the man could not have got far. "Where on earth has he hidden himself?" Julian muttered.

He went down to the clump of bushes, still holding his gun in readiness for instant use. The patch was but some thirty feet long by half as wide. He walked backwards and forwards among the low bushes, but the fugitive was certainly not there. Going to the end of the patch he could see plainly enough the track where the man had entered, for although there was little snow on the top of the ground it lay among the tufts of grass. He walked round the clump, but there were no signs of any footsteps leaving it. "This is the rummest thing I ever saw," he muttered; "the fellow can't have flown away; yet, he certainly has not walked off."

Thinking it over, an idea suddenly occurred to him. When sailing along the coast with Bill, the latter had one day pointed out to him a hole in the cliff some twenty feet above high-water mark. "Do you see that hole, Mr. Julian?"

"Yes, I see it plain enough. What of it?"

"Well, sir, if I owned all the goods that have been taken into that hole on dark still nights I should be a rich man."

"Do you mean to say that they run cargoes there, Bill?"

"Not kegs—they are too heavy and too awkward to get away—but laces, and silks, and such like. Many a lugger when she comes from abroad lands all them sorts of things here, and then sails away and takes her chance of running the rest of the cargo somewhere else."

"But how can anyone get up there? I see nothing like a path."

"There ain't no path, sir. The revenue men would have found it out long ago if there had been. The boat comes along, as I said, of a dark night, when there is no swell on, and the chaps inside show a tiny light to guide them to the spot. When the boat comes, they lower a rope down and haul the bales up; and then the boat goes back to the lugger, and she ups sail, and no one is the wiser."

"But what do they do with the stuff? I don't mean, where do they stow it, but how do they get it away?"

"There is a passage somewhere," Bill replied. "I don't know where it goes out. I reckon there ain't half a dozen men in Weymouth who do know. I should say, except the men whose business it is to take the goods inland and forward them to London, there is only one chap who is in the secret; and he is not in Weymouth now—he is in jail. That is Joe Markham. He is in for poaching. But for a good many years he sailed in one of those French luggers. Then, as I have heard, he was keeper of the cave for a bit; but he had to give it up—he was too well known to the coast-guard, and they kept too sharp an eye on him for him to venture to go out. He had had enough of the sea, and no doubt he had got some money laid by; anyhow, he took a cottage by the river, and took to poaching, more for devilment, I should say, than because he wanted the money. I expect he was well paid by the smugglers, for he used to get up half the stories to put them off the scent, and never missed being present when a run was made."

This conversation came back to Julian's memory, as he stood by the clump of bushes wondering what had become of the man that he had pursued, and it flashed upon him that the spot where he was standing could not be far from the smugglers' cavern, and that the entrance to this might very well be among these bushes. The man knew where that entrance was, and nothing was more likely than that he should make for it as a place of concealment until an opportunity occurred to get on board a lugger and cross the channel. It was a very likely place; men could come and go at night without risk of being seen or heard by any of the coast-guardsmen on the cliff, and would not be likely to encounter anyone within two or three miles of it. Years might pass without anyone happening to enter the bushes.

Laying down his gun, Julian began to search in earnest. It was half an hour before, feeling about in the coarse grass, he came upon a handle. He pulled at it, gently at first, then as it did not yield, he exerted his strength, and it gave way, and a section of the rough herbage rose, while three feet away it sank in the same porportion. Raising it higher, he saw that the trap-door—for such it was—was two feet wide by about five feet long and eighteen inches deep; it was, in fact, a deep tray pivoted on the centre and filled with earth, on which grass grew as freely as in the ground adjoining.

The greater portion of the trap was overhung by bushes, which grew so thickly round the part which sank that the probability was small indeed that anyone would tread upon it. Julian saw, too, that under the handle was a bolt that, when fastened, would hold the trap firmly down. No doubt the man in his haste had forgotten to fasten it before he descended. Looking down, Julian saw a circular hole like a well, evidently artificially made in the chalk; a ladder was fastened against one side.

Julian hesitated. Should he return to Weymouth, inform the authorities that he had traced the murderer of Mr. Faulkner to a place of concealment, and bring them there to arrest him, or should he go down and encounter him single-handed? Although of a fearless disposition, he would have decided on the more prudent course had it not been that to have done so, would have let the authorities into the knowledge of the smugglers' cave. Although he had determined to have nothing more to do with them, this he felt would be an act of treachery, for it was only because he had been believed by Bill to be absolutely trustworthy, that the latter had told him of the existence of this cavern and of the secret exit, and without that information he would never have searched for and discovered the trap-door. Then, too, the thought that the credit he would gain by the capture of the murderer single-handed would go far to efface the memory of the disgrace that had befallen him, helped to decide him.

He fetched his gun and slung it over his shoulder, got upon the ladder, and pulled the trap-door down behind him.

JULIAN FINDS HIMSELF A PRISONER AMONG THE SMUGGLERS

As he did so he found that it moved easily, and that he could push it up again without any difficulty, and feeling the bolt, discovered that it had been partially shot, but not sufficiently to catch fairly, although containing so far a hold of the frame, that it had torn a groove in the somewhat rotten wood with the force that he had used to raise it. He went down the ladder very cautiously, until, after descending for some thirty steps, his foot encountered solid ground. After a moment's consideration he knelt down and proceeded on his hands and knees. Almost immediately he felt the ground slope away in front of him. He got on to his feet again. Holding out his arms he found that the passage was about four feet wide, and he began to descend with extreme care, feeling his way along both walls. He had gone, he thought, about fifty yards when the passage made a sharp turn, still descending, and at a considerable distance ahead the light streamed in through a rugged hole. He walked more confidently now, and soon the light was sufficient to enable him to see the path he was following.

On arriving at the aperture, he saw that, as he expected, he was looking over the sea. On one side of the hole there was a shelf cut in the chalk. This was stained as if by oil, and he guessed at once that it was a look-out and a spot for signalling a craft in the offing. The path here turned again and ran parallel with the face of the cliff. There was no occasion to exercise care in walking now, as here and there the light streamed in through openings a few inches long. He now unslung his gun, stooped and took off his boots, and then proceeded noiselessly. The descent was considerable, and in some places steps had been cut. At last he arrived at a door. It was roughly but very solidly made, and would doubtless sustain an attack for some time before it yielded, and so would give time to the occupants, in case the trap-door was discovered, to make their escape by the lower entrance on to the beach. There was a latch to it. Lifting this quietly, he found the door yielded, and, holding his gun in his right hand ready to cover the fugitive the moment he entered, Julian threw the door wide open and sprang forward.

He had not calculated on a further descent, but the floor of the cave was five feet below him, and he fell heavily upon it, the gun going off as it struck the floor. Instantaneous as the fall had been, his eyes had taken in the scene. Several lanterns faintly lit up the cave; while in the centre a table, at which several figures were sitting, was illuminated by three or four candles. He was partly stunned by the heaviness of his fall, but vaguely heard shouts of surprise and alarm, and was, a minute later, roughly seized and dragged along. Then he felt that he was being tightly bound. For some minutes he was left to himself, but he could see three men with guns in their hands standing near the door by which he had entered, listening attentively. Presently he heard steps coming down the passage and two other men came through the door, shut and bolted it carefully, and then came down the steps into the cabin.

They spoke to their comrades as they came in, and the news was evidently satisfactory, for the men leaned their guns against the wall and came to the table. There was some talk for a few minutes, and then Julian was raised and placed in a sitting position on the head of a cask by the table. One of the men then addressed him in French. Julian, who by this time had recovered from the effects of his fall, shook his head. The other then spoke to the poacher, who had seated himself opposite Julian, and the latter then said:

"You are the young fellow who was tried in court three weeks ago, are you not?"

"Yes, I am."

"I thought so; I was there. It was the very day I got to Weymouth. Well, what the deuce are you doing here? You are the chap who has followed me all the way up the hill?"

Julian nodded.

"What did you follow me for?"

"Because I was in the road when you shot Faulkner. I heard the gun, and ran in and found him dead. I caught sight of you in the wood, and went in chase of you."

"What did you intend to do, you young fool?"

"I intended to capture you," Julian said fearlessly.

"What for? I have done you a good service as well as myself. You had no reason to bear him any good-will, and some of the men who were there told me that though Downes got you off, it was true that you were going to throw Faulkner into the fire."

"So I was; but he had just struck me and I was in a furious passion; but that was a different thing altogether to shooting a man in cold blood."

"He got me two years' imprisonment," the man said, "which to my mind was a good reason for shooting him when I got the chance; and another thing was, he would never leave us alone, but was always on our heels. There are two or three men in prison now that he got sent there, and eight more are waiting their trial. He made war on us, and I have turned the tables on him.

"I heard that you had been at several of the runs, and of course you are in with some of our fellows. How did you get to know about the entrance to this place?"

"I only knew that there was a cave here, that it was used by the smugglers, and that it had an entrance somewhere. The man who told me knew well that I was to be trusted, but it was only because you disappeared among those bushes, and that there were no footprints to show that you had left them, that it appeared to me that the passage might be there, and so I looked about until I found a handle to the trap-door."

"Why didn't you go and call the coast-guard? There was a station not a quarter of a mile away."

"Because I could not have done that without betraying the secret of the cavern. I found the entrance myself, but I should never have done so, if I had not been told about the cave and the secret passage, and I felt that it would be an act of treachery to betray it."

"And you were really fool enough to think that if you captured me single-handed I should walk with you like a lamb to the gallows?"

"I didn't intend to give you a chance of making a fight. I intended to rush straight in and cover you with my gun."

"Well, you have plenty of pluck, young fellow, if you haven't much wisdom; but if you think that after getting in here, I shall let you go out again to bring the constables down on me you are mistaken altogether."

CHAPTER IV.

THE SMUGGLER'S CAVE.

JOE MARKHAM had, as soon as he arrived, told the French smugglers that he had shot the magistrate who had for the last five or six years given them so much trouble and caused them so much loss, and who had, as the last affair showed, become more dangerous than ever, as he could only have obtained information as to the exact point of landing by having bribed someone connected with them.

"It was a case of his life or our business," he said. "If he had not been got out of the way we must have given up the trade altogether on this part of the coast; besides, he has been the cause, not only of several seizures of cargoes, but of the death of eight or ten of our comrades and of the imprisonment of many others. Now that he is out of the way we shall find things a great deal easier."

"It served him right," the leader of the party said, "and you have rendered good service; but what are you going to do? Do you think that any suspicion will fall upon you?"

"Yes; I have put myself in an awkward position, I am afraid. I thought that the job had been so well managed that it could never be traced to me, but when I got up to the top of the hill I saw a fellow just starting from the bottom. I did not think much of it at the time, but he came up so quickly after me that he must have run all the way up. He has chased me hard, and as he got nearer I could see that he had a gun too. He was not more than a quarter of a mile away when I got to the trap-door."

"Why didn't you hide yourself in the bushes and put a bullet into him, Markham?"

"For several reasons. In the first place, the gun might have been heard by some of those cussed revenue men. Then there would be an inquiry and a search. They would have seen by the direction he had been going, that he must have been shot from the bushes, and as no one would have been in sight when they ran up, the thing would have been such a puzzle to them that you may be sure they would have suspected there must be some hidden way out of the clump. Besides, they would probably have hunted every inch of the ground to see if they could find anything that would give them a clue as to who had fired the shot. That is one reason."

"And quite good enough without any others," the Frenchman said.

"Well, there was another one that went for almost as much with me. I shot down Faulkner because he was a curse to us all. He had imprisoned several of my pals, and done a lot of damage to the trade, and was likely to break it up altogether, besides which I had a big grudge against him on my own account. But I should not have liked to shoot down this fellow in cold blood. I had no feeling against him; he has done me no harm; I did not even know who he was. If he had overtaken me in the open, you may be sure that I should have made a fight of it, for it would have been my life against his. I don't pretend to be soft; there is little enough of that about me, and I have fought hard several times in the old days when we were surprised; but I could not have shot down that fellow without giving him a chance of his life. If there had not been the trap-door to escape by I should have stood up, given him fair warning, and fought it out man to man. As it was—" at this point the conversation had been arrested by the sudden entrance of Julian.

"Who is he?" the chief of the smugglers asked Joe when he had finished his conversation with the prisoner. "Is he a spy?"

"No; he is a young chap as lives down in the town. He is a pal of some of our friends there, and has been with them at the landings of goods. He was caught in that last affair, but got off because they could not prove that he was actually engaged in the business. He is an enemy of Faulkner's too; they had a row there, and Faulkner hit him in the face. You can see the mark still; and he would have thrown Faulkner on to the bonfire they had lit if he had not been prevented by some of the coast-guards. It is through what he had heard from our friends of this cavern, and there being an entrance to it somewhere, that he came to look for the trap-door. I certainly pushed the bolt forward when I came down, but I was in a hurry, so I suppose it could not have caught rightly."

"Well, what is to be done, Joe?"

"I don't know. You see he knows about my shooting Faulkner. I would trust him not to peach about this cavern or the trap-door, but I don't know as I would about the other thing. It seems to me that he is just as likely to be suspected of having a hand in it as I am. His row with Faulkner is the talk of the place, and when Faulkner is found with a bullet in him, he will be the first fellow to be suspected. Well, if that was so, and you see he would not be able to account for himself for three or four hours afterwards, he might be driven to peach on me to save his own life, and he would be obliged to give all the story about following me and coming down here. There would be an end of the best hiding-place in the country, and I should not be able to show my face on this side of the Channel again."

"I should say the safest plan would be to cut his throat and chuck him into the sea, and have done with it."

"No, I won't have that," the poacher said positively. "Your lugger will be in to-night, and we will take him across with us to France."

"That is all very well," one of the men said; "but what is to prevent his coming back again?"

"We could prevent it somehow or other. We could get up a tale that he was an English sailor we had picked up at sea, and hand him over to the authorities, and tell them his story was, that he had fallen overboard from an English ship of war. Then they would send him away to some place in the interior where they keep English prisoners of war, and there he might lie for years; perhaps never get back again. He does not know a word of French, as you saw when you spoke to him, so he can't contradict any story we may tell, and if by chance any questions should be asked, I can just say what suits us."

"He might ruin us all if he came back," the smuggler growled.

"It ain't likely that he will come back," the poacher said. "I have heard that they die off like flies in those prisons of yours; and, besides, I will guarantee, if he does, he will never split about this place. He is a gentleman, and I will get him to swear to me, and you may be sure he will not break his oath."

"But how about yourself?"

"Well, as he won't come back for some years, I will take my chance of that. He has got no evidence against me; it would be his word against mine. He would tell his story and I should tell mine, and mine would be the most likely. I should say I met him on the hills with his gun, and, knowing who I was, and what cause I had got to hate Faulkner, he told me that he had shot him, and asked me to get him on board a smuggler craft and across the Channel, and that I had done so: and that is all I should know about it. No, I am not afraid of anything he might say when he comes back again."

Julian had watched the speakers anxiously during this conversation. He was wholly ignorant of French, but from the tone and manner of the speakers, he gathered that the poacher was speaking in his favour. He had expected no mercy; his life was nothing to these French smugglers; and he was surprised to find the man, whose life he thought he held in his hand if released, apparently pleading his cause.

"Look here, young fellow!" the poacher said, turning towards him. "In the first place, these men are afraid that you may betray the existence of this place, and their opinion is that the best thing to make us safe would be to cut your throat and throw you out of the mouth of the cave into the sea. I told them that you knew of the cave from one of our friends, and could be trusted to keep the secret; at any rate they demand, in the first place, that you shall take an oath never to split about it."

"I will do that willingly enough," Julian said, with a great feeling of relief.

Joe Markham then dictated a terrible oath, which had been always taken by all those made acquainted with the existence of the cave, and this Julian repeated after him. The poacher then told the smugglers what Julian had sworn to.

"Now, young fellow, I may tell you that we are going to take you over to France to-night. You may think I shall be asking you to take another oath, like that, not to say anything against me, but I ain't going to. I shot the man, and I don't pretend to be sorry for it. He was a hard, bad chap, and he got what he deserved. I owed him a long score, not only for myself, but for others, and if I had not shot him, someone else would have done so sooner or later. I shall do what I can to prevent you coming back here, though I don't think you will say anything against me when you do come back. In the first place, like enough I shall take to the sea again, and may be settled in France before you return. In the next place, I may be dead; and, most of all, you have got no evidence against me. If I were here, and you told the story, of course I should say that it was a lie, and that you had shot the man yourself, and I had got you out of the way by sending you across to France in a lugger, so I think you will see that it is best to keep a quiet tongue in your head; anyhow I am ready to take my chance of it."

"They will be horribly alarmed when I don't get home to-night," Julian said.

"Well, they must be alarmed," the poacher said carelessly. "You have interfered in this business, which was none of yours, and you have got to take the consequences; you may think yourself a lucky fellow that you are not by this time drifting about on the tideway."

"I feel that," Julian said; "and though I did not understand a word of what you said, I am sure that it was owing to you that I am not there. I could not have promised that I would never say a word to anyone about you, because one can never tell how one may be placed; but, after what you have done, I think that I can safely promise that I will never go out of my way to denounce you."

"I don't want any promise about it," the poacher replied. "I had made up my mind to leave Weymouth, for, after having been in jail two years, I shall always have the constables as well as the revenue men keeping their eye on me, so I had intended all along to take to the lugger again, and live on board her as I did before, and I only stayed here until I could settle accounts with Faulkner. I have no doubt that they will suspect me of this business. There are plenty of men who know that I had sworn to be even with him, and my disappearance is sure to be put down to that. Now, in the next place, will you promise not to try to escape, because if you do, I will get them to take these ropes off you? I dare say you have been thinking that if you could get free you would make a run for the mouth of the cave and dive in, for it is about high-water now."

Julian had, in fact, been thinking so, but as he saw that unless he gave his promise he would have to remain in the cords that were cutting into his wrists, he at once took the required oath. Joe told the Frenchmen, and they then unfastened Julian's cords.

"We may as well carry up the bales at once," their leader said, "before it gets dark. It it no use giving anyone at sea a chance of seeing a light. Tell him to take one and come up with us. I am not going to leave him here by himself, promise or no promise."

The poacher translated the order to Julian. Some bales were taken out from beneath a tarpaulin at the end of the cave, and, each shouldering one, they proceeded up the passage until they reached the foot of the ladder. Here they laid the bales down, and then returned to the cave.

"Is that all?" Julian asked.

"Yes, those bales are worth a lot of money. There is fifteen hundred pounds worth of lace in one of them. The others are silks and satins, and worth another five hundred. To-night, when we hear the signal, I and three of the Frenchmen will go up. We shall find two men there, and shall carry the bales to a place a mile and a half away, where they will be hidden until it is convenient to send them up to London, or wherever they are going to dispose of them— that is their business; ours is finished when they hand us over the money for them. They will come at eight o'clock, and at ten the lugger will be off the coast here and send a boat ashore for us. So you have got five or six hours yet, and I should say the best thing you can do is to turn in and sleep till then. There are plenty of blankets in that corner and a pile of sheep-skins that you can sleep on."

Julian nodded, threw two or three of the sheep-skins down in a corner, rolled another up for a pillow, drew a blanket over him, and for the first time looked round the cave. It was lighted only by a small hole used as a lookout; at present a blanket hung before this. There was a door similar to that by which he had entered from above leading to the lower cave. How far that lower entrance might be below them Julian had no means of knowing, but from the view he had obtained of the sea through a large loophole he had passed in his descent, he did not think

that the cavern he was in could be less than seventy or
eighty feet above the water. The sole ventilation, as far as
he could see, was the current of air that found its way in
through the door from below, and passed up through that
above, and what could come in through the loop-hole sea-
wards. Doubtless in warmer weather both the doors stood
open, but were now closed more for warmth than for any
other purpose, although he had noticed that the lower one
had been bolted and locked after he had been first captured.

As he lay down he wondered how it was all going to end.
His position was at once perilous and uncertain. He had,
so far, escaped better than he could have expected, for from
the looks the Frenchmen had given him, he had no doubt
what his fate would have been had not the man he had been
chasing spoken in his favour. His life therefore seemed
for the present safe, but the future was very dark. The
poacher had spoken as if he was not likely to return for
some years. They surely could not intend to keep him on
board ship all that time. Could they mean to put him upon
some vessel sailing abroad? What a way Frank and his
aunt would be in! They would learn that he had started
for home early in the afternoon, and it would be absolutely
certain that he could not have strayed from the road nor
met with any accident coming along the valley. It would
certainly be awkward his being missed on the same day
Faulkner had been shot, especially as, according to the time
he had started for home, he would have come along the road
somewhere about the time the magistrate was shot.

It was a horrible thought that suspicion might fall upon
him. Those who knew him would be sure that he could
have had nothing whatever to do with the murder; still,
the more he thought of it the more he felt that suspicions
were certain to rise, and that he would find it extremely
difficult to explain matters on his return. The memory of

his quarrel with the magistrate was fresh in everybody's mind, and even his friends might well consider it singular that his words to Faulkner should so soon have been carried into effect. It is true that Joe Markham would be missing too, and that the man's own acquaintances would have no great difficulty in guessing that he had carried out his threats against Faulkner, but they would certainly not communicate their opinion to the constables, and the latter might not think of the man in connection with the murder, nor notice that he was no longer to be seen about the town.

Even were he himself free to leave the cave now and return to Weymouth, he would find himself in a most awkward position. There was, of course, no shadow of evidence against him save that he was known to have quarrelled with Faulkner, and must have been very near the spot the moment he was killed, but how could he explain six or seven hours' absence? He could but say that he had caught sight of a man in the plantation and followed him for miles among the hills, and had lost sight of him at last. He had not a shadow of evidence to produce in confirmation of his story; in fact there was no direct evidence either way. There could be no doubt he would have to remain under a cloud of suspicion. It was bad enough before, but this would be altogether intolerable, and it was perhaps best, after all, that he was to be taken away, and his future decided for him.

He should have gone anyhow, and no doubt he would be able to get some opportunity of writing to Frank and setting his mind at rest as to his safety, and telling him something about what had happened, and that he had been kidnapped and carried over to France. He had acted like a fool, no doubt, but Frank would understand why he had followed his first impulse and gone alone after the man who committed the murder, instead of going to the constables and telling them that some unknown man had killed the magistrate. One thing seemed certain, he should never be able to go back to Weymouth again unless the affair was cleared up, and he did not see how that ever could be.

At this point Julian's thoughts became confused. The voices of the men talking at the table seemed to get further and further away, and then he was conscious of nothing more until he heard a bell tinkle faintly somewhere overhead. There was a movement in the cave, and he sat up. All the men went out by the upper door. When they had left he got up and went to see if the lower door was so fastened that he could not open it. He had no idea of breaking his word, but did so out of curiosity rather than from any other feeling. He found that the bolts could be pulled back, but that the lock was a very strong one, and the jamb was, at the point where the bolt shot into it, covered with a piece of iron, so that no instrument could be used for forcing back the bolt.

"It may be," he thought, "that some other prisoner has been confined here at some time or other, or possibly this has been done in order that if the trap-door above should be found, and the revenue men come down that way, the smugglers in their flight might lock the door behind them and so have time to get away in a boat or along at the foot of the cliffs before their pursuers could get down to the lower entrance and open fire upon them."

Then he lay down again. He wondered whether the pull of the bell he had heard could be hidden in the grass like the handle of the trap. It might only be a very small knob, but he had looked so closely among the bushes that he wondered it had escaped him. In three or four minutes the French captain came down again, and walked across to where he was lying:

"*Pauvre diable!*" he muttered, and then went back to the

table, filled himself a glass of spirits and water, and lit his pipe. A moment later a thought seemed to strike him, and he came across to Julian again and touched him. He at once sat up. The Frenchman motioned him to come to the table, went to a cupboard, brought out a wooden platter with a large lump of cold beef and a loaf of bread and some cheese, poured him out a horn of brandy and water, and motioned him to eat. Julian attacked the food vigorously. He had had some lunch with his friends before starting for his walk back to Weymouth, but that had been nearly seven hours before, and his run across the hills in the keen air had given him a sharp appetite, so he did full justice to the food.

"This is not a bad fellow after all," he said to himself, as the smuggler, when he had finished, brought out a box of cigars and placed it before him. "He would have knocked me on the head without compunction, in the way of business; but now when he has concluded that I am not dangerous, he comes out as a good fellow." He nodded pleasantly to the Frenchman as he lit the cigar, which was an excellent one, and far better than any Julian had been accustomed to smoke with his associates in the billiard-room.

The Frenchman's thoughts were not dissimilar to his own. "He is a brave *garçon*," he said to himself, "and makes the best of things. He is a fine-looking fellow, too, and will be a big man in another year or two. It is a misfortune that we have got to take him and shut him up in prison. Why did he mix himself up in this affair of Markham? That is the way with boys. Instead of being grateful to the man that had killed his enemy, he must needs run after him as if he had done him an injury. Well, it can't be helped now; but, at least, I will make him as comfortable as I can as long as he is on board the lugger."

In another half-hour Joe Markham returned with the

French sailors. "There is a big stir down in Weymouth," he said to Julian. "I heard from our friend that the place is like a hive of bees. I tell you, Mr. Wyatt, that it is a lucky thing for you that you found the trap-door and came down here. You mayn't like being our prisoner; but it is a lot better than being in a cell down in Weymouth with a charge of murder hanging over you, which you would have been if you had gone straight back again."

"A charge of murder!" Julian repeated, springing to his feet. "How could such a charge be brought? It could not have been known so soon that I was missing. I must go back and face it. If I run away, now I have been openly accused, everyone will make sure of my guilt."

"Well, sir, I should say it is a sight better that they should suspect you, and you safely over in France, than that they should suspect you with you in their hands; but at any rate, you see you have no choice in the matter. You could only clear yourself by bringing me into it; though I doubt, as things have turned out, that that would help you a bit."

"I warn you that I shall make my escape, and come back again as soon as I can," Julian said passionately.

"Well, sir, if you have a fancy for hanging, of course you can do so; but from what I hear, hanging it would be, as sure as you stand there. There is a warrant out against you, and the constables are scouring all the country."

"But what possible ground can they have to go upon except that smuggling affair?"

"Well, if what our friend told me is true, they have very good grounds, as they think, to go on. He was talking with one of the constables, and he told him that Faulkner is not dead yet, though he ain't expected to last till morning. His servants came out to look for him when the horse came back to the house without him. A man rode into Weymouth for the doctor, and another went to Colonel Chambers and Mr. Harrington. By the time they got there Faulkner was conscious, and they took his dying deposition. He said that he had had a row with you a short distance before he had got to his gate, and that you said you would be even with him. As he was riding up through the wood to his house, he suddenly heard a gun and at the same moment fell from his horse. A minute later you came out from the wood at the point where the shot had been fired. You had a gun in your hand. Feeling sure that your intention was to ascertain if he was done for, and to finish him off if you found that he was not, he shut his eyes and pretended to be dead. You stooped over him, and then made off at full speed. Now, sir, that will be awkward evidence to get over, and you must see that you will be a long way safer in France than you would in Weymouth."

Julian sank down, crushed by the blow. He saw that what the poacher said was true. What would his unsupported assertion go for as against the dying man's deposition? No doubt Faulkner had stated what he believed to be the truth, though he might not have given quite a fair account of what had taken place in the road; still, there would be no cross-examining him as to what had passed there, and his statement would stand unchallenged. As things now stood, Julian's own story that he had pursued a man over the hills, and had lost him, would, wholly unsupported as it was, be received with absolute incredulity. He had been at the spot certainly at the time. He had had words with Faulkner; he had had a gun in his hands; he had come out and leaned over the wounded man within less than a minute of the shot being fired. The chain of evidence against him seemed to be complete, and he sat appalled at the position in which he found himself.

"Look here, youngster," the poacher said, "it is a bad

job, and I don't say it isn't. I am sorry for you, but I ain't so sorry as to go and give myself up and get hung in your place; but I'll tell you what I will do. When I get across to France I will draw up a statement and swear it before a magistrate, giving an account of the whole affair, and I will put it in a tin case and always carry it about with me. I will direct it to Colonel Chambers, and whenever anything happens to me it shall be sent to him. I am five-and-twenty years older than you are, and the life I lead ain't likely to give me old age. To make matters safer, I will have two copies made of my statement—one I will leave in the hands of one of our friends here. The craft I am in may be wrecked some day, or sunk by one of the cutters; anyhow, whichever way it comes, he is certain to hear of my death, and I shall tell him that when he hears of it he is to send that letter to Chambers."

"Thank you," Julian said earnestly. "It may not come for a long time, but it will be something for me to know that some day or other my name will be cleared of this horrible accusation; but I would rather have gone and faced it out now."

"It would be just suicide," the man said. "Weymouth ain't the only place in the world; and it is better for you to live out of it, and know you will get cleared some day, than to get hung, with only the consolation that perhaps twenty years hence they may find out they have made a mistake."

"It isn't so much myself I am thinking of as my brother and aunt. My going away and never sending them a word will be like confessing my guilt. It will ruin my brother's life, and kill my aunt."

"Well, I'll tell you what I will do," Markham said. "You shall write a letter to your brother, and tell him your story, except, of course, about this cave. You can say you followed me, and that I and some smugglers sprang on you and captured you, and have carried you across to France. All the rest you can tell just as it happened. I don't know as it will do me any harm. Your folks may believe it, but no one else is likely to do so. I don't mean to go back to Weymouth again, and if I did, that letter would not be evidence that anyone would send me to trial on. Anyhow, I will risk that."

"Thank you, with all my heart," Julian said gratefully. "I shall not so much mind, if Frank and Aunt get my story. I know that they will believe it if no one else does, and they can move away from Weymouth to some place where it will not follow them. It won't be so hard for me to bear then, especially if some day the truth gets to be known. Only please direct your letters to 'Colonel Chambers, or the Chairman of the Weymouth magistrates', because he is at least ten years older than you are, and might die long before you, and the letter might never be opened if directed only to him."

"Right you are, lad! I will see to that."

Just at this moment one of the sailors came down from the look-out above, and said that the signal had just been made from the offing, and that the lugger's boat would be below in a quarter of an hour. All prepared for departure; the lower door was unbolted, the lights extinguished, and they went down to the lower entrance. It was reached by a staircase cut in the chalk, and coming down into a long and narrow passage, at the further end of which was the opening Julian had seen from the sea. The party gathered at the entrance. In a few minutes a boat with muffled oars approached silently; a rope was lowered, a noose at its upper end being placed over a short iron bar projecting three or four inches from the chalk a foot or two inside the entrance.

The French captain went down first. Julian was told to

follow. The sailors and Markham then descended. A sharp jerk shook the rope off the bar, and the boat then rowed out to the smuggler, which was lying half a mile from shore. As soon as they were on board the sails were sheeted home, and the craft began to steal quietly through the water, towing the boat behind it. The whole operation had been conducted in perfect silence. The men were accustomed to their work; there was no occasion for orders, and it was not until they were another mile out that a word was spoken.

"All has gone off well," the captain then said. "We got the laces and silks safely away, and the money has been paid for them. The revenue cutter started early this morning, and was off Lyme Regis this afternoon, so we shall have a clear run out. We will keep on the course we are laying till we are well beyond the race, and then make for the west. We have sent word for them to be on the look-out for us at the old place near Dartmouth to-morrow night, and if we are not there then, the night after; if there is danger, they are to send up a rocket from the hill inland."

The wind was but light, and keeping a smart look-out for British cruisers, and lowering their sails down once or twice when a suspicious sail was seen in the distance, they approached the rocky shore some two miles east of the entrance to the bay at ten o'clock on the second evening after starting. A lantern was raised twice above the bulwark, kept there for an instant, and then lowered.

"I expect it is all right," the captain said, "or they would have sent up a rocket before this. Half-past eight is the time arranged, and I think we are about off the landing-place. Ah, yes, there is the signal!" he broke off as a light was shown for a moment close down to the water's edge. "Yes, there it is again! Lower the anchor gently; don't let it splash."

A light anchor attached to a hawser was silently let down into the water.

"Now, off with the hatches; get up the kegs."

While some of the men were engaged at this work, others lowered the second boat, and this, and the one towing behind, were brought round to the side. Julian saw that all the men were armed with cutlasses, and had pistols in their belts. Rapidly the kegs were brought up on deck and lowered into the boat.

"Ah, here comes Thompson!" the captain said, as a very small boat rowed up silently out of the darkness. "Well, my friend, is all safe?" he asked in broken English as the boat came alongside.

"Safe enough, captain. Most of the revenue men have gone round from here to the other side of the bay, where they got news, as they thought, that a cargo was going to be run. The man on duty here has been squared, and will be away at the other end of his beat. The carts are ready, a quarter of a mile away. I made you out with my glass just before sunset, and sent round word at once to our friends to be in readiness."

The boats started as soon as their cargoes were on board, and the work went on uninterruptedly for the next two hours, by which time the last keg was on shore, and the boats returned to the lugger. The men were in high spirits. The cargo had been a valuable one, and the whole had been got rid of without interruption. The boats were at once hoisted up, the anchor weighed, and the lugger made her way out to sea.

"What port do you land at?" Julian asked Markham.

"We shall go up the Loire to Nantes," he replied; "she hails from there. To-morrow morning you had best put on that sailor suit I gave you to-day. Unless the wind freshens a good deal we sha'n't be there for three or four days, but

I fancy, from the look of the sky, that it will blow up before morning, and, as likely as not, we shall get more than we want by evening. There is generally a cruiser or two off the mouth of the river. In a light wind we can show them our heels easily enough, but if it is blowing at all their weight tells. I am glad to be at sea again, lad, after being cooped up in that cursed prison for two years. It seems to make a new man of one. I don't know but that I am sorry I shot that fellow. I don't say that he didn't deserve it, for he did; but I don't see it quite so strongly as I did when I was living on bread and water, and with nothing to do but to think of how I could get even with him when I got out; besides, I never calculated upon getting anyone else into a mess, and I am downright sorry that I got you into one, Mr. Wyatt. However, the job is done, and it is no use crying over spilt milk."

Markham's prediction turned out correct. A fresh wind was blowing by the morning, and two days later the lugger was running along, close under the coast, fifteen miles south of the mouth of the Loire, having kept that course in order to avoid any British cruisers that might be off the mouth of the river. Before morning they had passed St. Nazaire, and were running up the Loire.

CHAPTER V.

FOLLOWING A TRAIL.

FRANK had started early for a walk with one of his school friends. Returning through the town at three in the afternoon, he saw people talking in groups. They presently met one of their chums.

"What is going on, Vincent?"

"Why, have you not heard? Faulkner, the magistrate, has been shot."

"Shot!" the two boys exclaimed. "Do you mean on purpose or accidentally?"

"On purpose. The servants heard a gun fired close by, and a minute later his horse galloped up to the door. Two men ran along the drive, and, not a hundred yards from the house, found him lying shot through the body. Three of the doctors went off at once. Thompson came back ten minutes ago, for some instruments, I believe. He stopped his gig for a moment to speak to the Rector, and I hear he told him that it might be as well for him to go up at once, as there was very little probability of Faulkner's living through the night."

"Well, I can't say that I am surprised," Frank said. "He has made himself so disliked, there are so many men who have a grudge against him, and he has been threatened so often, that I have heard fellows say dozens of times he would be shot some day. And yet I suppose no one ever really thought that it would come true; anyhow it is a very bad affair."

Leaving the other two talking together, Frank went on home. Mrs. Troutbeck was greatly shocked at the news.

"Dear, dear!" she said, "what dreadful doings one does hear of. Who would have thought that a gentleman, and a magistrate too, could have been shot in broad daylight within a mile or two of us. I did not know him myself, but I have always heard that he was very much disliked, and it is awful to think that he has been taken away like this."

"Well, Aunt, I don't pretend to be either surprised or shocked. If a man spends his life in going out of his way to hunt others down, he must not be surprised if at last one of them turns on him. On the bench he was hated; it was not only because he was severe, but because of his bullying way. See how he behaved in that affair with Julian. I can't say I feel any pity for him at all, he has sent many a man to the gallows, and now his time has come."

At five o'clock it was already dusk, the shutters had been closed, and the lamp lighted. Presently the servant entered.

"There is someone wants to speak to you, Master Frank."

Frank went out into the hall. The head of the constabulary and two of his men were standing there. Much surprised, Frank asked the officer into the other sitting-room.

"What is it, Mr. Henderson?" he said.

"It is a very sad business, a very sad business, Mr. Wyatt. Your brother is not at home, I hear?"

"No. Julian went over this morning to have a day's rabbit-shooting with Dick Merryweather. I expect it won't be long before he is back. There is nothing the matter with him?" he asked, with a vague feeling of alarm at the gravity of the officer's face.

"It is a very painful matter, Mr. Wyatt; but it is useless trying to hide the truth from you, for you must know it shortly. I hold a warrant for your brother's arrest on the charge of attempted wilful murder."

Frank's eyes dilated with surprise and horror.

"You don't mean—" he gasped, and then his faith in his brother came to his aid, and he broke off indignantly: "it is monstrous, perfectly monstrous, Mr. Henderson. I suppose it is Faulkner, and it is because of that wretched smuggling business that suspicions fall on him, as if there were not a hundred others who owe the man a much deeper grudge than my brother did; indeed he had no animosity against him at all, for Julian got the best of it altogether, and Faulkner has been hissed and hooted every time he has been in the town since. If there was any ill-feeling left over that matter, it would be on his part and not on Julian's. Who signed the warrant? Faulkner himself?"

"No; it is signed by the Colonel and Mr. Harrington. They took the dying deposition of Mr. Faulkner. There is no harm in my telling you that, because it must be generally known when your brother is brought up, but till then please do not let it go further. He has sworn that he overtook Mr. Wyatt two or three hundred yards before he got to his own gate. There was an altercation between them, and he swears that your brother used threats. He had a double-barrelled gun in his hand, and as Faulkner was riding up the drive to the house he was fired at from the trees on his left, and fell from his horse. Almost directly afterwards Mr. Wyatt ran out from the spot where the gun had been fired. Thinking he would finish him if he thought he was still alive, Mr. Faulkner closed his eyes and held his breath. Your brother came up and stood over him, and having satisfied himself that he was dead, ran off through the trees again."

"I believe it is a lie from beginning to end," Frank said passionately. "Julian had brought him into disgrace here, and the fellow invented this charge out of revenge. If it had been in the road, and Faulkner had struck Julian as he did before, and Julian had had his loaded gun in his hand, I don't say but that in his passion he might have shot him; still, I don't believe he would, even then. Julian is one of the best-tempered fellows in the world; still, I would admit that, in the heat of the moment, he might raise his gun and fire; but to say that he loaded his gun after Faulkner had gone on—for I am sure it was empty as he came along, as I have never known him to bring home his gun loaded—

and that he then went and hid behind a tree and shot a man down, why, I would not believe it if fifty honest men swore to it, much less on the oath of a fellow like Faulkner."

"I can't say anything about that, Mr. Wyatt; I have only my duty to do."

"Yes, I understand that, Mr. Henderson. Of course he must be arrested, but I am sure no one will believe the accusation for a minute. Oh!" he exclaimed, as a fresh idea struck him, "what was Faulkner shot with?"

"It is a bullet wound."

"Well, that is quite enough," Frank exclaimed triumphantly. "Julian had his double-barrelled gun with him, and had been rabbit-shooting; and if it had been he who fired it would have been with a charge of shot. You don't suppose he went about with a bullet in his pocket to use in case he happened to meet Faulkner, and have another row with him. Julian never fired a bullet in his life, as far as I know. There is not such a thing as a bullet-mould in the house."

The officer's look of gravity relaxed. "That is important, certainly," he said, "very important. I own that after hearing the deposition read it did seem to me that, as the result of this unfortunate quarrel, your brother might have been so goaded by something Mr. Faulkner said or did, that he had hastily loaded his gun, and in his passion ran across the wood and shot him down. But now it is clear, from what you say, that it is most improbable he would have a bullet about him, and unless it can be proved that he obtained one from a gunmaker or otherwise, it is a very strong point in his favour. I suppose your brother has not returned this afternoon?"

"No. I asked the servant, when I got home at three, whether he had returned, though I did not expect him back so soon, and she said that he had not come in, and I am sure he has not done so since."

"Then I will not intrude any longer. I shall place one of my men in front of the house and one behind, and if he comes home his arrest will be managed quietly, and we will not bring him in here at all. It will save a painful scene."

When the officer had left, Frank returned to his aunt.

"What is it, Frank?" she asked.

"Well, Aunt, it is a more absurd affair than the other; but, absurd as it is, it is very painful. There is a warrant out for the arrest of Julian on the charge of attempting to murder Mr. Faulkner."

Mrs. Troutbeck gave a cry, and then burst into a fit of hysterical laughter. After vainly trying to pacify her, Frank went out for the servant, but as her wild screams of laughter continued he put on his hat and ran for the family doctor, who lived but a few doors away. He briefly related the circumstances of the case to him, and then brought him back to the house. It was a long time before the violence of the paroxysm passed, leaving Mrs. Troutbeck so weak that she had to be carried by Frank and the doctor up to her room.

"Don't you worry yourself, Aunt," Frank said, as they laid her down upon the bed; "it will all come out right, just as the last did. It will all be cleared up, no doubt, in a very short time."

As soon as the maid had undressed Mrs. Troutbeck, and had got her into bed, the doctor went up and gave her an opiate, and then went down into the parlour to Frank, who told him the story in full, warning him that he must say nothing about the deposition of Mr. Faulkner until it had been read in court.

"It is a very grave affair, Frank," the old doctor said. "Having known your brother from his childhood, I am as convinced as you are that, however much of this deposition be true or false, Julian never fired the shot; and what you say about the bullet makes it still more conclusive, if that were needed—which it certainly is not with me. Your brother had an exceedingly sweet and even temper. Your father has often spoken to me of it, almost with regret, saying that it would be much better if he had a little more will of his own and a little spice more of temper. Still, it is most unfortunate that he hasn't returned. Of course, he may have met some friend in the town and gone home with him, or he may have stayed at Mr. Merryweather's."

"I don't think he can have stopped in the town anyhow," Frank said; "for the first thing he would have heard when he got back would have been of the shooting of Faulkner, and he would have been sure to have come home to talk it over with me. Of course, he may have stopped with the Merryweathers, but I am afraid he has not. I fancy that part of Faulkner's story must be true; he could never have accused Julian if he had not met him near his gate —for Julian in that case could have easily proved where he was at the time. No, I think they did meet, and very likely had a row. You know what Faulkner is; and I can understand that if he met Julian he would most likely say something to him, and there might then be a quarrel; but I think that his story about Julian coming out and looking at him is either pure fancy or a lie. No doubt he was thinking of him as he rode along; and, badly wounded as he was, perhaps altogether insensible, he may have imagined the rest."

"That is all quite possible," the doctor agreed; "but in that case Julian's not coming home is all the more extraordinary. If he met Faulkner between two and three o'clock, what can he have been doing since?"

This was a question Frank could not answer.

"I can't tell, sir," he said after a long pause; I really can't imagine. Still, nothing in the world would make me believe that Julian did what he is charged with."

Several times Frank went outside the door, but the constable was still there. At last, after sitting and looking at the fire for some time he put on his cap and went to the residence of the chief constable.

"Excuse me, Mr. Henderson, but I have been thinking it over ever since you left. Whoever did this murder did not probably return to the road, but struck off somewhere across the fields. There was snow enough in the middle of the day to cover the ground; it stopped falling at two o'clock, and has not snowed since. Might I suggest that in the morning a search should be made round the edge of the wood. If there are footprints found it might be of great importance."

"You are quite right, Mr. Wyatt, and I had already determined to go myself, with a couple of constables, at daylight."

"May I go with you, sir?"

"If you please. But you must remember that the evidence of footprints which we may find may be unfavourable to your brother."

"I have not the slightest fear of that," Frank said confidently.

"Very well, then, Mr. Wyatt. The two constables will be here at half-past seven, and I shall be ready to start with them at once. Should you by any chance be late, you will, no doubt, be able to overtake us before we get there."

The next morning Frank was at the office half an hour before the appointed time. Fortunately no snow had fallen in the night. The chief constable looked grave and anxious when the search began; Frank was excited rather than anxious. He had no fear whatever as to the result of the investigation; it would disclose nothing, he felt certain, to Julian's disadvantage. The continued absence of the latter was unaccountable to him, but he felt absolutely certain that it would be explained satisfactorily on his return.

The moment they got across the hedge into the fields skirting the wood the chief constable exclaimed:

"Stay, men; here are footprints by the edge of the trees! Do not come out until I have carefully examined them. Do you not think," he went on, turning to Frank, "that it would be much better that you should not go further with me, for you see I might have to call you as a witness?"

"Not at all, Mr. Henderson; whatever we find, I shall have no objection to being a witness, for I am certain that we shall find nothing that will tend to incriminate my brother. I see what you are thinking of—that these footprints were Julian's. That is my own idea too. At any rate, they are the marks of a well-made boot of large size, without heavy nails."

The constable nodded. "There are two sets," he said, "one going each way; and by the distance they are apart, and the fact that the heel is not as deeply marked as the rest of the print, whoever made them was running."

"Certainly," Frank agreed; "he ran up to the hedge and then turned. Why should he have done that?"

"Probably because he saw some vehicle or some persons walking along the road, and did not wish to be seen."

"Possibly so, Mr. Henderson; but in that case, why did he not keep among the trees both coming and going, instead of exposing himself, as he must have done running here; for the hedge is thin, and any one walking along, much less driving, could have seen him."

Mr. Henderson looked at Frank with a closer scrutiny than he had before given him.

"You are an acute observer, Mr. Wyatt. The point is

an important one. A man wishing to avoid observation would certainly have kept among the trees. Now, let us follow these footprints along; we may learn something further."

Presently they came to the point where Julian had come out from the wood.

"You see he was in the wood, Mr. Wyatt," the constable said.

"I quite see that," Frank said. "If these are the marks of Julian's boots—and I think they are—we have now found out that he came out of the wood at this point, ran for some purpose or other, and without an attempt at concealment, as far as the hedge; then turned and ran back again, past the point where he had left the wood. Now let us see what he did afterwards—it may give us a clue to the whole matter."

Fifty yards further they came on the spot where Julian had turned off on the poacher's track.

"There it is, Mr. Henderson!" Frank exclaimed triumphantly. "Another man came out of the wood here—a man with roughly-made boots with hob-nails. That man came out first; that is quite evident. The tracks are all in a line, and Julian's are in many places on the top of the other's. They were both running fast. But if you look you will see that Julian's strides are the longest, and, therefore, he was probably running the fastest."

"It is as you say, Mr. Wyatt. The lighter footprints obliterate those of the heavier boots in several places. What can be the meaning of this, and what can the second man have been doing in the wood?"

"The whole thing is perfectly plain to me," Frank said excitedly. "Julian was in the road, he heard the report of the gun close by in the wood, and perhaps heard a cry; he jumped over the hedge and made for the spot, and possibly, as Mr. Faulkner said, ran into the drive and stooped over him; then he started in pursuit of the murderer, of whom he may possibly have obtained a sight. There was not enough snow under the trees for him to follow the footprints, he therefore ran to the edge of the wood, and then to the road, in search of the man's track. Then he turned and ran back again till he came upon them leaving the wood, and then set off in pursuit.

"By Jove! Mr. Wyatt," the officer said, "I do think that your explanation is the right one. Give me your hand, lad; I had no more doubt five minutes ago that your brother had, in a fit of passion, shot Mr. Faulkner than I have that I am standing here now. But I declare I think now that he acted as you say. How you have struck upon it beats me altogether."

"I have been thinking of nothing else all the night, Mr. Henderson. I put myself in Julian's position, and it seemed to me that, hearing a gun fired so close at hand, even if he did not hear a cry, Julian, knowing how often the man had been threatened, might at once have run to the spot, and might have behaved just as Faulkner says he did. All that seemed to me simple enough; Julian's absence was the only difficulty, and the only way I could possibly account for it, was that he had followed the murderer."

"It was very imprudent," Mr. Henderson said gravely.

"Very; but it was just the sort of thing Julian would have done."

"But, however far he went, he ought to be back before this."

"That is what I am anxious about, Mr. Henderson. Of course he ought to be back. I am terribly afraid that something has happened to him. This man, whoever he was, must have been a desperate character, and having taken one life from revenge, he would not hesitate to take another to secure his own safety. He had a great advantage over Julian, for, as we know, his gun carried bullets, while Julian had nothing but small shot. Which way shall we go next, Mr. Henderson—shall we follow the track or go into the wood?"

"We will go into the wood; that will take us a comparatively short time, and there is no saying how far the other may lead us. But, before we do so, I will call up my two men, take them over the ground, and show them the discoveries we have made. It is as well to have as many witnesses as possible."

The two constables were called up and taken along the line of track, and the chief constable pointed out to them that the man with well-made boots was evidently running after the other. Then they entered the wood. Carefully searching, they found here and there prints of both the boots. They went out into the drive, and, starting from the spot where Mr. Faulkner had been found, made for a large tree some thirty yards to the left.

"Just as I thought," Mr. Henderson said. "Someone has been standing here, and, I should think, for some little time. You can see that the ground is kicked up a bit, and, though it was too hard to show the marks of the boots plainly, there are many scratches and grooves, such as would be made by hob-nails. Now, lads, search about closely; if we can find the wad it will be a material point."

After five minutes' search one of the men picked up a piece of half-burned paper. Frank uttered an exclamation of satisfaction as he held it up.

"Julian always used wads. This never came from his gun. Now let us go back to the tree, Mr. Henderson, and see which way the man went after firing the shot."

After careful search they found the heavy footprints at several spots where the snow lay, and near them also found traces of the lighter boots. The trees then grew thicker, but following the line indicated by the footprints, they came to the spot where he had left the wood.

"You see, Mr. Henderson," Frank said, "Julian lost the footprints just where we did, and bore a little more to the left, striking the edge of the wood between where the man had left it and the road. Now, sir, we have only to find the spot where Julian first left the road, and try to trace his footsteps from there to the spot where Mr. Faulkner was lying. We know that the shot was fired from behind that tree—and if my brother's footsteps miss this spot altogether, I think the case will be absolutely proved."

They went back into the road, and found where Julian had crossed the untrodden snow between it and the hedge, and had pushed his way through the latter. It was only here and there that footprints could be found; but, fortunately, some ten yards to the right of the tree there was an open space, and across this he had evidently run.

"You have proved your case, Mr. Wyatt," the chief constable said, shaking Frank cordially by the hand. "I am indeed glad. Whoever the man was who shot Mr. Faulkner, it was certainly not your brother. Now let us start at once on the tracks."

Frank's face became more serious than it had been during the previous search, as soon as they took up the double track across the fields. Before, he had felt absolutely confident that whatever they might find it could only tend to clear Julian from this terrible accusation; now, upon the contrary, he feared that any discovery they might make would confirm his suspicions that evil had befallen him. Scarcely a word was spoken as they passed along the fields.

"The man with the hob-nailed boots is taking to the hills," the chief constable remarked.

"I am afraid so, Mr. Henderson; and as they are bare of snow there will be no chance of our following him."

When they came to the point where the snow ended they stopped.

"There is an end of our search, Mr. Wyatt. We must return to the town. The magistrates will meet at eleven o'clock and I and the constables must be there. But I will send off two men directly we get back, to go along the cliffs and question all the men who were on duty yesterday afternoon as to whether they saw two men with guns crossing the hills, one being probably some distance behind the other. I think, perhaps, you had better come to the court. I don't say that it will be absolutely necessary, but I think it would be better that you should do so; and you see it would be useless for you to be hunting over those hills alone. As soon as the court is over I will take four men and will myself start to search for him. There is no saying whether we may not find some sign or other. I shall be glad if you will go with me; you have shown yourself a born detective this morning, for had you been trained to it all your life you could not have followed the scent up more unerringly."

"I will certainly go with you, Mr. Henderson, and I will be at the court-house. I would start at once for the hills, but I have had nothing to eat this morning, and, what is much more important, I want to ease my aunt's mind. Of course, she was as certain as I was that Julian had nothing whatever to do with this, but naturally it will be an immense relief to her to know that the suspicion of so dreadful a crime no longer rests on him."

When Frank returned home he found that Mrs. Troutbeck was so prostrated with the shock that she was still in bed, where the doctor had ordered her to remain. As soon, however, as she heard that Frank was back, she sent down for him to come up. Her delight was extreme when he told her of the discoveries he had made, and that the constables had no doubt the warrant for Julian's arrest would be withdrawn. She became anxious again when she found that Frank could give no satisfactory explanation of his long absence.

"I would not trouble about it, Aunt," he said, soothingly; "no doubt we shall hear of him before long. Let us be content that he has come well out of this terrible accusation, just as he did from the former charge, and let us hope that the explanation of his absence will be just as satisfactory when we hear it. Even if I thought that Julian had got into any trouble, it would be infinitely easier to bear than a knowledge that he was suspected of murder, for it would have been murder, Aunt. I heard just now that Faulkner died last night."

The meeting of magistrates was an informal one, as they agreed, directly they heard that Julian was not in custody, that they could proceed no further in the matter. Mr. Henderson, after answering their first question, followed them into their private room.

"So you did not lay hands on him last night," Colonel Chambers said. "We shall have to alter the warrant, for I find that Mr. Faulkner is dead."

"I think, gentlemen," the chief-constable said quietly, "that after you have heard what I have to tell, you will have to withdraw the warrant altogether."

"Eh! what? Do you mean to say, Henderson, that you think the young fellow did not fire the shot after all? I would give a hundred pounds if I could think so, but, with Faulkner's deposition before us, I don't see how there can be any possible doubt in the matter. Besides, I was present when he gave it, and though it may have been coloured a good deal by his feeling against young Wyatt, I am convinced that he believed, at any rate, that he was speaking the truth."

"I have no doubt he did, sir, and I had no more doubt than you have as to Mr. Wyatt's guilt; indeed, until his brother pointed out one very important fact, nothing would have persuaded me that he did not fire the shot. I don't say that it was at all conclusive, but it sufficed to show that the matter was by no means so certain as it seemed to be. I found him at the house when I went there to arrest his brother. Of course, the young fellow was greatly shocked when I told him the nature of the charge, and declared it to be absolutely impossible. So certain was he, that even when I told him the nature of Mr. Faulkner's depositions, he was more puzzled than alarmed. The first question he asked was whether Mr. Faulkner had been killed by shot or by a ball. When I said by a ball his face cleared up altogether. His brother, he said, and as we know, had been rabbit-shooting at Mr. Merryweather's. He would have had small shot with him, but young Wyatt said that he did not think his brother had ever fired a bullet in his life. He knew there was not such a thing as a bullet in the house. Mr. Wyatt could not possibly have known that he was likely to meet Mr. Faulkner on his way back from shooting, and therefore, unless upon the rather improbable theory that he went about with the intention of shooting Mr. Faulkner whenever he met him, and that he had bought a bullet in the town and carried it always about with him for the purpose, it was clear that he could not have fired that shot."

"There is something in that, Mr. Henderson. A good deal in it, I am ready to admit, but nothing that would really counteract the effect of Faulkner's direct testimony, given when he knew that he was dying."

"No, sir; still it is a point that I own I had entirely overlooked; however, that is not now so important. I will now tell you what has taken place this morning."

And he then related the story of the discovery of the tracks, that proved that Julian had not gone near the tree behind which the murderer had for some time been standing, and how, after running in and finding Mr. Faulkner's body, he had set out in pursuit of the scoundrel.

"I have the two constables outside who were with me, Colonel, and if you like to question them, they will, I am sure, confirm my statement in all respects."

"I am glad indeed to hear your story, Mr. Henderson," Colonel Chambers said warmly. "The lad's father was an old friend of mine, and it was terrible to think that his son could have committed such a dastardly crime. What you say seems to me quite conclusive of his innocence, and, at the same time, is not in any way in contradiction with the deposition. I give you very great credit for the manner in which you have unravelled this mystery."

"The credit, sir, is entirely due to Mr. Wyatt's brother. He had formed the theory that, as in his opinion his brother was certainly innocent of the crime, the only possible way in which he could account for his absence from home that night was that, upon hearing the gun fired so close at hand, Mr. Wyatt had at once run to the spot, found the body of Mr. Faulkner, and had then immediately started in pursuit of the murderer. Setting out with me on the search with this theory strongly fixed in his mind, young Wyatt seized at once every point that confirmed it, and pointed out to me that the man with heavy boots had crossed the fields at a run, and that the other had followed as soon as he came upon the footprints, after searching for them up and down by the edge of the wood. Once we had got this clue to follow up, the matter was then plain enough. The search through the wood showed us the whole circumstances of the case, as I have related them to you, just as plainly as if we had witnessed the affair. But if I had not been set upon the right trail, I say honestly that I doubt whether I should have unravelled it, especially as the snow is rapidly going, and by this afternoon the footprints will have disappeared.

"Well, as a matter of form, we will take down your statement, Mr. Henderson, and then take those of the constables."

"Young Mr. Wyatt is outside, if you would like to hear him, sir."

"Certainly we will," the Colonel said. "He must be a wonderfully shrewd young fellow, and I think we ought to take his statement, if only to record the part he played in proving his brother's innocence. But where is the brother, Mr. Henderson; hasn't he come back yet?"

"No, sir; and I own that I regard his absence as alarming. You see the murderer, whoever he is, was armed with a rifle, or at any rate with a gun that carried bullets, while Mr. Wyatt had only a shot-gun. Such a fellow would certainly not suffer himself to be arrested without a struggle, and when he found that he was being followed across the hills, would be likely enough to shoot down his pursuer without letting him get close enough to use his fowling-piece. I have sent two constables up to inquire of the coast-guard men along the cliffs whether they observed any man with a gun crossing the hills yesterday afternoon, and whether they heard a gun fired. As soon as you have before you the statements of the constables who were with me this morning, I intend to take them and two others and start myself for a search over the hills, and I am very much afraid that we shall come upon Mr. Wyatt's body."

"I sincerely hope not," Colonel Chambers said; "but I own that I can see no other way for accounting for his absence. Well, if you will call the clerk in, he will take down your statement at once. What do you think, Harrington? It seems to me that when we have got the four statements we shall be fully justified in withdrawing the warrant against young Wyatt."

"I quite think so, Colonel. You see, the facts will all come out at the coroner's inquest, and, when they do so, I think there will be a good deal of strong feeling in the place, if it is found that young Wyatt has been killed while bravely trying to capture Faulkner's murderer, while at the same time our warrant for his apprehension for the murder was still in force."

"Yes, there is a good deal in that, Harrington. If Faulkner had not died I think that it would have been best merely to hold the warrant over in order that when Wyatt comes back, if he ever does come back, all these facts might be proved publicly; now that will all be done before the coroner."

The statements of Mr. Henderson and the two constables were taken down. Frank was then called in.

"I congratulate you most heartily upon the innocence of your brother having been, to our minds, so conclusively proved, and, as Mr. Henderson tells us, chiefly owing to your shrewdness in the matter. Before you begin, you can repeat your opinion about the bullet that you pointed out to the chief-constable last night, in order that the point may be included in your statement. After that you can tell us the story of your search in the wood."

When Frank had finished, Colonel Chambers said: "This is a very awkward thing about your brother's disappearance. While giving him the fullest credit for his courage in following a desperate man armed with a rifle, it was certainly a rash undertaking, and I fear that he may have come to harm."

"I don't suppose, when he started, that it was so much the

idea of capturing the man, Julian had in his mind, as of seeing who he was. Had my brother come back with only the statement that some man unknown had shot Mr. Faulkner, his story might not have been credited. Certainly, in the teeth of Mr. Faulkner's depositions, it would not have been believed when there was no evidence to support it. Still, I don't suppose it had even entered Julian's mind that any suspicion could possibly fall upon him. I am greatly afraid that he has been killed or badly hurt; if not, I can see but one possible way of accounting for his absence. Mr. Faulkner was extremely active in the pursuit of smugglers, and had, we know, received many threatening letters. If the man was a smuggler, as seems to me likely, he may have gone to some place where he had comrades awaiting him, and, Julian pursuing him, may have been seized and made prisoner. You see, sir, he knew many of them, and, after the affair the other day, was probably regarded as a friend, and they may hold him in their keeping only until the man who fired the shot can get safely out of reach."

"I hope that this may prove so indeed," the magistrate said. "It is at any rate possible. And now we will detain you no longer, for Mr. Henderson told me that you were going to accompany them in their search among the hills. I see that it is just beginning to snow, which will, I fear, add to your difficulties."

For some days an active search was maintained, but no trace was discovered of Julian Wyatt, or of the man whom he had followed. From inquiries that had been instituted in the town, the chief-constable had learned that the man Markham, who had a few weeks before returned after serving out his sentence for poaching in Mr. Faulkner's preserves, had disappeared from his lodgings on the day of the murder and had not returned. As he was known to have uttered many threats against the magistrate, a warrant was issued for his arrest on the day after the coroner's jury, having heard the whole of the evidence, brought in a verdict that Mr. Faulkner had been wilfully murdered by a person or persons unknown.

CHAPTER VI.

A COMMISSION.

ABOUT a week after the coroner's inquest, the servant one evening brought in a letter that had been left at the door by a man who looked like a fisherman. Frank gave a shout of joy as he glanced at the address.

"It is Julian's handwriting, Aunt," he shouted, and then exclaimed, as Mrs. Troutbeck, who was on the sofa, gave a low cry and fell back fainting, "What an ass I am to blurt it out like that!" Then he rang the bell with a vigour that brought down the rope. "Here, Mary," he exclaimed, as the servant re-appeared at the door with a scared face, "Aunt has fainted; do what you can for her. I will run round for the doctor directly; but I must look at this letter first. It is from Mr. Julian."

"Lor', sir, that is good news!" the girl exclaimed, as she hurried across to her mistress. After the custom of her class, she had hitherto looked upon the matter in the darkest possible light, and had joined in the general conviction that Julian had been killed.

Julian's letter was written on board the smuggler.

"My dear Frank, I am afraid you must all have been in a horrible fright about me, and no wonder. I am a most unfortunate fellow, and seem to be always putting my foot in it, and yet really I don't think I was to blame about this.

In the first place, I may tell you that I am on board a French smuggler, that we have just entered the Loire, and that in a few hours we shall be at Nantes. The smugglers will bring this letter back to England, and as they say they shall probably sail again a few days after they get in, I hope it will not be very long before it comes to hand. And now as to how I got here."

Julian then related the story of the quarrel with Mr. Faulkner, of hearing the gun fired, of running in and finding the body, and of his pursuit of the murderer.

"After a long tramp on the hills he took to a place of hiding. I am bound by oath to afford no clue as to where that place is, and can only say that upon my following him in, I was pounced upon by some French smugglers who were there with him, and trussed up like a fowl. Then there was a discussion what to do with me, in which the man I had been following joined. Of course I did not understand the language, but I could see that the smugglers were in favour of cutting my throat for having discovered their hiding-place, and that the man himself was, contrary to what I should have expected, arguing in my favour. He had been a smuggler as well as a poacher, but although he had murdered Mr. Faulkner, and knew that I had pursued him for that crime, he undoubtedly saved my life. They first made me take an oath not to reveal their hiding-place, and then said that they should carry me over to France, and would take steps so that I should not return to England for some years.

"What those steps will be I cannot say, but I feel sure that they will in some way prevent my coming back for a long time. They can't keep me themselves, but may hand me over as a prisoner to the French authorities. Before we sailed, the man told me he had learnt that a warrant was out against me for the murder of Faulkner, and that

Faulkner had declared it was I who shot him. If I could possibly have escaped I would have come back to stand my trial, though I can see plainly enough that it might go very hard with me, for there would be only my word, which would go for nothing against Faulkner's accusation, and the fact of our quarrel. However, I would have come rather than disappear with this awful charge against me. The man has given me permission, not only to write and tell you this story, but even to give you his name, which is Joseph Markham. He had only been a short time out of prison, where he had been sent for poaching, and he killed Faulkner simply for revenge. He told me that he did not mind my getting his name as, in the first place, he had no idea of returning to Weymouth, and intended making France his home; and, in the second place, because, although you might believe my story, no one else would, and even if he showed himself in Weymouth, this letter, written by a man accused of the murder, would not be accepted for a moment against him. However, there is no doubt that the fellow has behaved extremely well to me, and I should be sorry to get him into trouble over this business with Faulkner, which is no affair of mine.

"You can, of course, show this letter to whom you like, but I don't expect anyone except you and Aunt to believe it. I have hopes of being cleared some day, for Markham has promised me to write out a full confession of his shooting Faulkner, and to swear to it before a French magistrate. He is going to write it in duplicate, and carry one copy about with him, directed to Colonel Chambers, or the senior magistrate at Weymouth, and to send the other copy to someone at home, who will produce it in case of his death in France, or by drowning at sea. I do not think that, if I get away, I shall return to England until I hear of his death. I am awfully sorry for you, old fellow, and for Aunt. But with this frightful accusation hanging over me, I don't think your position would be better if I were to come back and be hung for murder; and I see myself that the case is so strong against me that it would almost certainly come to that if they laid hands on me. I am specially sorry that this trouble should come upon you now, just as you were going to try to get a commission, for of course they could hardly give one to a fellow whose brother is accused of murder, and if they did, your position in the army would be intolerable. Now, good-bye, dear old Frank; give my fond love to Aunt, who has always been too good to me. If I get an opportunity I will write again, but I hardly fancy that I shall get a chance to do so, as, even if I were free to write I don't see how letters can be sent from France except through smugglers. God bless you, old fellow!

"Your unfortunate brother,

"JULIAN."

Happily, by the time he had finished reading the letter, the servant had succeeded in restoring Mrs. Troutbeck.

"It is exactly what we thought, Aunt. Julian was seized by smugglers, and has been taken over to France, and I am afraid it will be some time before he gets back again, especially as he believes that this charge is hanging over him. I won't read you the letter now, but to-morrow when you are strong enough you shall read it yourself. I must take it the first thing in the morning to Colonel Chambers, who will, I am sure, be very glad to hear that Julian is safe, for I know that he thinks he was shot by the man he pursued. He will be interested, too, and so will Mr. Henderson, at seeing how exactly we were right in the conclusions we arrived at."

Mrs. Troutbeck was quite satisfied with the explanation, and was at once taken up to bed by the servant, while

Frank, seeing that it was as yet but eight o'clock, put on his cap and ran to Mr. Henderson's. The latter was at home, and received with great pleasure the news that Julian was alive. He read the letter through attentively.

"If we had seen the whole thing happen, we could not have been closer than we were in our conclusion as to how it all came about. Well, the news that it is Markham who shot Mr. Faulkner does not surprise me, for, as you know, I have already a warrant out against him on the charge. I fear that there is little chance that we shall lay hands on him now, for he will doubtless learn from some of his associates here of the evidence given at the coroner's inquest, and that your brother has been proved altogether innocent of the crime. I can understand that, believing, as he did, the evidence against Mr. Wyatt to be overwhelming, he had no great objection to his giving his name; for, as the matter then stood, your brother's story would only have been regarded as the attempt of a guilty man to fix the blame of his crime on another. As it has turned out, the letter is a piece of important evidence that might be produced against Markham, for all the statements in it tally with the facts we have discovered for ourselves. Still I congratulate you most heartily. I certainly thought that your brother had been murdered, though our efforts to find any traces of the crime have failed altogether. I am afraid, as he says, it will be a long time before he manages to get away; still, that is a comparatively unimportant matter, and all that I can hope is that this fellow Markham will come to a speedy end. Of course you will show this letter to everyone, for now that nobody believes for a moment that your brother was Mr. Faulkner's murderer, everyone will be glad to hear that the mystery is cleared up, and that he is simply in France instead of being, as all supposed, buried in some hole where his body would never be discovered.

"All that can possibly be said against him now is that he behaved rashly in following a desperate man instead of coming back to us for assistance; but I quite see that, under the circumstance of his relations with the magistrate, he was doubly anxious to bring the latter's murderer to justice, and, as we now know, the latter would certainly have got away unsuspected had your brother not acted as he did."

Colonel Chambers was equally pleased when Frank called upon him the next morning, and begged him, after showing the letter to his friends, to hand it over to him for safe-keeping, as, in the event of Markham ever being arrested, it would be valuable, if not as evidence, as affording assistance to the prosecution.

"Do you think, Colonel Chambers, that they will be able to keep Julian away for a long time?"

"If his supposition is a correct one, and they intend to hand him over to the French authorities as a prisoner of war, it may be a long time before you hear of him. There are many towns all over France where English prisoners are confined, and it would be practically impossible to find out where he is, or to obtain his release if you did find out, while the two nations are at war. There are very few exchanges made, and the chances of his being among them would be very small. However, lad, things might have been a great deal worse. This tremendous war cannot go on for ever. Your brother is strong and healthy; he seems to be, from all I hear, just the sort of fellow who would take things easily, and although the lot of prisoners of war, whether in England or France, cannot be called a pleasant one, he has a fairer chance than most, of going through it unharmed.

"The experience may be of benefit to him. Of course, when this matter first began, I made close enquiries in several quarters as to his character and habits. I need not say that I heard nothing whatever against him; but there was a sort of consensus of opinion that it was a pity that he had not some pursuit or occupation. As you know, he mixed himself up to some extent with smugglers, he spent his evenings frequently in billiard-rooms, and altogether, though there was nothing absolutely against him, it was clear that he was doing himself no good."

"He had given up the billiard-table," Frank said. "He promised me that he would not go there any more, and I am sure he wouldn't."

"I am glad to hear it, lad; still I think that this experience will do him good rather than harm. He was a kindly, good-tempered, easy-going young fellow, a little deficient, perhaps, in strength of will, but very generally liked, and with the making of a fine man about him; and yet he was likely, from sheer easiness of temper and disinclination to settle down to anything, to drift with the stream till he ruined his life. That is how I read his character from what I have heard of him, and that being so, I think this complete break in his life may ultimately be of considerable benefit to him."

"Perhaps it will, sir. A better brother never lived, but he may have been too ready to fall in with other people's views. I think that it was a very great pity that he did not apply for a commission in the army."

"A great pity," Colonel Chambers agreed. "A young fellow who will start in pursuit of a desperate man who is armed with a gun, would be the sort of fellow to lead a forlorn hope. And what are you going to do, Frank?"

"I am going to try and get a commission, sir, now that Julian is completely cleared. I shall set about it at once. I am sixteen now. Colonel Wilson, with whom my father served in Spain, wrote at his death, and said that if either of us wished for a commission, he would, when the time came, use his influence to get him one, and that after father's services he was sure there would be no difficulty about it."

"None whatever. Colonel Wyatt's sons have almost a right to a commission. If you will write to Sir Robert Wilson at once, and let me know when you get his reply, I will write to a friend at the Horse-guards and get him to back up the request as soon as it is sent in."

Three weeks later Frank received an official document, informing him that he had been gazetted to the 15th Light Dragoons, and was to join the depôt of his regiment at Canterbury immediately. Mrs. Troutbeck had been consulted by Frank before he wrote to Colonel Sir R. Wilson. As it had, since Julian decided not to enter the army, been a settled thing that Frank should apply for a commission, she had offered no objection.

"It is only right, my dear," she said, with tears in her eyes and a little break in her voice, "that one of my dear brother's sons should follow in his footsteps. I know that he always wished you both to join the army, and as Julian had no fancy for it, I am glad that you should go. Of course it will be a trial, a great trial to me; but a young man must go on his own path, and it would be wrong indeed for an old woman like me to stand in his way."

"I don't know, Aunt, that it is so. That is my only doubt about applying for the commission. I can't help thinking that it is my duty to stay with you until Julian comes back."

"Not at all, Frank. It would make me much more unhappy seeing you wasting your life here, than in knowing you were following the course you had marked for yourself. I shall do very well. Mary is a very good and attentive girl, and I shall get another in to do most of her work, so that she can sit with me and be a sort of companion. Then, you know, there are very few afternoons that one or other of my friends do not come in for an hour for a gossip, or I go in to them. I take a good deal of blame to myself for all this trouble that has come to Julian. I think that if, three years ago, I had pressed it upon him that he ought to go into the army, he would have done so; but certainly anything that I did say was rather the other way, and since he has gone I see how wrong I was, and I certainly won't repeat the mistake with you. Even now Julian may come back long before you go. I don't mean before you go away from here, but before you go out to join your regiment, wherever that may be. You are sure to be a few months at the depôt, and you know we have agreed to write letters to Julian, telling him that the matter is all cleared up, and that everyone knows he had nothing to do with the murder, so of course he will try to escape as soon as he gets one of them."

"Yes, when he gets one, Aunt. I will give the letters to men who are, I know, connected with the smugglers, and possibly they may be taken over, but that is a very different thing from his getting them. We may be sure that the smugglers who have taken Julian over will not trouble themselves about detaining him. They would never go to all the bother of keeping and watching him for years. If they keep him at all it will be on board their craft, but that would be a constant trouble, and they would know that sooner or later he would be able to make his escape. If they have handed him over to the French authorities he may have been taken to a prison hundreds of miles from Nantes, and the smugglers would not know where he was and would be unable to send a letter to him. No, Aunt, I feel confident that Julian will come home, but I am afraid that it will be a long time first, for as to his escaping from prison, there is no chance whatever of it. There are numbers of English officers there; many of them must be able to speak French well, and the naval officers are able to climb ropes and things of that sort that Julian could not do. It is very rare indeed that any of them, even with these advantages, make their escape, and therefore I cannot hope that Julian will be able to do so."

"Well, then, my dear, I must wait patiently until he does. I only hope that I may be spared to see him back again."

"I am sure I hope so, Aunt. Why should you always call yourself an old woman? when you know that you are not old in years. Why, you said last birthday that you were fifty-nine, and it is only because you are such a hand at staying indoors, and live such a quiet life, that it makes you think yourself old. I should think this war won't last very much longer. If it does, all the men in Europe will be used up. Of course, as soon as peace is made Julian will be sent home again."

The same day that the post brought Frank the news of his commission, it brought a letter from Colonel Wilson saying that he was at present in town, and giving him a warm invitation to come up and stay with him for a week, while he procured his necessary outfit. A fortnight later Frank arrived in town and drove to Buckingham Street, where Colonel Wilson was lodging. He received Frank very kindly, and when the lad would have renewed the thanks he had expressed in the letter he had written on receiving the news of his having obtained his commission, the colonel said:

"It was a duty as well as a pleasure. Your father saved my life at Aboukir. I had been unhorsed and was guarding myself as well as I could against four French cuirassiers, who were slashing away at me, when your father rode into the middle of them, cut one down and wounded a second, which gave me time to snatch a pistol from the holster of my fallen horse and to dispose of a third, when the other rode off. Your father got a severe sabre wound on the arm and a slash across the face. Of course, you remember the scar. So you see the least I could do, was to render his son any service in my power. I managed to get you gazetted to my old regiment, that is to say, my first regiment, for I have served in several. I thought, in the first place, my introduction would to some extent put you at home tnere. In the second, a cavalry man has the advantage over one in a marching regiment that he learns to ride well, and is more eligible for staff appointments. As you know, I myself have done a great deal of what we call detached service, and it is probable that I may in the future have similar appointments, and, if so, I may have an opportunity of taking you with me as an aide. Those sort of appointments are very useful. They not only take one out of the routine of garrison life and enable one to see the world, but they bring a young officer's name prominently forward, and give him chances of distinguishing himself. Therefore I, as an old cavalry man, should much prefer taking an assistant from the same branch, and indeed would almost be expected to do so. From what I hear, I think that, apart from my friendship for your father, you are the kind of young fellow I should like with me."

Frank looked rather surprised.

"I had a letter," Colonel Wilson went on, "from Colonel Chambers, who was a captain in the 15th when I joined. He spoke in very high terms of you, and sent a copy of the proceedings and reports connected with the murder of that magistrate, and said that it was almost entirely due to your sharpness that your brother was cleared of the suspicion that had not unreasonably fallen upon him, and the saddle put upon the right horse. There is a sort of idea that any dashing young fellow will do for the cavalry, and no doubt dash is one of the prime requisites for cavalry officers, but if he is really to distinguish himself and be something more than a brave swordsman, more especially if he is likely to have the opportunity of obtaining a staff appointment, he needs other qualities, for on a reconnaissance a man who has a quick eye, good powers of observation and thoughtfulness, may send in a report of a most valuable kind, while that of the average young officer might be absolutely useless.

"Having said this much, I would advise you strongly to devote a couple of hours a day regularly to the study of French and German. You may find them invaluable, especially if you are engaged on any diplomatic mission, and much more useful at first than the study of writers on military tactics and strategy. There will be plenty of time for that afterwards. At Canterbury you will have no difficulty in finding a master among the many French *émigrés*, and as there are at present two or three troops of one of our German Hussar regiments there, and some of these men belong to families who preferred exile and service in the ranks to living under French domination, you may find a soldier who will be glad enough to add to his pay by a little teaching. A draft went out only a fortnight or so since to your regiment, and you are therefore likely to be some time at Canterbury before you are ordered out, and as the time in a garrison town hangs heavily on hand, a little steady work will help to make it pass not unpleasantly."

"I will certainly do so, sir. We had a French master at school. It was not compulsory to learn the language, but I thought it might be useful if I went into the army, and so took it up. I don't say that I can speak well at all, but I know enough to help me a good deal."

"That is right, lad. Ah, here is supper! I am sure you must want it after being eighteen hours on the outside of a coach in such weather as this, though I daresay as far as food went you did not do badly."

"No, sir; there was plenty of time at the stopping-places for meals, and as I was well wrapped up the cold was nothing."

Frank, however, could not deny that he felt very stiff after his journey, and was not sorry to retire to bed as soon as he had eaten his supper. There were few men in the army who had seen so much and such varied service as Colonel Sir Robert Wilson. Joining the army in 1793, he served through the campaigns of Flanders and Holland. In 1797, having attained the rank of captain, he was detached from his regiment and served on Major-general St. John's staff during the rebellion in Ireland. Two years later he rejoined his regiment and proceeded to the Helder, and was engaged in all the battles that took place during that campaign. On the Convention being signed he purchased a majority in one of the regiments of German Hussars in our service. He was then sent on a mission to Vienna, and having fulfilled this, went down through Italy to Malta, where he expected to find his regiment, which formed part of General Abercrombie's command. He joined it before it landed in Egypt, and served through the campaign there. He then purchased his lieutenant-colonelcy, and exchanged into the 20th Light Dragoons. He was with that portion of his regiment which formed part of Sir David Baird's division, and sailed first to the Brazils and then to the Cape of Good Hope, which possession it wrested from the Dutch.

On his return to England he was directed to proceed on the staff of Lord Hutchinson to Berlin, but on his arrival at Memel was despatched to the Russian headquarters as British commissioner. He continued with the Russian army during the next two campaigns, and on the signature of the treaty of Tilsit returned to England, and made several journeys to St. Petersburg with confidential despatches, and brought to England the first news that the Czar had concluded an alliance with Napoleon and was about to declare war against England. In 1808 Sir Robert Wilson was sent to Portugal to raise the Portuguese legion, and, acting independently as a Brigadier-general, rendered very valuable services, until in 1809 the legion was absorbed in the Portuguese army. He was now waiting for other employment.

The colonel went out with Frank after breakfast next morning and ordered his uniform and equipments. Frank was well supplied with money, for by the terms of his father's will either of his sons who entered the army was entitled to draw two hundred pounds a year to pay for outfit, horse, and as allowance until he came of age, when he would receive his share of the capital. Mrs. Troutbeck had, when he said good-bye to her, slipped a pocket-book with bank-notes for a hundred pounds into his hands.

"Money is always useful, Frank," she said, when he protested that he was amply supplied, "and if you should ever find that your allowance is insufficient write to me. I know that you are not in the least likely to be extravagant or foolish, but you see what a scrape your brother has got into, without any fault of his own, and you may also find yourself in a position where you may want money. If you do, write to me at once."

After the orders had been given, Sir Robert Wilson took Frank about London to see some of the sights. At dinner he asked him many questions as to his studies and amusements, and the way in which his day was generally spent. After dining at Sir Robert's club they returned to his lodgings.

"I am very pleased, Frank," he said as he lighted a cigar, "both with what I have heard of you and with what I see for myself. Now I will speak to you more freely than I did before, but mind, what I say is strictly confidential. Government have obtained secret information which points surely to the fact that Napoleon is meditating an offensive war against Russia. He is accumulating troops in Germany and Poland out of all proportion to the operations he has been carrying on against Austria. When that war will break out is more than I or anyone can say, but when it does take place I have Lord Wellesley's promise that I shall go out there in the same position I held during their last war, that is, as British commissioner with the Russian army. Now, lad, in that position I shall be entitled to take a young officer with me as my assistant, or what, if engaged on other service, would be called aide-de-camp. One cannot be everywhere at once, and I should often have to depend upon him for information as to what was taking place at points where I could not be present.

"He would, too, act as my secretary. It may possibly be a year before Napoleon's preparations are completed; but even in a year I should hardly be justified in choosing so young an officer from my old regiment, unless he had some special qualifications for the post. Now, for your father's sake, Frank, and because I like you and feel sure that you are just the man I require, I should like to take you, but could not do so unless you had some special knowledge that I could urge as a reason for applying for you. There is only one such qualification that I know of, namely, that you should be able to speak the Russian language. When I spoke to you about learning French and German I did so on general principles, and not with a view to this, for it did not seem to me that I could possibly select you to go with me on this service; but I have since thought it over, and have come to the conclusion that I could do so, if you did but understand Russian. It is a most difficult language, and although I can now get on with it fairly after my stay out there, I thought at first I should never make any headway in it. It would, therefore, be of no use whatever for you to attempt it unless you are ready to work very hard at it, and to give up, I should say, at least four hours a day to study."

"I should be quite ready to do that, sir," Frank said earnestly, "and I thank you indeed for your kindness. But who should I get to teach me?"

"That we must see about. There are, I have no doubt, many Russian Poles in London who speak the language well, and who have picked up enough English for your purpose. The Poles are marvellous linguists. We will go to-morrow to the headquarters of the Bow Street runners. They are the detectives, you know, and if they cannot at once put their hands upon such a man as we want, they will be able to ferret out half a dozen in twenty-four hours. One of these fellows you must engage to go down to Canterbury and take lodgings there. They are almost always in destitute circumstances, and would be content with very moderate pay, which would not draw very heavily on your resources. Thirty shillings a week would be a fortune to one of them. Even if this war should not come off—but I have myself no doubt about it—the language might in the future be of great value to you. I don't suppose there is a single officer in the English army, with the exception of myself, who knows a word of Russian, and in the future it might secure you the position of military attaché to our embassy there. At any rate it will render it easy for me to secure you an appointment on my mission when it comes off, and in that case you will be a witness of one of the most stupendous struggles that has ever taken place. You think you can really stick to it, Frank? You will have, no doubt, to put up with a good deal of chaff from your comrades on your studious tastes."

"I sha'n't mind that, sir. I have often been chaffed at school, because I used to insist on getting up my work before I would join anything that was going on, and used to find that if I took it good-temperedly, it soon ceased."

The next day they went to Bow Street. Sir Robert's card was sufficient to ensure them attention, and several of the detectives were questioned. One of them replied, "I think that I know just the man. He occupies an attic in the house next to mine. He is a young fellow of four-and-twenty, and I know he has been trying to support himself by giving lessons in German, but I don't think that he has ever had a pupil, and I believe he is nearly starving. His landlady told me that he has parted with all his clothes except those that he stands upright in. Of late he has been picking up a few pence by carrying luggage for people who land at the wharves. I have not spoken to him myself, but she tells me that he is a perfect gentleman, and though sometimes, as she believes, he has not so much as a crust of bread between his lips all day, he regularly pays his rent of a Saturday."

"I should think that he would be just the man for us. Would you see him when you go home this afternoon, and ask him to come to No. 44 Buckingham Street, either this evening at nine, or at the same hour to-morrow morning? I have written my address on this card."

At nine o'clock that evening the landlady came upstairs and said, rather doubtfully, that a young man had called to see Sir Robert, and that he had one of Sir Robert's cards.

"That is right, Mrs. Richards. I was expecting him."

The Pole was brought up. He was a pale young man, dressed in a thin suit of clothes that accorded but ill with the sharp frost outside. He bowed respectfully, and said in very fair English, "I am told, sir, that you wish to speak to me."

"Take a seat, sir. By the way, I do not know your name."

"Strelinski," the man said.

"I am told that you are desirous of giving lessons in languages."

"I am, sir, most desirous."

"Mr. Wyatt, this gentleman here, is anxious to learn Russian."

The man looked with some surprise at Frank. "I should be glad to teach it, sir," he said doubtfully, "but Russian is not like French or English. It is a very difficult language to learn, and one that would require a good deal of study. I should not like to take money without doing something in return, and I fear that this gentleman would be disappointed at the small progress he would make."

"Mr. Wyatt has just obtained a commission, and he thinks that as there are few, if any, officers in the army who speak it fluently, it might be of great advantage to him. He is, therefore, prepared to work hard at it. I myself," he went on in Russian, "speak it a little, as you see; I have already warned him of the difficulty of the language, and he is not dismayed. He is going down to Canterbury to join the depôt of his regiment in the course of a few days, and he proposes that you should accompany him and take a lodging there."

The young man's face had a look of surprise when he was addressed in the Russian language, and Frank saw a faint flush come across his face and tears flow to his eyes as he heard the offer.

"What terms would you ask? He might require your services for a year."

"Any terms that would keep me from starving," the man said.

"May I ask what you were in your own country, Mr. Strelinski?"

"I was educated for the law," the Pole said. "I took my degree at the University of Warsaw, but I was suspected of having a leaning towards the French—as who had not, when Napoleon had promised to deliver us from our slavery—and had to fly. I had intended at first to enter one of the Polish regiments in the French service, but I could not get across the frontier, and had to make north, getting here in an English ship. The war between you and France prevented my crossing the sea again, and then I resolved to earn my living here, but—" and he stopped.

"You have found it hard work. I can quite understand that, Mr. Strelinski. It is terribly hard for any foreigner, even with good introductions, to earn a living here, and to one unprovided with such recommendations well-nigh impossible. Please to sit here for a moment. Frank, come into the next room with me."

"Well, what do you think?" he asked when they were alone.

"I should think that he will do splendidly, sir, and his being a gentleman will make it very pleasant for me. But I should not like to offer him as little as thirty shillings a week."

"I have no doubt that he would be delighted with it, Frank, but as he will have to pay his lodgings out of it and furnish his wardrobe, we might say two pounds, if you can afford it."

"I can afford it very well, sir. My aunt gave me a hundred pounds when I came away from home, and that will pay for it for one year. I am sure I shall like him."

"He impresses me very favourably too," Sir Robert said, "and perhaps I may find a post for him here if we go out, though we need not think of that at present. Well, let us go in to him again. I have no doubt that the poor fellow is on thorns."

"I have talked it over with Mr. Wyatt," he went on when they had returned to the sitting-room; "he will probably require your services for a year, though possibly he may have to join his regiment sooner than that. He is willing to pay two pounds a week for your services as his instructor. Will that suit you?"

"It is more than sufficient," the Pole said in a broken voice. "For half of that I could keep myself."

"Yes, but there will be your lodgings to pay, and other matters; and if you are willing to accept two pounds, which appears to us a fair rate of remuneration, we will consider that as settled. It is a cold night, Mr. Strelinski. You had better take a glass of wine and a biscuit before you venture out."

He fetched a decanter of port and a tin of biscuits from the sideboard, and placed them in front of him; then he made a sign to Frank to leave the room. In a few minutes he called him back again. Frank found the Pole standing with his hat in his hand ready to leave. There was a look of brightness and hope in his face, which was a strong contrast to his expression on entering. He bowed deeply to Sir Robert, and took the hand that Frank held out to him.

"You have saved me," he said, and then, without another word, turned and left the room.

"I have insisted upon his taking ten pounds on account of his salary, as I told him that he must have warm clothes and make a decent figure in Canterbury. You are to deduct ten shillings a week from his pay till it is made up. The poor fellow fairly broke down when I offered it to him. There is no doubt that he is almost starved, and is as weak as a rat. He is to come to-morrow at twelve o'clock. I have business that will take me out all day, so you can have a quiet chat with him and break the ice."

CHAPTER VII.

A FRENCH PRISON.

JULIAN WYATT had expected that there would be some formalities on his arrival at Nantes—that he should probably be taken before a court of some sort,—and he determined to make a protest, and to declare that he had been forcibly brought over from England. At the same time he felt that to do so would make little difference in his position. When Holland was overrun with the French, all English residents were thrown into prison, and the same thing had happened after the short peace; still he determined to make the effort, for he thought that as a civilian he might not be placed in a military prison, and might, therefore, have a better chance of making his escape. He had, however, no opportunity for protest or remonstrance. The captain of the lugger and two of his men went ashore as soon as the craft was moored alongside the quay.

A quarter of an hour later they returned with a sergeant and two soldiers. The captain pointed him out to the sergeant. The latter crossed the plank on to the deck, put his hand on Julian's shoulder, and motioned to him to follow him ashore.

"Good-bye, young fellow!" Markham said, as, feeling the uselessness of protest or resistance, Julian moved towards the plank. "I am very sorry for you, but there is nothing else to do, and you will be as well there as anywhere, for you couldn't show your face in Weymouth. I will keep my promise, never fear; and some day or other everyone shall know that you had nothing to do with giving that fellow the end he deserved."

Julian was marched along the quay for some distance, and then through the streets till they came to a large building. The sergeant rang the bell at the gate. When it was opened he entered with Julian, leaving the two soldiers without. A sub-officer of the prison came up, and the sergeant handed to him a paper, which was an order signed by the mayor for the governor of the prison to receive an English sailor, name unknown, age twenty-one, who had been picked up at sea by the master of the French lugger *Lucille*. The official gave a receipt to the sergeant for the prisoner, and a warder then led Julian away to a vaulted hall, where some forty or fifty men were either lying on some straw or were walking up and down in the endeavour to warm themselves. Julian saw at once that they were English sailors, although their clothes were for the most part ragged and torn.

"Hulloa, mate!" one of them said as the door closed behind him. "Have you come all alone? For the most part we arrive in batches. Where do you hail from, and what was your ship?"

"I hail from Weymouth," Julian replied cheerfully, his habit of making the best of things at once asserting itself. "I don't know that I can be said to belong to any ship, but I made the passage across in a French smuggling lugger, the *Lucille*. I suppose I ought to feel indebted to them, for they brought me across without asking for any passage-money; but they have played me a dirty trick here, for they have handed me over to the authorities, as far as I can understand the matter, as a man-of-war sailor they have picked up."

"What were you doing on board?" another sailor asked. "Did you have to leave England in a hurry?"

"I left in a hurry because I could not help it. Going across the hills I came quite accidentally upon one of the smugglers' hiding-places, and was seized before I had time to say a word. There was a little discussion among themselves as to what they would do with me, and I should have had my throat cut if an Englishman among them had not known that I was friends with most of the fishermen there, and had been present once or twice when a cargo was run. So they finally made up their minds to bring me over here, and as they feared I might, if I returned, peach as to their hiding-place, they trumped up this story about me, and handed me over to the French to take care of."

"Well, that story will do just as well as another," one of the sailors laughed. "As to their taking care of you, beyond looking sharp that you don't get away, the care they give you ain't worth speaking of. We are pretty nigh starved, and pretty nigh frozen. Well, there is one thing, we shall get out of it in two or three days, for we hear that we are all to be marched off somewhere. A batch generally goes off once a fortnight."

"Are you mostly men-of-war's men?"

"None of us, at least not when we were taken, though I reckon most of us have had a spell at it one time or other. No; we all belong to two ships that were captured by a couple of their confounded privateers. The one I belonged to was bound for Sicily with stores for some of the troops stationed there; the other lot were on their way to the Tagus. They caught us off Finisterre within a couple of days of each other. We both made a fight of it, and if we had been together when they came up, we might have beaten them off; but we had not any chance single-handed against two of them, for they both carried much heavier metal than we did. I don't think we should have resisted if we had not thought that the noise of the guns might have brought one of our cruisers up. But we had no such luck, and so here we are."

"I suppose, lad, you haven't got anything to pay your footing with? They did not leave us a *sou* in our pockets, and I don't suppose the smugglers were much more generous to you."

"Yes, they were," Julian said. "I have a guinea and some odd silver. I will keep the odd silver for the present, for it may come in handy later on; but here is the guinea, and if there are any means of getting anything with it, order what you like."

There was a shout of satisfaction, followed by an animated debate as to how the money should be spent. Julian learnt that there was no difficulty in obtaining liquor in the prison, as one of the warders had permission to sell it in quantities not exceeding one glass, for which the charge was four *sous*, and also that prisoners with money could send out for food. After much discussion, it was finally settled that forty-five pints of soup and the same number of rations of rum should be obtained. The soup was but three *sous* a pint, which would leave them enough for a tot of grog all round next day. One of them, who had been first mate on board— for Julian found that only the masters had separate treatment as officers—went across to the man who supplied liquor. The warder soon returned with him, carrying four bottles, a large stone jar of water, and two or three small tin cups. The mate, who spoke French pretty fluently, had a sharp argument with him as to the amount in French money that he should receive as change out of the guinea; and as he had learnt from one of the last batch that had been sent away, the proper rate of exchange in the town, he finally got the best of it, and the work of serving out the liquor then began.

A few of the sailors tossed off their allowance without water, but most of them took it half and half, so as to make it go further. Undoubtedly if the warder would have sold more than one allowance to each man the whole of the guinea would at once have been laid out, but he was firm on this point. Soon afterwards the prisoners' dinner was brought in. It consisted of a slice of black bread to each man and a basin of very thin broth, and Julian was not surprised at the hungry look that he had noticed on the men's faces.

"Pretty poor fare, isn't it, mate?" one of them said as he observed the air of disfavour with which Julian regarded his rations. "It has been a matter of deep calculation with these French fellows as to how little would do just to keep a man alive, and I reckon they have got it to a nicety. This is what we have three times a day, and I don't know whether one is most hungry when one turns in at night, or when one turns out in the morning. However, we shall be better off to-night. We get our supper at six, and at eight we shall get in that stuff you paid for. It is a precious deal better than this, I can tell you; for one of our chums managed to hide two or three shillings when they searched us, and got some in, and it was good, and no mistake; and they give half a slice of bread with each pint. It is better bread than this black stuff they give us in prison. Though an English dog would turn up his nose at it, still it helps to fill up."

The second supper was voted a great success, and after it was eaten, the men, cheered by its warmth, and freed for a time from the annoying feeling of hunger they generally experienced, became quite merry. Several songs were sung, but at the conclusion of a grand chorus an armed warder came in and ordered them to be silent.

"If the governor hears you making that row," he said, "you will have one of your meals cut off to-morrow."

The threat was effectual, and the men lay down in the straw as close as they could get to each other for warmth, as by this means the thin rug each had served out to him sufficed to spread over two bodies, and their covering was thus doubled. Julian had really another guinea besides the silver in his pocket, but he had thought it better to make no mention of this, as in case of his ever being able to make his escape, it would be of vital service to him. The following day there was another council over the ten francs still remaining. A few would have spent it in another allowance of rum all round, but finally, by an almost unanimous vote, it was determined that fifteen clay pipes should be obtained, and the rest laid out in tobacco. The forty-five were solemnly divided into three watches. Each member of a watch was to have a pipe, which was to be filled with tobacco. This he could smoke fast or slow as he chose, or, if he liked, could use the tobacco for chewing. At the end of half an hour the pipes were to be handed over to the next watch, and so on in regular order until evening.

This plan was carried out, and afforded unbounded satisfaction, and many loudly regretted that it had not been thought of at first, as the money spent on grog would have largely extended the time the tobacco would hold out. So jealous did the men become of their store of tobacco that the mate was requested to fill all the pipes, as some of the men in helping themselves rammed their pipes so closely that they held double the proper allowance of tobacco. This treat at once established Julian as a popular character, and upon his lamenting, when talking to the mate, his inability to speak French, the latter offered to teach him as much as he could. Directly he began three or four of the younger sailors asked to be allowed to listen, a school was established in one corner of the room, and for several hours a day work went on, both master and pupils finding that it greatly shortened the long weary hours of idleness.

Three weeks passed without change. Then they were

told that next morning they would be marched away to make room for another batch of prisoners that had been brought into the fort that afternoon. All were glad of the change, first, because it was a change, and next, because they all agreed they could not be worse off anywhere than they were at Nantes. They were mustered at daybreak, formed up in fours, and with a guard of twenty soldiers with loaded muskets marched out from the prison gates. The first day's journey was a long one. Keeping along the north bank of the Loire, they marched to Angers, which they did not reach until night was falling. Many of the men, wholly unaccustomed to walking, were completely worn out before they reached their destination, but as a whole, with the exception of being somewhat footsore, they arrived in fair condition. Julian marched by the side of the first mate, and the lesson in French was a long one, and whiled away the hours on the road.

"It would not be difficult for us, if we were to pass the word down, to fall suddenly on our guards and overpower them," the mate said in one of the pauses of their talk. "A few of us might be shot, but as soon as we had knocked some of them over and got their arms, we should easily make an end of the rest. The difficulty would be what to do afterwards."

"That is a difficulty there is no getting over," Julian said. "With the exception of yourself, there is not one who speaks French well."

"I don't speak it well," the mate said. "I know enough to get on with, but the first person that I addressed would see at once that I was a foreigner. No; we should all be in the same boat, and a very bad boat it would be. We should all be hunted down in the course of twenty four hours, and I expect would be shot twelve hours afterwards. I think that instead of sending twenty men with us they might safely have sent only two, for it would be simply madness to try to escape. If one alone could manage to slip off there would be some chance for him. There is no doubt that the Bretons are bitterly opposed to the present state of things, and have not forgotten how they suffered in their rising early in the days of the Republic. They would probably conceal a runaway, and might pass him along through their woods to St. Malo or one of the other seaports, and thence a passage across might be obtained in a smuggler, but it would be a hazardous job."

"Too hazardous for me to care to undertake, even if I got the chance to slip away," Julian said.

"You are right, mate; nothing short of a big reward would tempt any of the smugglers to run the risk of carrying an escaped prisoner out of the country; and as I have not a penny in my pocket, and nothing to draw on at home —for there is only my pay due up to the date we were captured when we were only eight days out—I should not have the slightest chance of getting away. No; I shall take whatever comes. I expect we are in for it to the end of the war, though when that will be is more than any man can tell."

They were marched into the prison at Angers, where they were provided with a much more bountiful meal than they had been accustomed to, a good allowance of straw, and two blankets each. To their great satisfaction they were not called at daybreak, and on questioning one of the warders who brought in their breakfast, the first mate learnt that after the march to Angers it was customary to allow a day's rest to the prisoners going through. They were ready for the start on the following morning, and stopped for that night at La Flèche. The next march was a long one to Vendôme, and at this place they again halted for a day. Stopping for a night at Beaugency, they marched to Orleans, where was a large prison. Here they remained for a week. The guards who had accompanied them from Nantes left them here at Orleans and returned by water.

From Orleans they struck more to the north, and after ten days' marching arrived at Verdun, which was, they learned, their final destination. Here there were fully a thousand English prisoners, for the most part sailors. The greater portion of them were lodged in wooden huts erected in a great court-yard surrounded by a high wall. The food was coarse, but was much more abundant than it had been at Nantes. The newly arrived party were quartered together in one of the huts.

Night and day sentries were posted on the wall, along which a wooden platform, three feet from the top, permitted them to pass freely; on this sentry-boxes were erected at short intervals. As soon as their escort had left them, the new-comers were surrounded by sailors eager to learn the last news from England—how the war was going on, and what prospect there was of peace. As soon as their curiosity was satisfied, the crowd speedily dispersed. Julian was struck with the air of listless indifference that prevailed among the prisoners, but it was not long before he quite understood it. Cut off from all news, without hope of escape or exchange, it was difficult for even the most light-hearted to retain their spirits.

As sailors, the men were somewhat better able to support the dull hopelessness of their lives than others would have been. Most of them were handy in some way or other, and as they were permitted by the authorities to make anything they could, they passed much of their time in working at something or other. Some cut out and rigged model ships, others knitted, some made quilts from patches purchased for a trifle by the warders for them in the town, some made fancy boxes of straw, others carved walking-sticks, paper-cutters, and other trifles.

Each day, two or three of their number had permission to go down into the town to sell their own and their comrades' manufactures, and to buy materials. There was a fair sale for most of the articles, for these were bought not only by the townspeople, but by pedlars, who carried them through the country. The prices obtained were small, but they afforded a profit over the money laid out in materials, sufficient to purchase tobacco and other little luxuries—the introduction of spirits into the prison being, however, strictly forbidden. Of more importance than the money they earned, was the relief to the tedium of their life in the work itself. Julian found a similar relief in studying French. There were some among the prisoners who spoke the language far better than did the mate, and after three months' work with the latter, Julian was advised by him to obtain a better teacher. He found no difficulty in getting one, who spoke French really well, to talk with him three or four hours a day on condition of being supplied with tobacco during that time; and as tobacco was very cheap, and could be always bought from the soldiers, Julian's store of money was not much diminished by the outlay.

He himself had now regularly taken to smoking; not at first because he liked it, but because he saw how much it cheered and comforted his comrades, who, however, generally used it in the sailor fashion of chewing. Escape was never talked of. The watch kept was extremely strict, and as on getting outside of the walls of the court-yard, they would but find themselves in a town girt in by walls and fortifications, the risk was altogether too great to be encountered. It had been attempted many times, but in the great majority of cases the fugitives had been shot, and their bodies had always been brought back to the prison in order to impress the others with the uselessness of the attempt. A very few, indeed, had got away; at least, it was supposed that they had done so, as their bodies had not been brought back; but it was generally considered that the chances were enormously against their being able to make their way over the wide extent of country between Verdun and the sea, and then to succeed in obtaining a passage to some neutral port, from which they could make their way to England. Several times offers of freedom were made to such of the prisoners as volunteered to enter the French army or navy, but very few availed themselves of them.

At the end of ten months, Julian was able to speak French fluently. Large bodies of troops were continually marching through the town bound for the east, and the prisoners learned from the guards that the general belief was that Napoleon intended to invade Russia.

"I have a good mind to enlist," Julian said one day, to his friend the mate. "Of course, nothing would persuade me to do so if it were a question of fighting against the English. But now that I have learnt French fairly, I begin to find this life horrible, and am longing intensely to be doing something. There are the reasons that I have already told you of why, even if I were free, I could not go home. I might as well be taking part in this campaign as staying in prison. Besides, I should have infinitely better chances of escape as a soldier than we have here, and if I find I don't like it, I can at least try to get off."

"Well, placed as you are, Wyatt, I don't know that I should not be inclined to do the same. At any rate, you would be seeing something of life, instead of living like a caged monkey here. Of course, as you say, no one would dream of such a thing if one would have to go to Spain to fight our fellows there. Still, if by any chance, after this Russian business, your regiment was ordered back to

France, and then to Spain, you would at any rate have a fair chance of escaping on such a journey. I would not do it myself, because I have a wife at home. One hopes, slight as the chance seems to be, that some day there will be a general exchange of prisoners. But as you can't go home, I don't know but that it would be a good plan for you to do what you propose. At any rate, your life as a soldier would be a thousand times better than this dog's existence."

"I could put up with that for myself, but it is awful seeing many of the men walking about with their heads down, never speaking for hours, and the pictures of hopeless melancholy. See how they die off, not from hunger or fever, for we have enough to eat, but wasting away and dying from home-sickness, and because they have nothing to live for. Why, of the forty-five of us who came up together, ten have gone already; and there are three or four others who won't last long. It is downright heartbreaking; and now that I have no longer anything to keep my thoughts employed a good part of the day, I begin to feel it myself. I catch myself saying, What is the use of it all? it would be better make a bolt and have done with it. I can quite understand the feelings of that man who was shot last week. He ran straight out of the gate; he had no thought of escape; he simply did it to be shot down by the sentries, instead of cutting his own throat. I don't believe I could stand it much longer, Jim; and even if I were certain of being killed by a Russian ball I think I should go."

"Go then, lad," the man said. "I have always thought that you have borne up very well; but I know it is even worse for you than it is for us sailors. We are accustomed to be cooped up for six months at a time on board a ship, without any news from outside; with nothing to do save to see that the decks are washed, and the brasses polished, except when there is a shift of wind or a gale

But to anyone like yourself, I can understand that it must be terrible; and if you feel getting into that state, I should say go by all means."

"I will give you a letter before I enlist, Jim; and I will get you, when you are exchanged, to go down with it yourself to Weymouth, and tell them what became of me, and why I went into the French army. Don't let them think that I turned traitor. I would shoot myself rather than run the risk of having to fight Englishmen. But when it is a choice between fighting Russians and going out of my mind, I prefer shouldering a French musket. I will write the letter to-day. There is no saying when they may next call for volunteers; for, as you know, those who step forward are taken away at once, so as to prevent their being persuaded by the others into drawing back."

The next day Julian wrote his letter. He recapitulated the arguments he had used to the mate, and bade Frank and his aunt a final farewell. "I may, of course, get through the campaign," he said. "The French soldiers here seem to think that they will sweep the Russians before them, but that is their way. They talked of sweeping us out of the Peninsula, and they haven't done it yet; and there is no doubt that the Russians are good soldiers, and will make a big fight of it. I hope you won't feel cut up about this, and really I care little whether I leave my bones in Russia or not. It may be twenty years or even longer before that fellow Markham's letter arrives to clear me. And until then I cannot return to England, or at any rate to Weymouth; indeed, wherever I was, I should live with the knowledge that I might at any moment be recognized and arrested. Therefore while others here have some hope of a return home, either by an exchange of prisoners or by the war coming to an end, I have nothing to look forward to. So you see, old fellow, that it is as well as it is.

"I have to earn my own living somehow, and this way will suit me better than most. Only, of one thing be sure, that if at the end of the Russian war I return alive, and my regiment is sent where there is a chance of fighting our people, I shall take an opportunity of deserting. As I have told you, I can speak French fairly well now, and after a few months in a French regiment I shall be able to pass as a native, and should have a good chance of making my way somehow through the country to the frontier. My idea at present is that I should make for Genoa and ship there as a sailor on board an Italian vessel, or, better still, if we happen to be masters of the place, or our fleet near, should either enlist in one of our regiments, or ship on board one of our men-of-war. I should, of course, take another name, and merely say that I had been captured by the French at sea, had been a prisoner at Verdun, and had managed to get free, and make my way across the country. Probably in any case I shall do this when the regiment returns from Russia. Two or three years' absence, and a fair share of the hardships of a soldier's life, and a disguise, might enable me without detection to travel down to Weymouth and see Aunt, and learn if there had been any news from Markham.

"Whether I shall find you there or not I can't tell. I have but little hope that you will be able to get a commission. This affair of mine will be, I fear, an absolute bar to that. But, wherever you may be, I shall do my best to find you out, after I have seen Aunt. This will be given you by a good fellow named Jim Thompson. He has been a first mate, and has been a good friend to me ever since I have been over here. If he is exchanged, he will bring it to you; if not, he will give it to one of the men who is exchanged, to post it on his arrival in England. I shall direct it both to you and Aunt, so that if you are away from Weymouth she will open it. God bless you both!"

Three days later a notice was posted in the prison saying that any of the prisoners who chose to volunteer for service in Germany were at liberty to do so. They would not be called upon at any future time for service against British troops, but would have the liberty to exchange into regiments destined for other service. Eight men, including Julian, came forward, when, an hour later, a French officer entered and called for volunteers. Julian had already announced his intention of doing so to his comrades in the hut, and to his other acquaintances.

"You see," he said, "we shall not be called upon for service against the English, and I would rather fight the Russians than stay in this place for years."

Hitherto the men who had volunteered had been hooted by their fellow-prisoners as they went out, but the promise that they should not be called upon for service against British troops made a great difference in the feeling with which the offer was regarded, and had it not been for the hope that everyone felt that he should ere long be exchanged, the number who stepped forward would have been greatly increased. A strong French division had marched into Verdun that morning, and the new volunteers were all divided among different corps. Julian, who now stood over six feet, was told off to a Grenadier regiment. A uniform was at once given to him from those carried with the baggage of the regiment, and the sergeant of the company in which he had been placed took him to its barrack-room.

"Comrades," he said, "here is a new recruit. He is an Englishman who has the good sense to prefer fighting the Russians to rotting in prison. He is a brave fellow, and speaks our language well, and I think you will find him a good comrade. He has handed over twenty francs to pay his footing in the company. You must not regard him as a traitor to his country, my friends, for he has received from the colonel a paper authorizing him to exchange into a regiment destined for other service, in case, after we have done with the Russians, we should be sent to some place where we should have to fight against his countrymen."

In half an hour Julian felt at home with his new comrades. They differed greatly in age: some among them had grown grizzly in the service, and had fought in all the wars of the Republic and Empire; others were lads not older than himself, taken but a month or two before from the plough. After they had drunk the liquor purchased with his twenty francs, they patted him on the back and drank to the health of Jules Wyatt, for Julian had entered under his own surname, and his Christian name was at once converted to its French equivalent. With his usual knack of making friends, he was soon on excellent terms with them all, joined in their choruses, and sang some English songs whose words he had as an exercise translated into French, and when the men lay down for the night on their straw pallets it was generally agreed that the new comrade was a fine fellow and an acquisition to the company.

The division was to halt for two days at Verdun, and the time was spent, as far as Julian was concerned, in the hands of a sergeant, who kept him hard at work all day acquiring the elements of drill. On the third morning the regiment marched off at daybreak, Julian taking his place in the ranks, with his knapsack and firelock. After the long confinement in the prison he found his life thoroughly enjoyable. Sometimes they stopped in towns, where they were either quartered in barracks or billeted on the inhabitants; sometimes they slept under canvas or in the open air, and this Julian preferred, as they built great fires and gathered round them in merry groups. The conscripts had by this time got over their home-sickness, and had caught the martial enthusiasm of their older comrades. All believed that the Grande Armée would be invincible, and fears were even expressed that the Russians would not venture to stand against them. Some of the older men, however, assured them that there was little chance of this.

"The Russians are hardy fighters, comrades," one of the veterans said. "*Parbleu!* I who tell you, have fought against them, and they are not to be despised. They are slow at manœuvring, but put them in a place and tell them to hold it, and they will do it to the last. I fought at Austerlitz against the Austrians, and at Jena against the Prussians, and in a score of other battles in Germany and Italy, and I tell you that the Russians are the toughest enemies I have met, save only your Islanders, Jules. I was at Talavera, and the way your people held that hill after the cowardly Spaniards had bolted and left them, and at last rolled us down it, was a thing I don't want to see again. I was wounded and sent home to be patched up, and that is how I come to be here marching against Russia instead of being under Soult in Spain. No, comrades, you take my word for it, big as our army will be, we shall have some tough fighting to do before we get to Moscow or St. Petersburg, whichever the Little Corporal intends to dictate terms in."

"It is as you say, Victor," one of the other veterans said, "and it is all the better. It would be too bad if we had to march right across Europe and back without firing a shot, but I, who know the Russians too, feel sure that that will never be."

Many a merry martial song was sung at the bivouac fires, many a story of campaigns and battles told, and no thought of failure entered the minds of anyone, from the oldest veteran to the youngest drummer-boy. Of an evening, after halting, Julian generally had half an hour's drill, until, three weeks after leaving Verdun, he was pronounced fit to take part in a review under the eyes of the Emperor himself. His readiness to oblige, even to undertaking sentry duty for a comrade who had grown footsore on the march, or was suffering from some temporary ailment, his cheeriness and good temper, had by this time rendered him a general favourite in the company, and when he was dismissed from drill the veterans were always ready to give him lessons with the sabre or rapier in addition to those he received from the *maître d'armes* of the regiment. Julian entered into these exercises with great earnestness. Quarrels between the men were not infrequent, and these were always settled by the sabre or straight sword, the officers' permission being necessary before these duels took place. It was seldom that their consequences were very serious. The *maître d'armes* was always present, and put a stop to the fight as soon as blood was drawn. At present Julian was on the best terms with all his comrades, but he felt that, if he should become involved in a quarrel, he of all men must be ready to vindicate his honour and to show that, Englishman as he was, he was not a whit behind his comrades in his readiness to prove his courage. Thus, then, he worked with ardour, and ere long became able to hold his own even with the veterans of the regiment.

CHAPTER VIII.

PISTOL PRACTICE.

"YOU are a rum fellow, Wyatt," one of the captains of the depôt of his regiment said to Frank a fortnight after he joined.

"How am I rum?"

"Why, about that Russian fellow. I never heard of a

young cornet setting-to to work like a nigger, when there is no occasion in the world for him to do so."

"There is no absolute occasion perhaps, but you see Russian may be very useful some day."

"Well, yes, and so might any other out-of-the-way language."

"It is an off-chance, no doubt; still it is better to be doing something that may turn out useful than to be walking up and down the High Street or playing billiards. I don't spend much time over it now, for there is a good deal to do in learning one's work, but when I once get out of the hands of the drill-sergeant and the riding-master I shall have a lot of time to myself, and shall be very glad to occupy some of it in getting up Russian."

"Of course it is your own business and not mine, Wyatt; but I am afraid you won't find things very pleasant if you take a line of your own and don't go with the rest."

"I have no wish not to go with the rest," Frank protested. "When there is anything to be done, whether it is hunting or any sort of sport, I shall certainly take my share in it; but don't you think yourself, Captain Lister, that it is much better for a fellow to spend part of his time reasonably than in lounging about, or in playing billiards or cards?"

"I don't say that it isn't better, Wyatt, but that is hardly the question. Many things may be better than others, but if a fellow doesn't go with the run he gets himself disliked, and has a very hard time of it."

"I used to hear a good deal of the same thing when I was at school," Frank said quietly, "but I don't think I was disliked for sticking to work sometimes, when other fellows were playing. Surely when one is from morning till night with other men, it can matter to no one but himself if he gives two or three hours a day to work."

"It does not matter to anyone, Wyatt. I am quite willing to grant it, but for all that, I am afraid, if you stick to it, you will have to put up with a great deal of chaff, and not always of a good-natured kind."

"I can put up with any amount of chaff," Frank replied; "I mean chaff in its proper sense. Anything that goes beyond that, I shall, I hope, be able to meet as it deserves. Perhaps it would be better if I were to take half an hour a day off my Russian studies and to spend that time in the pistol-gallery."

Captain Lister looked at him earnestly. "I think you will do, youngster," he said approvingly, "that is the right spirit. There is a lot of rough fun and larking in a regiment, and the man that goes through it best, is he who can take a joke good-temperedly as long as it does not go beyond the bounds of moderation, but who is ready to resent any wilful insult; but I think you would be very wise to do as you say. Half an hour in a pistol-gallery every day is likely to be of vastly more use to you than any amount of Russian. The reputation that a man is a crack shot with a pistol will do more than anything in the world to keep him out of quarrels. Here at the depôt at any rate, where the fellows are for the most part young, it would certainly save you a good deal of annoyance if it were known that, although not by any means a quarrelsome fellow, you were determined to put up with nothing beyond good humoured jokes. Well, lad, I don't want to interfere with your hobby, only I advise you not to ride it too hard, at any rate at first. When the men all know you and get to like you, and see that, apart from this fancy of yours, you are an all-round good fellow, as I can see you are, they will let you go your own way. At any rate, as captain of your troop, I will do all I can to make things pleasant for you, but don't forget about the pistol practice. At a depôt like this, where there are half a dozen regiments represented, you will meet with a larger proportion of disagreeable men than you would in your own ante-room. You see, if colonels have such men, they are glad enough to rid the regiment of them by leaving them at the depôt, and any serious trouble is more likely to come from one of them than from anyone in your own regiment."

"I will take your advice, certainly," Frank said; "the more so that the time spent in learning to be a good shot with a pistol will be most useful in a campaign, even if there is no occasion ever to put it to the test when at home."

"There is a gunsmith in St. Margaret's Street. It is a small shop, but the man, Woodall is his name, has got a long shed that he uses as a pistol-gallery, a quarter of a mile out beyond the gate. He is an admirable shot himself as well as an excellent workman, and you can't do better than go to him. Tell him that you want to become a good shot with the pistol, and are willing to pay for lessons. If he takes you in hand it won't be long before he turns you out as a fair shot; whether you ever get beyond that depends on nerve and eye, and I should think that you have no lack of either."

"I hope not," Frank said, with a smile. "At any rate I will see him this afternoon."

"Put on your cap at once, and I will go down with you," Captain Lister said; "and mind, I think if I were you I should say nothing about it at the depôt until he tells you that he has done with you. Knowing that the man is a learner might have just the opposite effect of hearing that he is a crack shot."

In a quarter of an hour they arrived at the gunsmith's. "Woodall," Captain Lister said, "my friend, Mr. Wyatt, who has lately joined, has a fancy for becoming a first-rate pistol shot."

"He couldn't have a more useful fancy, Captain Lister. My idea is, that every cavalry-man—trooper as well as officer—should be a dead shot with a pistol. The sword is all very well, and I don't say it is not a useful weapon, but a regiment that could shoot—really shoot well—would be a match for any three French regiments, though they were Boney's best."

"He wants you take him in hand yourself, Woodall, if you can spare the time to do so; of course, he is ready to pay you for your time and trouble, and would meet you at any hour you like to name in the afternoon at your shed."

"All right, sir! It is a rum thing to me that, while every officer is ready to take any pains to learn the sword exercise, they seem to think that pistol-shooting comes by nature, and that, even on horseback, in the middle of the confusion of a charge, you have only got to point your pistol and bring down your man. The thing is down-right ridiculous! It will be a pleasure to teach you, Mr. Wyatt. I should say, from your look, you are likely to turn out a first-rate shot."

"It won't be for want of trying if I don't," Frank replied.

"If you will take my advice, sir, you will learn to shoot with both hands. For a civilian who never wants to use a pistol except in a duel, the right hand is all that is necessary, but for a cavalry-man, the left is the useful hand. You see an officer always carries his sword in his right hand, and if he has got to shift it to his left before he can use his pistol, he could never use it at all, if hard pressed in a fight. Another thing is, that the left side is the weak side of a horseman. His sword is all right in defending him if attacked on the right, but if he is attacked on the left he is fighting under a big disadvantage. He has much more difficulty in guarding himself on that side, and he has nothing like the same reach for striking as he has on the other."

"That is quite true, now I come to think of it," Frank said; "though I never gave it a thought before. Yes, I see that the left hand is the most useful one, and I will practise with that as well as with the other. Well, what hour will suit you?"

"It don't make much difference to me, sir; the evenings are getting longer; you can see well enough until five."

"Well, then, shall we say half-past four?"

"Half-past four will suit very well, Mr. Wyatt. It is four o'clock now, so if you like to take your first lesson to-day I will meet you at the shed in half an hour. You cannot miss the place, it is on the right side of the road and stands by itself, and there is my name over the door."

"Thank you; I will be there," Frank replied.

"I may as well come with you, Wyatt," Captain Lister said. "I will fire a few shots myself, for I have had no practice for the last two years, and I have a fancy to see what I can do with my left hand. I have never tried with it, and I quite agree with Woodall that it is the left hand that a cavalry-man should use."

Frank was a good deal surprised at first to see how much more difficult it was to hit a mark, even at the distance of twelve paces, than he imagined that it would be. Woodall would not allow him to take aim.

"You will never get a chance to do that, Mr. Wyatt, in a fight; you have got to whip out your pistol, to throw up your arm and fire. It has got to be done by instinct rather than by aim. It is all very well to aim when you are on your feet and standing perfectly steady, but on a horse half-mad with excitement, and perhaps going at a gallop, you could no more hold your arm steady on a mark than you could fly. Put down the pistol for a time. Now you know, sir, when you point at a thing with your first finger extended, however quickly you do it, you will be there or thereabout, and it is the same thing if you have got a pistol in your hand. You see that black patch on the wall to the right of the target. Now turn your back to it. Now, when I give the word, turn on your heels, and the moment your eye catches that patch throw up your arm with your forefinger extended and point to it. When you get it up there, hold it as steady as you can. Now, sir!"

Frank did as he was ordered.

"Now, sir, look along your arm. You see you are pointing very nearly at the centre of the patch. You are just a little high. Now try it with your left. There, you see, you are not quite so accurate this time—you are six inches to the left of the patch, and nearly a foot high. Remember that it's always better to aim a little low than a little high, for the tendency of the hand in the act of pulling the trigger is to raise the muzzle. Now, sir, try that half a dozen times, using the hands alternately. Very good! Now take this empty pistol—no, don't hold it like that! Not one man in twenty, ay, not one in a hundred, holds a pistol right, they always want to get the first finger on the trigger. Now, you want the first finger to point with, the second finger is quite as good to pull with, in fact better, for going straight, as it does, with the arm, there is less tendency to throw up the muzzle. Now take it like this; you see my fore-finger lies along in the line of the barrel, that is the really important point. Get into the way of always grasping your pistol so that the first finger is in an exact line with the barrel, then, you see, just as your finger naturally follows your eye and points at the spot, so your pistol must be in the same line. It is best to have the middle and third fingers both on the trigger, and the little finger and thumb alone grasping the butt.

"You will find that a little difficult at first, but you will soon get accustomed to it, and your little finger will rapidly gain strength, and, you see, the hold of your first finger along the barrel helps the other two to steady it. By having the middle and third fingers both on the trigger, you give a pressure rather than a pull to it, and they will soon come to give that pressure at the very moment when the first finger gets on the mark aimed at. Now try it half a dozen times with the pistol unloaded, and after pressing the trigger keep your hand and arm in as nearly the same position, so as to see if it is pointing truly at the mark. Very good! Now try with the left hand. There, you see, that hand is not so accustomed to its work, and though you might have hit the target, I doubt if either of the shots would have struck the inner circle. Now we will try with the pistol loaded."

Six shots were fired alternately with the right and left hand. Those of the former were all within a few inches of the bull's-eye, while none of the others went wide of the outside.

"Very good, indeed," the gunsmith said. "I don't hesitate to say that in a very short time you will become a fair shot, and at the end of the three months, if you practise regularly, a first-class one. Your hand is very steady, your eye true, and you have plenty of nerve. Now, sir, I should advise you to keep that unloaded pistol in the drawer of your table, and whenever you have nothing else to do, spend five minutes in taking quick aims at marks on the wall, using your hands alternately. Now, Captain Lister, will you try a few shots?"

Taking a steady aim Captain Lister put his bullets almost every time into the bull's-eye, but, to Frank's surprise, when he came to try quick firing in the way he had himself done, the captain's shooting was much less accurate than his own.

"It is a question of eye," the gunsmith said next day, when Frank was alone with him. "You see Captain

Lister's shooting was fair when he took a steady aim, but directly he came to fire as he would in action, and that without the disturbing influences of excitement and of the motion of his horse, he was nowhere. He did not even once hit the target in firing with his left hand. He would certainly have missed his man and would have got cut down a moment later, and even with his right hand his shooting was very wild."

Captain Lister himself was evidently disconcerted at finding how useless his target practice would be to him in the field, and, two or three times in the next week, went with Frank to practise. He improved with his right hand, but did not seem to obtain any accuracy in firing with his left; while Frank, at the end of a month, came to shoot as well with one hand as with the other.

Frank worked steadily at Russian, and although he found it extremely difficult at first, soon began to make progress under his teacher, who took the greatest pains with him. He soon got over the good-tempered chaff of the subalterns of his detachment, who, finding that he was at other times always ready to join in anything going on, and was wholly unruffled by their jokes, soon gave it up. They agreed among themselves that he was a queer fellow, and allowed him to go his own way without interference. At the end of three months he was discharged from drill and riding-school, and had thenceforth a great deal more time on his hands, and was able to devote three hours of a morning and two of an afternoon to Russian.

He was delighted with his master, whom he came to esteem highly, finding him a most intelligent companion as well as an unwearied teacher. Strelinski, indeed, would have been glad to have devoted twelve hours a day instead of five, could Frank have afforded the time. He was a very different man now to what he was when he had first called at Sir Robert Wilson's lodgings. He looked well and happy; his cheeks had filled out, and he carried himself well; he dressed with scrupulous care, and when Frank had no engagement with his comrades, the Pole accompanied him on long rides on his spare charger, he having been accustomed to riding from his childhood. From him Frank learned a great deal of the state of things in Poland and Russia, and gained a considerable insight into European politics, besides picking up a more intimate colloquial knowledge of Russian than he gained at his lessons. Of an evening Frank not unfrequently went to parties in the town. The gallant deeds of our troops in Spain had raised the military to great popularity throughout the country, and the houses of all the principal inhabitants of Canterbury were hospitably opened to officers of the garrison.

Many of the young men preferred billiards and cards in the mess-room, but Frank, who declined to play billiards, and had not acquired sufficient skill at cards to take a hand at whist, was very glad to accept these invitations. He specially enjoyed going to the houses of the clergy in the precincts of the cathedral; most of them were very musical, and Frank, who had never heard much music at Weymouth, enjoyed intensely the old English glees, madrigals, and catches performed with a perfection that at that time would have been hard to meet with except in cathedral towns.

After three months the gunmaker no longer accompanied Frank to his shooting-gallery.

"It would be robbing you to go on with you any longer, Mr. Wyatt. When a man can turn round, fire on the instant and hit a penny nine times out of ten at a distance of twelve paces, there is no one can teach him anything more. You have the best eye of any gentleman I ever came across, and in the twenty years that I have been here I have had hundreds of officers at this gallery, many of them considered crack shots. But I should go on practising, if I were you, especially with your left hand. It is not quite so good as the right yet, although very nearly so. I will come down once a week and throw up a ball to you or spin a penny in the air; there is nothing like getting to hit a moving object. In the meantime you can go on practising at that plummet swinging from the string. You can do that as well by yourself as if I were with you, for when you once set it going it will keep on for five minutes. It is not so good as throwing up a penny, because it makes a regular curve; but shooting, as you do, with your back to it, and so not able to tell where it will be when you turn round, that don't so much matter."

"What is the best shooting you ever heard of?"

"The best shot I ever heard tell of was Major Rathmines. He could hit a penny thrown up into the air nineteen times out of twenty."

"Well, I will go on practising until I can do that," Frank said. "If a thing is worth doing it is worth doing well."

"And you will do it, Mr. Wyatt; there is nothing you could not do with practice."

"There is one thing I wish you would do for me—that figure you have got painted as a target is ridiculous. I wish you would get some one who has an idea of painting to do another figure. I want it painted, not standing square to me, but sideways, as a man stands when he fights a duel. I want it drawn with the arm up, just in the same position that a man would stand in firing. I hope I shall never be called upon to fight a duel. I think it is a detestable practice; but unfortunately it is so common that no one can calculate on keeping out of it—especially in the army."

"Well, sir, you need not be afraid of fighting a duel, for you fire so mighty quick that you would be certain of getting in the first shot, and if you got first shot there would be an end of it."

"Yes, but that would be simple murder—neither more nor less, whatever people might call it—and I doubt whether, accustomed as I am to fire instantly the moment I catch sight of a thing, that I could help hitting a man in the head. Now what I want to become accustomed to is to fire at the hand. I should never forgive myself if I killed a man. But if ever I did go out with a notorious duellist who forced the duel upon me, I should like to stop his shooting for the rest of his life. So I want to be able to hit his hand to a certainty. Of course the hand is an easy enough mark, and by getting accustomed to the height and the exact position it would be in, I should get to hit it without fail."

"A very good idea, sir. The hand is not much of a mark when holding a pistol, still it is a good bit bigger than a penny piece, and you would soon get to hit it just as certainly."

For the next three months Frank fired fifty shots a day—twenty-five with each hand—and at the end of that time could hit a penny thrown up by Woodall, eighteen times out of twenty.

"That is good enough," he said; "now I shall only practise once a week, to keep my hand in."

Frank had not been without an incentive to gain exceptional proficiency with a pistol. Although he got on very well with his comrades of his own depôt, there was a captain of a lancer regiment who had not unfrequently taxed his patience to its farthest limit. The man was a noted duellist, and was known to be a dead shot. On the strength of this, he was in the habit of making remarks so offensive, that they would have at once been taken up, if uttered by anyone else in barracks. For the last two months he had made a special butt of a young cornet, who had recently joined the depôt of the Dragoons. He was a pleasant lad, with plenty of spirit and pluck, but he had a slight impediment in his speech, although when giving the word of command he never hesitated. It was this defect that was the object of Captain Marshall's ill-natured remarks. The lad tried to laugh them off and to ignore the offensiveness of the tone, but he felt them deeply, and confided to Frank—to whom he had specially taken—that he could not stand it much longer.

"I never used a pistol in my life until you advised me the other day to take some lessons from Woodall, and of course he would put a bullet through my head; but I can't help that. As it is, everyone must think me a coward for standing it, and at any rate I can show them that I am not that."

"Don't you mind, Wilmington," Frank said one day, "and don't make a fool of yourself. You put up with it a little longer, and something may occur to put a stop to it. He may go away on leave, or he may get a hint that he had better retire from the service. I have heard that it is likely enough that he will get a hint the next time he has an affair of this sort. The last two were with civilians, and I believe that is the reason why so few accept our invitations to mess; but I fancy if he gets into trouble again with one of ourselves he will have to go."

"Well, I will try to go on a little longer if you say so, Wyatt, but—"

"There are no 'buts' in it, Wilmington. You must give me your word of honour that you will go on as you have done. Don't be afraid of anyone thinking you a coward. There is no cowardice in refusing to fight a man who is so much your superior in skill that it would be nothing short of suicide in standing up against him. I have a private reason for believing that it won't last long."

"In that case I will give you my word of honour, Frank.'

A week later there was an unusually large party at mess. the depôts were very strong, and some forty officers sat down; and it being a guest night, four or five civilians were present. Dinner went on without incident until one of the mess waiters asked Wilmington whether he would take sirloin of beef or goose. He replied, "B-b-b-b-beef." There happened to be a slight lull in the conversation at the moment, and Wilmington's effort to get the word out made him raise his voice so that it was generally heard.

"Waiter," Captain Marshall said loudly, "bring me some g-g-g-g-goose."

Wilmington's face flushed and then turned deadly pale. He looked appealingly at Frank, who was sitting next to him. The latter whispered, "Remember your word of honour. Get up and leave the room." There was a dead hush from those present as the young cornet rose and left the room, and then a low murmur of indignation. Captain Marshall looked round searchingly, as if to pick out one of those who had thus shown signs of resentment. But directly the door closed upon Wilmington, Frank rose to his feet.

"I wish, Mr. President," he said in a clear, steady voice, "to ask you, whether a man who, relying upon his skill with the pistol, wantonly insults another, is not a blackguard and unfit for the society of gentlemen?"

Had a thunderbolt fallen in the room those present could not have been more surprised. Some of Frank's comrades knew that he often went to Woodall's shooting-gallery to practise with the pistol, but they had no idea that he had attained any great skill in its use, and their impression when he spoke was that he must have gone out of his mind thus publicly to insult Marshall. The latter was at least as much astonished as anyone else. He started as if struck with a blow, and then, leaning across the table, he said in a low voice to Frank, who was sitting just opposite to him:

"Of course, you are prepared to answer to me for this, Mr. Wyatt?"

"Certainly," Frank said carelessly; "and at any time you please."

There was a strange hush in the dining-room until the cloth was removed. The guests, under one excuse or another, took their departure almost immediately after the king's health had been drunk; the officers talked in low tones together and very soon rose from the table.

"Will you act for me, Captain Lister?" Frank said, going up to him quietly.

"Certainly, lad; but this is a horrible business. If it had been merely an ordinary quarrel the colonel would have interfered to stop it, but after what you said before us all, and with strangers present too, I am afraid it must go on. You must be mad, lad. I have not seen you shoot since that first evening when we went down, and two or three times shortly afterwards. Woodall told me that you were getting on well; but however well you may have got on, you can be no match with a pistol for a man like Marshall; and you may be sure he won't spare you after so public an affront."

"I must take my chance," Frank said quietly. He had himself begged the gunmaker to say little to anyone about his shooting. "Come across to my quarters. I suppose he will be sending over there at once."

They had just taken their seats when there was a hurried knock on the door, and Wilmington came in, pale and agitated.

"This cannot go on, Wyatt!" he exclaimed. "You put me on my word of honour and then take it up yourself. Don't you see that I am hopelessly disgraced in letting you be Marshall's victim for what he said of me. I shall go to him and insist upon my right to take the matter up myself."

"Sit down a minute, Wilmington, and be reasonable. If I get shot you can, if you like, go out and get shot next day. But I don't mean to get shot. There is one broad distinction between you and me—you can't shoot, and I can. Marshall could kill you without the slightest risk to himself, and I flatter myself that if I chose to do so, I could kill him with the same certainty. I shall not choose to do so. I don't want the blood of any man—not even of a ruffian like this—to rest upon my head. I shall simply prevent him from ever fighting another duel."

Captain Lister and the young cornet gazed at Frank as if they doubted his sanity.

"Do you quite know what you are saying, lad?" the former said kindly, after a pause. "You don't look as if you had been taking anything before dinner, and we know that you are always abstemious at mess; still you are talking strangely."

"I daresay you think so," Frank replied with a smile. "You fancy the excitement of this quarrel has a little turned my head. But it has not done so. In the first place, I have learnt to be so quick in firing that I am sure to get first shot."

"Yes, you might do that, lad," Captain Lister said sadly; "but it would be the very worst thing you could do. With a hurried shot like that it would be ten to one you missed him, and then he would quietly shoot you down."

"Not only shall I not miss him," Frank replied, "but I will lay you any wager you like that I will carry off his trigger-finger, and probably the second and third. Feel my hand. You see I am perfectly cool—as cool as I shall be to-morrow—and I do not think there is anything wild about my eye. It is simply as I say: I am a first-rate shot—

probably as much better than Marshall as he is better than Wilmington. Ah, here is his man! Please arrange it for to-morrow morning, if possible. The sooner it is over the better."

Captain Lister nodded and went out. He returned in a quarter of an hour.

"It is to come off to-morrow," he said, "at six o'clock. It is to be in the field outside the wall, on the other side of the town. I have told my man to have the dog-cart ready at half-past five. It did not take us long to arrange matters. His second is Rankin, of his regiment; and I don't think he liked the job at all. He began by saying:

"'I am afraid, Captain Lister, that there is no chance of our arranging this unhappy business. Nothing short of a public apology, and the acknowledgment that Mr. Wyatt was in liquor when he uttered the words, will satisfy my principal, and I had great difficulty in bringing him even to assent to that.'

"I said that you had not the most remote idea of making any apology whatever. Therefore, we had only to arrange the preliminaries of a meeting.

"This was soon done. I could see that the young fellow was very much cut up over the affair, and that he had undertaken to act for Marshall because he was afraid to refuse. It did not take us five minutes altogether. I looked in at the doctor's after we separated, to ask him to go with us.

"'It is none of my aid you are likely to want, Captain Lister," he said, "and I protest against the whole affair; it is nothing short of cold-blooded murder. Still, of course I will go.'

"And now, lad, let us hear something more about your shooting."

"It is just as I told you, Captain Lister. I suppose I

have an unusually good eye and steady hand, and have a sort of natural aptitude for shooting. Woodall said that he considered me as good a shot as any man in the country, if not better. I am afraid we mustn't fire a pistol here, or I think I could convince you."

"No, we mustn't fire in barracks at this time of the evening, Wyatt. But if you are as good as that, the prospects are better than I thought they were. What can you do, lad?"

"I can hit a penny spun up into the air eighteen times out of twenty with my right hand, and sixteen or seventeen with my left."

"Is that so! Well, that ought to be good enough for anything," Lister said. "It sounds almost miraculous. Now, let us have a look at your pistols, lad."

"They are all right," Frank said. "I was using them this afternoon, and cleaned them when I came back."

"And you really mean to aim at his hand?"

Frank nodded.

"Well, of course, if you go a little high or a little low you will still have him; but if you go an inch or two wide you may miss him altogether. I would much rather, lad, that you aimed at the body. The fellow has never shown mercy to anyone, and there is no reason why you should show mercy to him."

"Don't be afraid of my missing it." And Frank spoke so confidently that his hearers felt satisfied he must at least have some good foundation for his faith in his skill.

"Well, I think you had better turn in now, Wyatt. Will you come across and have a cup of coffee with me before you start?"

"Thank you. Will you mind sending your servant across to call me at a quarter to five? I am not at all good at waking myself."

"All right, lad! I don't think I am likely to get much sleep."

"Don't say much to the others when you go out," Frank said. "You can tell them that, from what I say, it won't be such a one-sided affair as they seem to think."

"All right! I will tell them as much as that, for they are in such a state of mind about it that it would be kind to give them a little consolation."

"By the way, Captain Lister, do I go out in uniform or in mufti?"

"In mufti, lad. Put on a gray or dark-coloured suit. Gray is the best; but, above all, don't take a coat with conspicuous buttons or anything to catch the eye, that would be a fatal mistake. Good night, lad! I shall turn in in better spirits than I expected to do."

Wilmington did not speak, but grasped Frank's hand warmly.

"Don't come out to-morrow," Frank said.

"I couldn't," the lad replied in a broken voice, "but I shall see you before you start."

"The major will come on with the doctor," Captain Lister said, as, after taking their coffee next morning, they went out to the trap standing at the door. Frank looked round the barrack yard, but no one was about. "I sent them all away before you came, Wyatt. The lads all looked so woebegone that I put it to them whether they considered that the sight of their faces was likely to improve your nerve. As to young Wilmington, he was like a ghost. I had almost to threaten to put him under arrest before I could persuade him to go without seeing you. No one will be there but the major. He told me that he considered it his duty to represent the regiment, but he quite approved of all the others staying away. He said the fewer there were present at an infamous business like this the better. By the way, I made a condition with Rankin that you were to be placed back to back, and neither was to move until the signal was given; and I insisted that this should be by pistol shot, as otherwise you could not both see the signal equally well. I said that this was fairer than for you to stand face to face, and would increase the chances of the affair not being a fatal one."

"Thank you, Lister. I was wondering whether you had made that condition, for if we stood ready to fire he might draw his trigger before I did, and things might go quite differently to what I had decided on. A bad marksman might hold his fire, but Marshall would rely so implicitly on his skill that he would be sure to try and get first shot; for if I fired first and missed, he would know that the feeling against him if he shot me down afterwards would be very strong."

"Now jump up, lad; I will take the reins. All right!"

The soldier servant standing at the head of the horse released the hold of the reins, swung himself up behind as the horse started and they drove out through the barracks gates, followed by the eyes of all Frank's comrades, who, as soon as they heard the sound of the wheels, ran to their windows or doors to take, as they believed, their last look at him. They had, indeed, obtained slight consolation from the words with which Captain Lister had sent them off to their quarters—"Keep up your spirits, lads. There is many a slip between the cup and the lip, and I have strong hopes that the affair is not going to turn out as bad as you fancy."

CHAPTER IX.

A DUEL.

CAPTAIN LISTER was very much more nervous than his principal as they drove on to the ground. In spite of Frank's confidence he could not bring himself to believe that the young fellow could be a match for a practised duellist, although he had, after he had left Frank's room the evening before, gone into the town and knocked up the gunmaker, who had sometime before gone to bed. When, however, Captain Lister confided to him the nature of his errand, he fully confirmed what Frank had said.

"Of course, I have not seen him stand up before a man with a pistol in his hand," he said, "but as far as shooting goes I would back him against any man in England; and I don't think, Captain Lister, that you need be afraid of him in the matter of nerve. Pistol shooting depends upon two things—nerve and eye; and he could never be the shot he is if he had not an extraordinary amount of both qualities. I will wager that he will be as cool as a cucumber. How are they to stand?"

"Back to back, and to turn at the signal of a pistol shot."

"Then he is all right, Captain. You need not worry about him. He is as quick as lightning, and he will get first shot, never fear, and more than that, I wouldn't mind betting that he carries off one of the fellow's fingers."

"Why, how do you know that?" Captain Lister asked in surprise. "He can't have been here since I left him."

"No, sir, he has not been here; but he told me that if he ever got into a duel he would aim at his opponent's hand, and he has been practising specially for that. He had a target made on purpose, but that did not please him, and we rigged out an arm holding a pistol and fixed it to the target just in the position it would be if the painted figure were firing at him. We had to have a rough sort of hand made of iron, for it would have cost a fortune if it had been made of anything else. Sometimes he would have it painted white, sometimes gray, sometimes black, either of which it might be, if a man wore gloves, but it did not make any difference to him; and I have seen him hit it twenty times following, over and over again."

All this had been very reassuring to Captain Lister, and if it had not been for Marshall's reputation he would have gone to the place of meeting feeling confident that all would go well; but the fact that it was Frank's first duel, while Marshall had been in some eight or ten affairs, prevented his feeling otherwise than nervous as to the result. They were first upon the ground; the major and doctor arriving two minutes later.

"You may as well tell the major, Captain Lister, that he need not be alarmed. He is looking terribly anxious, and so is the doctor."

Captain Lister nodded, and went up to them as they dismounted from the gig. "I fancy that it is going to be all right, doctor," he said, "Wyatt tells me so himself, and what he says is confirmed by Woodall, the gunsmith. It seems the lad is an extraordinarily good shot. I told you last night that he had been practising a good deal, but I did not like to raise your hopes too high until I had seen Woodall. I will bet you a guinea that Wyatt comes out of it all right."

"I could not bet on it, Lister, though I would pay the guinea with greater pleasure than I ever felt at winning one; but I hear that Marshall is a very quick shot."

"So is Wyatt, major, and as the young 'un has been

practising regularly, I fancy he will be as quick as, or quicker than the other."

"Well, I hope to heaven that it may turn out so. Nothing would please me more than that Wyatt should put a ball into the fellow's head. Men like him are a curse to the army."

"I don't think he will put a ball in his head, major, but I shall not be surprised if he carries off one of his fingers. He has conscientious scruples about killing the man, and he is going to aim at his hand."

The Major shook his head. "I am afraid that settles it, Lister. It may do for a good shot to try experiments of that sort with a bad one, but not against a man like Marshall. It would be far better for him to aim at the body. That is a good big mark, and if he is as good a shot as you say, and is quick enough to pull his trigger first, it would make matters safe; but as to aiming at his hand, it would be sheer madness. You tell him what I think of it. Ah! here come the others."

As soon as Captain Marshall and his second alighted, the latter came forward and spoke to Captain Lister. They talked for a minute together and then proceeded to choose the ground. This was quickly done, as there were no trees, and it being a cloudy morning neither party would have any advantage from the light. The two cases of pistols were then examined. They were of the same calibre and about the same weight, and Marshall's second at once agreed to Captain Lister's proposal that each should fire with his own pistol, so that neither should be placed at the disadvantage of using a weapon that he was unaccustomed to. Captain Lister proposed that they should toss which of the two seconds should fire the signal, but Rankin said, "I would rather not do it, Captain Lister. I need hardly tell you that I would give anything not to be here in my present capacity, and I would very much rather that a third party should fire it—either your major or the surgeon.

Lister went across to the major, who at once consented to give the signal. The pistols were then loaded, the ground measured, and the principals placed in position. The major took two pistols—one loaded with ball, the other with powder only, and then placed himself some ten paces on one side of the line of fire.

"Now," he said, "gentlemen, I shall say 'Are you ready?' and on receiving no answer shall fire; but mind I am determined that if either of you makes a move to turn, or raises his arm by as much as an inch from his side before he hears the shot, I will shoot him down at once. Do you both understand that?"

Both answered "Yes".

He waited a moment, and then said "Are you ready?" Then a second later he fired. Both the antagonists turned swiftly on their heels, their arms going up as they did so. Then the two shots rang out. They seemed almost simultaneous; but Captain Lister, whose eyes were fixed on Marshall, saw that his hand jerked in the act of firing, and that his ball must have flown high. At the same moment his pistol fell to the ground, and he staggered back a pace. Then, with an exclamation of fury, he caught his right hand in his left, and stood rocking himself in pain. His second and the surgeon ran up to him.

"Are you hit, Marshall?" the former said.

"Of course I am hit!" he said savagely. "You don't suppose I should have dropped the pistol if I hadn't been. I believe that young villain has carried off one of my fingers."

"I must protest against this language, Marshall," Lieutenant Rankin said indignantly. "I am bound to bear testimony that your opponent has acted extremely well, and that his conduct has been that of an honourable gentleman."

At this moment Captain Marshall turned deadly pale, and would have fallen had not Rankin and the doctor caught him, and lowered him gradually to the ground.

"He will do no more shooting," the surgeon said grimly, "the ball has carried off his trigger finger. Cut his coat-sleeve off, Rankin. Don't you see he is bleeding a great deal? Lister, please bring me those bandages at once."

Captain Lister,—who had, as soon as he saw Marshall's pistol fall, run up to Frank and grasped his hand warmly, saying, "Thank heaven, my dear lad, that it has turned out as you said it would! I congratulate you with all my heart,"—at once ran to fetch the bandages, and they all gathered round the wounded man, Frank turning very white as he saw him lying insensible.

"What is it, doctor? I aimed at his hand. I hope it has not done any serious damage, except there." The latter was too busy to answer. "Bring the tourniquet," he said to Rankin, and as he ran off he looked up at the major.

"The ball evidently struck the first finger on the knuckle, and went in between the first and middle finger and then ran up the wrist and along the arm, and has gone out, as you see, above the elbow, cutting an artery as it went, and smashing the bone just above the elbow. The first thing is to stop the bleeding."

He took the tourniquet from Rankin, and applied it two or three inches above the elbow, and continued to screw until the rush of blood ceased. Then he bandaged the arm and hand and fastened it across Marshall's chest. "That is all I can do now," he said. "I think there is no doubt I shall have to amputate above the elbow; but we will take him back first. I wish we had a stretcher."

"We have a stretcher," the major said. "I told off four men with one half an hour before we started. I thought we should want it to bring Wyatt back." He put a whistle to his lips and blew loudly. A minute later four troopers ran out from behind a cottage a hundred yards away. They had, no doubt, been furtively observing the combat, for there was an expression of gladness and triumph on their faces as they arrived.

"Lay Captain Marshall on the stretcher," the surgeon said. "Lift him carefully and carry him to his quarters. I will drive on at once and get things ready. I suppose, Mr. Rankin, you will go with him. You had better cover him up with a rug. Have either of you any brandy? I forgot to bring any with me."

"I have a flask," the major replied. "I will get it for you at once."

"We may as well be off, Wyatt," Captain Lister said to Frank; "it is of no use your waiting here any longer. We can do no good."

"I am sorry he is hurt so," Frank said, as they drove off.

"Then you will be the only man that is," Captain Lister replied. "You have rid the army of a pest; that is to say, you have rendered him harmless. Possibly he may not retire. There are plenty of men in the service who have lost an arm; however, I should think he will go. The disgrace will be worse to him than the wound."

"Still, I am heartily sorry that I hurt him so much," Frank repeated. "I meant to take off one or two of his fingers, and spoil his shooting for the rest of his life; but I never thought of the ball going up his arm as it did."

"Well, if you had not hit him where you did, you would be lying on that stretcher now. It was a close thing between the two shots, not more than a fifth of a second, I should say, and if you had only hit him in the body, I have no doubt that he would have fired before he fell; and if ever a man meant to kill another, he did. I could see it in his eye, as he stood there waiting for the signal. Well, Wyatt, you can stop in the army until you get to be a general, but one thing is morally certain, that after this affair no one will venture to insult you, and your first duel is likely to be your last."

"I sincerely trust so," Frank said gravely. "I think I can say that assuredly I shall never be the first to insult anyone else, and that if ever I fight again, it will, as in this case, not be in my own quarrel."

As they drove along the straight road towards the barracks, they saw a number of men clustered outside the gate.

"They are on the look-out," Captain Lister said. "They will have heard from the mess waiters the news of the quarrel last night, and I don't suppose there was a soul in barracks that did not know what our errand was when we drove out this morning. I expect if you had been killed they would have had to move either the Lancers' depôt or ours away from Canterbury, for the men of the two regiments would have been sure to have fought whenever they met each other."

As soon as they were near enough to the gates for their figures to be made out, there was a sudden movement among the men. Several took off their caps and waved them, while others threw them into the air.

"This is not exactly discipline, Wyatt," Captain Lister said, with a smile; "but it shows conclusively enough that you are a favourite with the men."

There were roars of cheering as they went in through the gates, in spite of Captain Lister holding up his hand and shaking his head. As they drove across the barrack square to Frank's quarters the subalterns came rushing out. "Glad indeed to see you back again, Wyatt," the first who ran up exclaimed; "so it was arranged without fighting after all?"

"Not at all, Macalister," Captain Lister replied, as he reined in the horse at Frank's door. "Wyatt did exactly what he told me he was going to do—carried off Marshall's trigger-finger. But the bullet did what he had not intended it should—ran up the arm and smashed it above the elbow, and the doctor says that he thinks the arm will have to come off."

A shout of satisfaction rose from the group, and Wilmington grasped Frank's hand as he leapt down.

"Thank God that you are safe, Wyatt!" he exclaimed. "I should never have forgiven myself if anything had happened to you. Of course, what you said last night cheered me a good deal, but I could hardly help thinking afterwards that you had made the best of it for that purpose."

"No, I did not, Wilmington. I felt absolutely confident that I should hit him on the hand. Now, I want some breakfast; I ordered it to be ready before I started."

"Well, you are a cool hand, Wyatt," Lister said. "If we ever get into a hand-to-hand affair with the French, I hope you will take me under your protection."

"We will see about it," Frank laughed. "Well, come up now. I ordered the breakfast for two, and I see Smith is bringing the dishes across from the kitchen."

"Oh, I say, Wyatt, you must let the rest of us up too. We can't wait to hear all about it until you have done."

"Come up, by all means. There is really nothing to tell you."

However, as the breakfast was being eaten, Captain Lister answered all questions.

"So he did not take it well," one of the subalterns said. "That is just what you would expect from a fellow like that."

"I don't think we should be too hard on him in that respect. It is very trying to any man's temper when he makes absolutely sure of doing a thing and is beaten by a novice. It was surprise, no doubt, as well as pain—and I fancy the pain was pretty sharp—that caused him to lose his temper. I expect that if he had been fighting with an old hand whom he thought dangerous, he would have borne the wound in a very different way. Now, look here, lads, there is one thing that you must bear in mind. Don't treat this affair as if it were a sort of triumph for the corps. I have no doubt that all the fellows in the Lancers will be every bit as much pleased as we are, at the way things have turned out; but we must not assume that. I should say you had much better not make any allusion to the affair, unless others speak to you about it. Of course, it will make a great deal of talk; there is no getting over that. But don't let it be a subject to be discussed in the mess-room. Duels between officers of different regiments have, before now, led to a lot of bad feeling, and I have known one such duel lead to half a dozen others. The Lancers are in no way to blame for Marshall's conduct; but, if they found any disposition among us to crow over it, it might give rise to ill-feeling, which would be bad enough if it were merely two regiments in garrison together, but would be a terrible nuisance in a depôt where there is a common mess. Therefore, when the matter is talked over, as it is sure to be, it is best to let the talking be done by others, and to keep your own mouths closed. Wyatt is the last fellow in the world to wish to pose as a conquering hero."

"Thank you, Lister," Frank said. "I am sure I never wish to hear the thing mentioned again. I have taken a lot of pains to become a good shot, and it seems that I have a natural aptitude that way. There is nothing more to feel boastful about than if nature had made me a giant, and I had thereby been able to thrash a man of ordinary strength. I am very glad that I have put it out of Marshall's power to bully other men, and, as he had several times done, to force them into duels, when his skill gave him such an advantage that it was nothing short of murder. I think that I shall go across to the major, and ask him to give me a fortnight's leave. I have not been away since I joined, and I had a letter yesterday saying that my aunt was not very well; so I should like to run down to Weymouth to see her."

"It would be a very good plan, Wyatt, and I am sure the major will give you leave at once."

When he had finished his breakfast, Frank went across to the major's quarters.

"I have not had time to congratulate you yet, Wyatt," the major said warmly, as he entered. "You have rendered a service to the army in general, and to our regiment in particular; for it would have been a nasty thing if it had got about that one of us had been grossly insulted without taking the matter up. If you had not interfered, the commandant told me that he should have reported the matter at headquarters. Had Wilmington taken it up, he would have refused to let the matter go on, until he had received an answer from the Horse-guards; and he would have done the same in your case, if you had not used such strong language. Your words practically forced Marshall into challenging you. Still, although we, who were present, should all have approved of Wilmington's not being allowed to throw away his life by going out with Marshall, one can't deny that it would have caused unpleasantness. Men who only heard that one of our fellows had put up with a gross insult without taking any steps, and had, so to speak, sheltered himself under the authority of the commandant, would have considered it an ugly business, and we should have found it very unpleasant when we joined the army in Spain. Therefore, we all feel very much indebted to you for having championed the honour of the regiment. You are a marvellous shot, lad, and you will have one satisfaction, which is, that when this affair is talked about, and it is known that you said beforehand that you intended to take off Marshall's trigger-finger, and that you did it, there is no chance of your ever being forced into a quarrel as long as you remain in the army."

"Thank you, Major. I have just come across to ask you if you will allow me a fortnight's leave of absence. I really want to pay a visit to my aunt at Weymouth, and I think it will be a very good plan for me to get away from here until this affair has blown over a little."

"A very good plan indeed, my lad. Certainly, you can have your leave. I will draw it out this moment, and take it over to the commandant, who will, I am sure, countersign it at once. Which way do you think of going?"

"I think I will go by the coach, that comes along here at twelve o'clock, to Dover; that is, if I see in the paper that there is any hoy sailing for the west this evening or to-morrow. The wind is in the east, and, with luck, I should get down there sooner than by going up to town and taking the coach."

"Here is the list of sailings," the major said, taking up a broad-sheet from a side table. "Yes, the hoy *Keepsake* will sail, weather permitting, from Dover this evening for Plymouth, touching at Southampton and Weymouth. That would just suit you. You had better not have more than a fortnight, for I think it likely we may get orders for the two troops to sail before long. Be sure and leave your address at the orderly-room."

From the major's, Frank went straight to Strelinski's lodging, and told him that he would have a fortnight's holiday.

"I do not want it," the Pole said; "but I am glad that you should have one, for you have been working very hard lately, and it is now nearly nine months since you came down here."

"I will get you to write an account of my progress, Strelinski. I told Sir Robert Wilson that he should have one every three months, and the third is nearly due now. He was very pleased at your last report."

"This will be even better, for you have been able to give a good deal more time to it, since you have not had so many drills. Besides, progress is not so manifest at first, until one is able to converse a little; after that it goes on rapidly."

Strelinski at once sat down and wrote the report.

Frank read it with some interest, for Strelinski was not in the habit of saying what he thought of his progress.

"I think you have made this too strong," he said, as he laid it down.

"Not at all," the Pole replied. "We are able to talk freely now, and it is very seldom that you are at a loss for a word. I can say conscientiously that you are now able to converse rapidly and well in it. I could not say that your writing leaves nothing to be desired. Having acquired it so much by ear and conversation, you are not perfect in your grammar or construction when you write it; but that is of little consequence. Sir Robert Wilson will naturally write in his own language, and is not likely to have despatches to send in Russian. You are quite fit to act as an interpreter, to deliver messages, and to carry on any ordinary conversation. There is a report that there has been a duel this morning, and that an officer was carried through the town on a stretcher."

"Yes. The wound is not a very serious one, but he will probably lose his forearm."

"And it was you who hit him," the Pole said quietly.

"How do you know that, Strelinski?"

"I guessed it. You have told me how you were practising, and how well you were getting on. I guessed you had some special purpose for taking so much pains, and you did not come in yesterday evening as usual. Then, too, you tell me he was hit in the arm, and you mentioned the other day that you were practising at that, and showed me the iron hand you had had made to hold a pistol."

"Well, yes, it was I. The fellow insulted a young comrade in my regiment, knowing well that he could not shoot; so I took it up, and there was an end of it."

"I am glad I knew nothing about it until it was all over. I should have been very unhappy if I had known that you were going to risk your life."

"I do not think there was any risk in it. As I told you, I have practised shooting very quickly, and felt sure that I should get first shot, and knew that there was no chance of my missing. The man was a dangerous fellow, and has fought many duels, but he will not now fight any more; and he will, I should think, leave the service. Well, I must not stay any longer, for I go by the twelve-o'clock coach, and have to write a letter to Sir Robert Wilson before I start."

Frank caught the coach without difficulty, and on arriving at Dover went down and took his berth on board the hoy.

"We shall start at eight sharp," the skipper said.

"I will be on board in good time. I think you are likely to have a quick passage."

"Yes, if the wind holds we shall be at Southampton tomorrow evening. I shall get out the cargo by torchlight, for with this wind I don't want to lose an hour. I don't know how much there will be to take in, but I reckon anyhow that we shall be off by nine o'clock in the morning, and if we have luck shall be at Weymouth before dark."

Frank went on shore to the hotel and dined, and spent the time until the hour fixed for sailing in going over the fortifications. The voyage was a quick and pleasant one, and although the accommodation was rough it was vastly superior to that which he had been accustomed to when going out in the fishing-boats. The skipper's calculations as to time were verified, and they entered the river at Weymouth forty-eight hours after leaving Dover. Mrs. Troutbeck was delighted to see Frank. He had indeed written a fortnight before, saying he hoped to be able before long to get a few days' leave and should come down to see her, and she was therefore not greatly surprised at his arrival.

"You have grown a good deal, my dear boy," she said after they had chatted together for some time, "but you are not changed so much as I expected."

"Well, Aunt, I don't see how I can change much till the hair begins to grow on my face. Putting on uniform doesn't in itself make one a man; but of course I feel older, and I think I have grown a bit. But there is no chance of my ever shooting up like Julian. Of course, you have heard nothing from him, Aunt, or you would have written to me at once!"

"Nothing, Frank. That fisherman, Bill, came in the other day and said he had only heard what we knew before, that he had been sent to gaol, and that he had been marched away with a batch of prisoners somewhere inland. The smugglers could not learn what prison they had gone to. They said that the people at Nantes did not know that, as the guards who went with them from there only received orders to take them a short distance, and they were then handed over to other soldiers, who went so much further with them, and as their escort might be changed a dozen times not even the officials at Nantes had an idea where they were taken to at last."

"No news of Markham, Aunt?"

"Only that he is one of the regular crew of that French lugger now."

Frank looked up all his old friends and spent a pleasant week. His visit did his aunt a great deal of good, and the servant told him that she was quite a different woman since he had come home again.

"She missed you wonderful, Master Frank, and though she used to go about as usual, she did not seem to take an interest in things as she did before. I expect, now that she has seen you again, and has perked up a bit, she will fall into her old ways more regular. Now she has heard from you all about what you are doing, and your friends, and such like, and she knows that you are well and not changed, she will feel more comfortable, and won't be always worriting herself. Mr. Henderson often comes in and talks about you, and that always seems to do her good. And Colonel Chambers, he looks in sometimes, and she tells me that they both think a great deal of you, and of course that pleases her; and she looks forward wonderful to your letters coming regular once a week. I don't think you need trouble yourself about her, Master Frank. She has not really much the matter with her; only you know it was always her way to worrit about things, and you can't expect her to be otherwise, and I do think your coming here will do her a lot of good."

Two mornings later one of the coast-guard came in. "Captain Downes will be glad, sir, if you will go on board; there is something particular that he wants to speak to you about."

Frank at once put on his hat.

"We had a sharp fight with the smugglers last night, your honour," the sailor said as they started. "We had been cruising about for two days to the west, and yesterday morning we made out to sea and held east, and at ten o'clock came into Swanage Bay. We came upon the lugger that has fooled us so many times, and for once we caught her napping. They were at work unloading a cargo when we came up, and she did not make us out until we were within a couple of cables'-length of her, then she slipped and ran; I expect she would have shown us her heels as usual, but we gave her a broadside, and that big spar of hers came down with a run, and we were alongside in no time. They made a tough fight of it, but pretty nigh half her crew were ashore with the kegs. Howsomever we were not long in beating them below, though two or three of our chaps were pretty badly hurt, and three of theirs killed before the scrimmage was over. We did not trouble about the chaps ashore. I expect they were accounted for all right, for we heard some pistol shots there, but we came back here at once with the lugger, and got in two hours ago."

"Are the prisoners all French?" Frank asked eagerly.

"Ay, sir, just as French as can be. I was one of the party as took them ashore and lodged them in jail; and there was no doubt about their all being French. They had all got rings in their ears; besides, you could tell from the cut of their jib that they were Frenchies."

In ten minutes Frank stepped on to the deck of the *Boxer*. Captain Downes met him there. "I congratulate you, Mr. Wyatt," he said warmly. "I suppose you have been hearing that we had a sharp tussle with the smugglers, and at last captured that confounded lugger that has given us so much trouble for the past two years. Though I am mightily pleased at that, I am more pleased still that among those on board was that fellow Markham. He fought like a tiger. I reckon he knew that his neck was in a noose, for he would, of course, have heard from his friends here that the matter of Faulkner's murder had been cleared up, and there was a warrant out against him. Well, he got a pistol shot in his chest, and after it was all over we found that he was pretty near gone. As soon as a lantern was put to his face two or three of the men knew him at once, and I went up to him. He was pretty well past speaking, but as I stooped over him he said, 'You have got me this time, Captain Downes, and no mistake. Well, it don't make much matter; I was getting sick of the life. You look in the pocket of my jacket when I am gone, and you will find a letter there. I swore to young Wyatt that I would clear him of that charge of shooting Faulkner. I shot him myself, and I have put it all down there.'

"He died a quarter of an hour later, and here is the letter. I am going to take it over to Colonel Chambers, but I thought you would like to go with me. Of course, your brother was really cleared of all suspicion, but it is just as well to have got it under the real man's own hand."

"I am delighted, Captain Downes. When I was told, as I came along, of the lugger being captured, I hoped that you might possibly have something like this to tell me, for I had heard, since I came here, that he was still on board her, and as it was not likely he would risk going ashore, I thought perhaps you had got him prisoner. But this is better altogether, for if he had been put on trial for Faulkner's murder, he would, no doubt, have accused Julian, and though I think the evidence was strong enough to fix the guilt on the man, there might have been some who would have believed what he said. Now it will be altogether cleared up. Though when Julian will be found and brought home is more than anyone can say."

"Well, we need not trouble about that, lad, just at present. He is cleared, which is the principal thing, and sooner or later he is sure to find his way back again."

Frank landed with Captain Downes. Taking a trap they

drove to the magistrate's, where fortunately they found Mr. Henderson, who had gone up to arrange for the examination of the prisoners. Both were greatly pleased when, on the letter being opened, it was found to contain a full confession of the murder, attested by a French magistrate, and corroborating in every respect the facts contained in Julian's letter, and as proved by the evidence given at the coroner's inquest. "I will give this letter to the Weymouth paper to insert," Colonel Chambers said, "and will send copies to the London papers, with a few lines recalling the facts of the murder and the proofs that had accumulated of Markham's share in it, and which show beyond all doubt the *bona-fides* of the confession."

"Thank you very much, Colonel," Frank said. "I only wish I knew where to send a copy to Julian."

"I am sure I wish that you could do so," the colonel said. "Poor fellow! he has paid dearly indeed for his well-meant though rash attempt to seize Faulkner's murderer. I shall have finished my business in two or three minutes, and shall be glad if you will stop to have a chat with me."

As soon as the magistrate had concluded his talk with Mr. Henderson, and the latter had gone off to carry out the arrangements, Colonel Chambers turned to the captain and said, "Have you seen any of the London papers, Downes?"

"No, Colonel. I have had enough to think of this morning since we moored up. Is there anything of importance in them?"

"Nothing perhaps extraordinarily important, but something certainly interesting at the present moment. Here is the *Morning Herald*. This is the item: 'Our correspondent at Canterbury states that much excitement has been lately caused in military circles there by an affair of honour—'" "Oh, that is too bad!" Frank broke in hotly— "'between an officer of the Lancers, Captain M—l, and a cornet of the 15th Light Dragoons, Mr. W—t. It is said that Captain M—l has been engaged in several similar encounters, and is famous for his skill with the pistol. The affair began, we understand, at a mess-dinner of the cavalry depôt a few days since, at which several well-known gentlemen of the town were present. Captain M—l used insulting language to a recently-joined young officer of the Dragoons. Mr. W—t took the matter up hotly, and rising, denounced Captain M—l in such strong language that a duel became inevitable. In view of the youth and supposed inexperience of Mr. W—t, the affair was regarded with extreme disapprobation by the officers of Captain M—l's regiment, as well as by those of the Dragoons. It seems, however, that Mr. W—t had for some time been practising with the pistol under the tuition of our respected townsman, Mr. Woodall the gunsmith, and before the parties met he confided to the officer who acted as his second that he intended to aim at his opponent's trigger finger and so to incapacitate him from further adventures of the kind. Extraordinary as it may appear, this intention was carried out. Captain M—l not only lost his finger, but the bullet passed up his arm and broke it above the elbow. We understand that the limb has been successfully amputated by the surgeons of the two corps. This singular feat on the part of the young officer, when opposed to so skilled a duellist as Captain M—l, has created a profound sensation throughout the garrison.'

"Well, Master W—t, what have you to say to that?"

"I don't know that I have anything to say to it, Colonel," Frank replied, "except that it is a great nuisance that such a thing should be talked about. I suppose I have a good eye and a steady hand. I have practised steadily every day since I joined, and have got to shoot pretty straight. The man was a notorious bully, and if the young fellow he had insulted had gone out with him, it would have been nothing short of murder; and yet if he had not gone out with him I believe he would have shot himself, rather than suffer the disgrace of putting up with an insult. So as I felt pretty certain that I could disable Marshall without having to do him any serious injury, I took it up and hit him in the hand as I intended to."

"Well, Downes," Colonel Chambers said, "it seems to me that these two brothers are born to get into adventures, and to get well out of them. However, Frank, although you have acted very creditably, and must certainly be a wonderful shot with a pistol, don't do this sort of thing too often."

"I am not going to, sir. I hope that I shall never fight a duel again, and I didn't practise for that, but to be able to use my pistols on service."

Three days later Frank said good-bye to his aunt and friends, and returned to Canterbury, travelling this time by coach, as no craft happened to be sailing for Dover.

CHAPTER X.

SMOLENSK.

JULIAN'S regiment arrived at Konigsberg early in March, and found that it was to form part of Ney's division. The whole country round had been turned into an enormous camp, and every town was the centre round which a great array of tents was clustered. The troops were of many nationalities—French, Poles, Bavarians, Saxons, Prussians, Austrians, and even Spanish. Never since the hordes of

Attila swept over Europe had so vast an army been gathered. The total force collected for the invasion of Russia amounted to 651,358 men, of whom some 520,000 were infantry, 100,000 cavalry, and the remainder artillery and engineers. They had with them 1372 guns.

April passed without any movement. The troops became impatient, and even the veterans, whose confidence in Napoleon was implicit, shook their heads.

"We ought to be across the frontier before this," an old sergeant of Julian's company said to him, as they smoked a pipe together over two mugs of German beer.

"It isn't that I think there will be much fighting, for what can Russia do against such an army as this? They say Alexander has been busy since the peace of Tilsit, but at that time he could scarce place 50,000 men in the field. No one fears the Russians; but it is a big country, and they say that in winter the cold is horrible. We shall have long distances to march, and you know how much time is always wasted over making a treaty of peace. If we are to be back again before winter we ought to be off now. Of course, the Emperor may mean to hold St. Petersburg and Moscow until next spring, and I daresay we could make ourselves comfortable enough in either place; but when you come to winter six hundred and fifty thousand men, and a couple of hundred thousand horses, it is a tremendous job; and I should think the Emperor would send all this riff-raff of Spaniards, Germans, and Poles back, and keep only the French as a garrison through the winter. Still, I would much rather that we should all be back here before the first snow falls. I don't like these long campaigns. Men are ready to fight, and to fight again, twenty times if need be, but then they like to be done with it. In a long campaign, with marches, and halts, and delays, discipline gets slack, men begin to grumble; besides, clothes wear out, and however big stores you take with you, they are sure to run short in time. I wish we were off."

But it was not until the 16th of May that Napoleon arrived at Dresden, where he was met by the Emperor and Empress of Austria, the Kings of Prussia and Saxony, and a host of archdukes and princes, and a fortnight was spent in brilliant fêtes. Napoleon himself was by no means blind to the magnitude of the enterprise on which he had embarked, and entertained no hopes that the army would recross the frontier before the winter. He had, indeed, before leaving Paris, predicted that three campaigns would be necessary before lasting terms of peace could be secured. Thus an early commencement of the campaign was of comparatively slight importance; but, indeed, the preparations for the struggle were all on so great a scale that they could not, with all the energy displayed in pushing them forward, be completed before the end of June.

Thus, then, while Napoleon delayed in Paris and feasted at Dresden, the roads of Germany were occupied by great hosts of men and enormous trains of baggage waggons of all descriptions, moving steadily towards the Russian frontier. On the 12th of June Napoleon arrived at Konigsberg. Ney's division had marched forward a fortnight before, and the Emperor on his route from Konigsberg to the frontier reviewed that division with those of Davoust and Oudinot, and also two great cavalry divisions.

To oppose the threatening storm Alexander had gathered three armies. The first, stationed in and round Wilna under General Barclay de Tolly, comprised 129,050 men; the second, posted at Wolkowich, and commanded by Prince Bagration, numbered 48,000; the third had its headquarters at Lutsk, and was commanded by Count Tormanssow; while the reserve, which was widely scattered, contained 34,000 men. Thus the total force gathered to oppose the advance of

Napoleon's army of 650,000 was but 211,050. It had, too, the disadvantage of being scattered, for it was impossible to foresee by which of the several roads open to him, Napoleon would advance, or whether he intended to make for St. Petersburg or Moscow.

During the next few days the divisions intended to form the advance moved down towards the Niemen, which marked the frontier, and on the 24th of June three bridges were thrown across the river near Kovno, and the passage began. The French cavalry drove off the Cossacks who were watching the passage, and the same evening the Emperor established his headquarters at Kovno, and the corps of Davoust, Oudinot, and Ney crossed the bridges, and with the cavalry under Murat, composing altogether a force of 350,000 men, marched forward at a rapid pace on the 26th for Wilna, seventy-five miles distant. It was not until a few days before Napoleon crossed the frontier that the Russians obtained any definite information as to the force with which he was advancing, and their commander-in-chief at once saw that it would be hopeless to attempt to oppose so large a body. A great mistake had been committed in occupying a position so near the frontier, but when the necessity for retreat became evident, no time was lost in carrying it into effect, and orders were despatched to the commanders of the various armies to fall back with all speed. Thus, although the French accomplished the wonderful feat of marching seventy-eight miles in two days, which was done in the hope of falling upon the Russians before they had time to concentrate, they found the town already evacuated, and the whole of the immense magazines collected there destroyed.

Almost simultaneously with the passage of the Niemen by the three corps under the French marshals, those of Prince Eugene and the other generals also crossed, but further south, and also advanced at full speed in hopes of interposing between the three Russian armies, and of preventing their concentration. For the next week the French pressed hard upon the rear of the retreating Russians, but failed to bring on a battle, while they themselves suffered from an incessant downpour of rain which made the roads well-nigh impassable. The commissariat train broke down, and a hundred pieces of cannon and 5000 ammunition waggons had to be abandoned. The rain, and a bitterly cold wind that accompanied it, brought on an epidemic among the horses, which were forced to depend solely upon the green rye growing in the fields. Several thousands died; the troops themselves suffered so much from thirst and hunger that no less than 30,000 stragglers fell out from the ranks and spread themselves over the country, burning, ravaging, plundering, and committing terrible depredations. Such dismay was caused by their treatment that the villages were all abandoned, and the whole population retired before the advance of the French, driving their flocks and herds before them, and thus adding greatly to the difficulties of the invaders.

The greater portion of these straggling marauders belonged not to the French corps, but to the allies, who possessed none of the discipline of the French soldiery, and whose conduct throughout the campaign was largely responsible for the intense animosity excited by the invaders, and for the suffering that afterwards befell them.

As the pursuit continued even Napoleon's best soldiers were surprised at their failure to overtake the Russians. However long their marches, however well planned the operations, the Russians always out-marched and out-manœuvred them. It seemed to them almost that they were pursuing a phantom army, a will-o'-the-wisp, that eluded all their efforts to grasp it, and a fierce fight between the rear-guard of Barclay de Tolly's army and the advance-guard of

Murat's cavalry, in which the latter suffered severely, was the only fight of importance, until the invaders, after marching more than half-way to Moscow, arrived at Witebsk.

Nevertheless they had suffered severely. The savage ferocity with which, in spite of repeated proclamations and orders, the invading army treated the people, had exasperated the peasantry almost to madness, and, taking up arms, they cut down every straggler, annihilated small parties, attacked baggage trains, and repeated in Russia the terrible retaliation dealt by the Spanish guerrillas upon their invaders.

On the right of the French advance there had been heavier fighting. There General Schwarzenberg with his 30,000 Austrians had advanced against the third Russian army, under Tormanssow. A brigade of the division under Regnier, which was by Napoleon's order marching to join Schwarzenberg, entered Kobrin, where it was surrounded by Tormanssow, and after a brave resistance of nine hours, in which it lost 2000 killed and wounded, the remainder, 2300 in number, were forced to surrender. Tormanssow then took up a strong position with his 18,000 men, and awaited the attack of the united forces of Schwarzenberg and Regnier, 38,000 strong.

The battle lasted all day, the loss on either side being between four and five thousand. Tormanssow held his position, but retired under cover of night. On the 3rd of August the armies of Barclay and Bagration at last succeeded in effecting a junction at Smolensk, and towards that town the French corps moved from various quarters, until 250,000 men were assembled near it, and on the 15th of August Murat and Ney arrived within nine miles of the place.

Smolensk, a town of considerable size, on the Dnieper, distant 280 miles from Moscow, was surrounded by a brick wall thirty feet high and eighteen feet thick at the base, with loopholed battlements. This wall formed a semicircle of about three miles and a half, the ends resting on the river. It was strengthened by thirty towers, and at its forts was a deep dry ditch. The town was largely built of wood. There were no heavy guns upon the walls, and the city, which was completely commanded by surrounding hills, was in no way defensible, but Barclay de Tolly felt himself obliged to fight.

The greatest indignation prevailed in Russia at the retreat of the armies without attempting one determined stand, the abandonment of so large a tract of country to the French, and the suffering and ruin thereby wrought among the population of one of the richest and most thickly-peopled districts of Russia. Barclay's own plan had been to draw the enemy farther and farther into the country, knowing that with every mile of advance their difficulties would increase and their armies become weakened by fatigue, sickness, and the assaults of the peasantry. But the continued retreats were telling upon the spirit of his own troops also. To them the war was a holy one. They had marched to the frontier burning to meet the invader, and that, from the moment of his crossing the Niemen, they should have to retreat, hunted and harassed like beaten men, goaded them to fury. The officers were no less indignant than the men, and Barclay found that it was absolutely necessary to make a stand.

The French were as eager as the Russians to fight, and when it became known that the enemy seemed determined to make a stand at Smolensk they were filled with exultation. Ney's corps was the first to appear before the town, and took up its position on rising ground a short distance from the suburbs lying outside the wall and next to the river. Davoust's corps was to his right, Poniatowski's division came next, while Murat with his cavalry division completed the semicircle.

"The Russians must be mad," was the comment of the veterans of Julian's regiment. "The place is of no strength; the artillery will breach the walls in no time. They have but one bridge by which to retreat across the river, and we shall soon knock that to pieces with our guns on the right, and shall catch all who are in the town in a trap."

The obstinate resistance, however, that had been given by the Russians to the attacks on their rear-guard had impressed the invaders with a respect for their foes, that was in strong contrast to the feeling entertained when they crossed the frontier, save only among the soldiers who had met the Russians before, and who knew with what dogged valour they always fought, especially when on the defensive.

"It is going to be tough work, Jules, I can tell you," one of them said to Julian, whose English birth was now almost forgotten, and who, by the good temper he always manifested, however long the marches and however great the fatigues, had become a general favourite. "I guess we are only going to fight because the Russians are tired of retreating, just as we are tired of pursuing them. They can gain nothing by fighting here. We outnumber them tremendously. The great bulk of their army lies on the heights on the other side of the river, and there is nothing to prevent their retreating to some strong position, where they might give battle with advantage. On the other hand, there is no reason why we should fight here. We have come down thirty or forty miles out of the direct road to Moscow, and if, instead of doing so, we had crossed the river, and had gone straight on, the Russians must have evacuated the town and pushed on with all speed in order to get between us and Moscow. But this marching about without getting a battle discourages men more even than defeat, and I hope that it will do something to restore discipline among the Germans and Austrians, ay, and among our own troops too.

I have been through a number of campaigns, and I have never seen such disorder, such plunder, such want of discipline as has been shown since we entered Russia. I tell you, Jules, even a defeat would do us good. Look at the Russians; they never leave a straggler behind them, never a dismounted gun, while the roads behind us are choked up with our abandoned guns and waggons, and the whole country is covered with our marauders. I should be glad if one of the brigades was ordered to break up into companies and to march back, spreading out across the whole country we have traversed, and shooting every man they met between this and the frontier, whether he was French, German, Austrian, or Pole."

"It has been terrible," Julian agreed, "but at least we have the satisfaction of knowing that Ney's corps d'armée has furnished a smaller share of stragglers than most of the others."

"That is true enough, but bad is the best, lad. Some of our battalions are nearly all young soldiers, and I can't say much for their conduct, while the seven battalions of Spaniards, Wurtembergers, and men from the Duchy of Baden have behaved shamefully, and I don't think that the four squadrons of Polish cavalry have been any better. We have all been bad; there is no denying it; and never should we have conquered Germany, crushed Prussia, and forced Austria to submit, had our armies behaved in the way they have done of late. Napoleon would soon have put a stop to it then. He would have had one or two of the worst regiments drawn up, and would have decimated them as a lesson to the rest. Now his orders seem to go for nothing. He has far too much on his mind to attend to such things, and the generals have been thinking so much of pressing on after the enemy that they have done nothing to see the orders carried into effect. It was the same sort of thing that drove the Spaniards into taking to the mountains, and causing us infinite trouble and great loss of life. Fortunately, here we are so strong that we need fear no reverse, but if a disaster occurred I tell you, Jules, we should have good cause to curse the marauders who have converted these lazy peasants into desperate foes."

"I should think we ought not to lose many men in taking that town, sergeant. There seem to be no guns on the walls. We have the suburbs to cover our advance, and, attacking them on all sides, as we shall do, we ought to force our way in without much trouble."

"It would seem so, lad; yes, it would seem so. But you know in Spain it once cost us five days' fighting after we got inside a town. I allow it was not like this. The streets were narrow, the houses were of stone, and each house a fortress, while, as you can see from here, the streets are wide and at right angles to each other, and the houses of brick, and, I fancy, many of them of wood. Still, knowing what the Russians are, I would wager we shall not capture Smolensk with a loss of less than ten thousand men, that is if they really defend it until the last."

The following day, the 16th of August, a cannonade was kept up against the walls by the French artillery, the Russians replying but seldom. The next morning it was discovered that Prince Bagration had marched with his army from the hills on the other side of the river to take post on the main Moscow road so as to prevent the position being turned by the advance of a portion of the French army by that route. During the night Barclay had thrown two pontoon bridges across the river in addition to the permanent bridge. At daybreak a dropping fire broke out, for both Davoust and Ney had sent bodies of troops into the suburbs, which they had entered without opposition, and these now opened an irritating fire on the Russians upon the wall. At eight o'clock the firing suddenly swelled into a roar. Doctorow, the Russian general in command of the troops in the town, made a sortie, and cleared the suburbs at the point of the bayonet. Napoleon, believing that the Russian army was coming out to attack him, drew up Ney and Davoust's troops in order of battle, with 70,000 infantry in the first line, supported by Murat's 30,000 cavalry.

Partial attacks were continued against the suburbs, but the Russians obstinately maintained themselves there. Finding that they showed no signs of advancing to attack him, Napoleon at two o'clock gave orders for a general assault, and the whole of the French troops advanced against the suburbs. The attack of Ney's corps was directed against the Krasnoi suburb, which faced them, and against an advanced work known as the citadel. For two hours a terrible struggle went on. The Russians defended all the suburbs with desperate tenacity, every house and garden was the scene of a fierce encounter, men fought with bayonet and clubbed muskets, the cannon thundered on the heights, and Poniatowski established sixty guns on a hill on the French right, but a short distance from the river, and with these opened fire upon the bridges. It seemed that these must soon be destroyed and the retreat of the Russian troops in Smolensk entirely cut off. In a short time, however, the Russians on the other side of the river planted a number of guns on a rise of equal height to that occupied by Poniatowski's artillery, and as their guns took his battery in flank, he was ere long forced to withdraw it from the hill.

It was only after two hours' fighting that the Russians withdrew from the suburbs into the town itself, and as the bridges across the river had not suffered greatly from the fire of the great French battery, Barclay sent

Prince Eugene of Wurtemberg across to reinforce the garrison. As soon as the Russians retired into the town a hundred and fifty guns opened fire on the wall to effect a breach, and at five a desperate assault was made upon one of the gates, which was for a moment captured, but Prince Eugene charged forward with his division and recaptured it at the point of the bayonet. The French shell and grape swept the streets and set fire to the town in a score of places, and several of the wooden roofs of the towers upon the wall were also in flames. After a pause for a couple of hours the French again made a serious and desperate assault, but the Russians sternly held their ground, and at seven o'clock made a sortie from behind the citadel, and drove the French out of the Krasnoi suburb. At nine the cannonade ceased. The French fell back to the position from which they had moved in the morning, and the Russians reoccupied the covered ways in front of the wall to prevent a sudden attack during the night.

"What did I tell you, Jules?" the old sergeant said mournfully, when the shattered remains of the regiment fell out and proceeded to cook their food. "I said that the capture of that town would cost us 10,000 men. It has cost Ney's corps alone half that number, and we have not taken it; and yet we fought well. Had every man been as old a soldier as myself they could not have done their duty better. *Peste!* these Russians are obstinate brigands."

"It was desperate work," Julian said, "more terrible than anything I could have imagined. How anyone escaped alive is more than I can say. Every wall, every house seemed to be fringed with fire. I heard no word of command during the day; all there was to do was to load and fire—sometimes to rush forward when the rest did so, sometimes to fall back when the Russians poured down upon us. Shall we begin again to-morrow?"

"I suppose so," the sergeant replied. "We certainly sha'n't march away until we have taken it. Perhaps the enemy may evacuate it. The whole town is a sea of flames; there is nothing to fight for, and next time we shall no doubt breach the walls thoroughly before we try. You see, we undervalued the Russians, and we sha'n't make that mistake again. Well, lad, we have both got out of it without serious damage, for that bullet you got through your arm will soon heal up again, but there is one thing, if you remain in the army for the next twenty years you are not likely to see harder fighting."

That night, indeed, Smolensk was evacuated by the Russians, contrary to the wishes of both officers and men, Prince Eugene and General Doctorow declaring that they could hold on for ten days longer. This might doubtless have been done, but Barclay was afraid that Napoleon might sweep round and cross the river somewhere to his left, and that in that case he must fall back, and the town would have to be evacuated in the daytime when the enemy could sweep the bridges with their fire. By three o'clock in the morning the whole force in the city had crossed, and the bridges were burnt behind them. The flames acquainted the French with the fact that the city had been evacuated, and at daybreak they entered the town, and soon afterwards their skirmishers opened fire on the Russians on the other side of the river. At eight o'clock a Spanish brigade crossed the river waist deep, and entered the suburb known as St. Petersburg, on the right bank; but they were at once attacked; many were killed or taken prisoners, and the rest driven across the river again.

General Barclay then withdrew his army to the heights, wishing to tempt the enemy to cross, intending to give them battle before all had made the passage; but Napoleon kept his troops in hand, except that his artillery maintained a fire to the right against the Russians. At eight o'clock in the evening some skirmishers crossed the river, and fires shortly broke out in St. Petersburg, and in an hour several hundred houses, extending for a mile along the river, were in a blaze, while those in Smolensk were still burning fiercely. At night the Russians again fell back. The direct road lay parallel with the river, but as it was commanded by the enemy's guns General Barclay directed the force, divided into two columns, to march by cross-roads. These led over two steep hills, and, owing to the harness breaking, these roads soon became blocked, and the march was discontinued till daylight enabled the drivers to get the five hundred guns and the ammunition trains up the hills.

The French, finding that the Russian army was going off, crossed the river in force and furiously attacked their rear-guard, and tried to penetrate between it and the main body of the army, but Prince Eugene's division was sent back to assist General Korf, who commanded there. In the meantime two columns of the French moved along the main road to Moscow with the evident intention of heading the Russian army at Loubino, the point where the cross-road by which they were travelling came into it. This they might have accomplished owing to the much shorter distance they had to travel and the delays caused by the difficulty of getting the guns over the hills, but a small Russian corps under Touchkoff had been sent forward to cover that point. Ney had crossed the river early by two bridges he had thrown over it, and Touchkoff, as he saw this force pressing along the main road, took up a position where he covered Loubino, and for some hours repulsed all the efforts of the French to pass.

At three o'clock the pressure upon Touchkoff became so severe that several regiments from Barclay's column, which was passing safely along while he kept the road open for them, were sent to his assistance, and the fight continued. Napoleon believed that the whole Russian force had taken post at Loubino, and sent forward reinforcements to Ney. The woods were so thick that it was some time before these reached him, the guns of one of the columns being obliged to go a mile and a half through a wood before they could turn, so dense was the growth of the trees. Ney now pressed forward with such vigour that Touchkoff was driven from his position in advance, upon the village itself, where he was again reinforced by four infantry battalions, two regiments of cavalry, and heavy guns. Murat with his cavalry endeavoured to turn the Russian left, but the two Russian cavalry regiments, supported by their artillery, maintained their ground. Soon after five o'clock the French had received such large reinforcements that the Russians were forced to give way, and were in full retreat when Barclay himself arrived upon the scene, and rallied them. The battle was renewed, and the last effort of the French was repulsed by a charge with the bayonet by the Russian grenadiers.

In the charge, however, General Touchkoff, by whose valour the Russian army had been saved, was carried too far in advance of his men, and was taken prisoner. It was not until midnight that the rear of Barclay's column emerged from the cross-road, in which it had been involved for twenty-four hours. In this fight the French and Russians lost about 6000 men each. Had Junot joined Ney in the attack on Touchkoff's force the greater part of the Russian army must have been destroyed or made prisoners.

The Russian army now pursued its march towards Moscow unmolested save by some attacks by Murat's cavalry. Ney's corps d'armée had borne the brunt of the fighting at Loubino, and had been diminished in strength by another 4000 men. In this battle, however, Julian's regiment, having suffered so heavily in the attack at Smolensk, was one of those held in reserve. Napoleon was greatly disappointed at the escape of the Russian army from his grasp. Only 30,000 Russians had been engaged both in the action in their rear and in that at Loubino, while the whole of the French army round Smolensk, with the exception of the corps of Junot, had in vain endeavoured to break through the defence and to fall upon the main body of the army so helplessly struggling along the road.

In the attack on Smolensk 12,000 of Napoleon's best soldiers had fallen. Loubino cost him 6000 more, and although these numbers were but small in proportion to the total strength of his army, they were exclusively those of French soldiers belonging to the divisions in which he placed his main trust. It was now a question with him whether he should establish himself for the winter in the country he occupied, accumulate stores, make Smolensk a great depôt that would serve as a base for his advance in the spring, or move on at once against Moscow. On this point he held a council with his marshals. The opinion of these was generally favourable to the former course. The desperate fighting of the three previous days had opened their eyes to the fact that even so great a force as that led by Napoleon could not afford to despise the Russians. The country that was at present occupied was rich. There were so many towns that the army could go into comfortable quarters for the winter, and their communications with the frontier were open and safe. It was unquestionably the safer and more prudent course.

With these conclusions Napoleon agreed in theory. It had originally been his intention to winter in the provinces that he had now overrun, and to march against St. Petersburg or Moscow in the spring. He had, however, other matters besides those of military expediency to consider. In the first place, the Poles were exasperated at his refusal to re-establish at once their ancient kingdom, a refusal necessitated by the fact that he could not do so without taking from Austria and Prussia, his allies, the Polish districts that had fallen to their share. Then, too, the Poles felt the terrible pressure of supporting the army still in Poland, and of contributing to the vast expenses of the war, and were the campaign to continue long their attitude might change to one of open hostility. In the next place, the conclusion of peace, brought about by the efforts of England, between both Sweden and Turkey with Russia, would enable the latter to bring up the whole of the forces that had been engaged in the south with the Turks, and in the north watching the Swedish frontier, and would give time for the new levies to be converted into good soldiers and placed in the field.

Then, too, matters were going on badly in Spain. He could place but little dependence upon Austria, Prussia, or Germany. Were he absent another year from France he might find these countries leagued against him. Therefore, although recognizing the justice of the arguments of his marshals, he decided upon pushing on to Moscow, and establishing himself there for the winter. He did not even yet recognize the stubbornness and constancy of the Russian character, and believed that the spectacle of their ancient capital in his hands would induce them at once to treat for peace. The decision was welcome to the army. The general wish of the soldiers was to get the matter over, and to be off home again. The obstinacy with which the Russians fought, the rapidity with which they marched, the intense animosity that had been excited among the peasants by the cruel treatment to which they had been exposed, the recklessness with which they threw away their lives so that they could but take vengeance for their sufferings, the ferocity with which every straggler or small detachment that fell into their hands was massacred—all these things combined to excite a feeling of gloom and anxiety among the soldiers.

There were no merry songs round the bivouac fires now; even the thought of the plunder of Moscow failed to raise their spirits. The loss of so many tried comrades was greatly felt in Ney's division. It had at first numbered over 40,000, and the losses in battle and from sickness had already reduced it by more than a fourth. Even the veterans lost their usual impassive attitude of contentment with the existing state of things.

"What I don't like," growled one of the old sergeants, "is that there is not a soul in the villages, not a solitary man in the fields. It is not natural. One gets the same sort of feeling one has when a thunderstorm is just going to burst overhead. When it has begun you don't mind it, but while you are waiting for the first flash, the first clap of thunder, you get a sort of creepy feeling. That is just what the sight of all this deserted country makes me feel. I have campaigned all over Europe, but I never saw anything like this."

A growl of assent passed round the circle, and there was a general repetition of the words, "It is not natural, comrade. Even in Spain," one said, "where they hate us like poison, the people don't leave their villages like this. The young men may go, but the old men and the women and children remain, and the priest is sure to stop. Here there is not so much as a fowl to be seen in the streets. The whole population is gone—man, woman, and child."

"It makes one feel," another said gloomily, "as if we were accursed, infected with the plague, or something of that sort."

"Well, don't let us talk about it," another said with an effort at cheerfulness. "There is Jules, he is the merriest fellow in our company. Come here, Jules. We are all grumbling. What do you think of things?"

"I don't think much about them one way or the other," Julian said as he came up. "We have not a great deal further to go to Moscow, and the sooner we get there the better. Then we shall have the satisfaction of seeing some people."

"Yes, Jules, that is what is vexing us, that everyone runs away at our approach."

"And no fools either," Julian replied, "considering the villainous way in which they have been harried. Even peasants have some feeling, and when they are treated like wild beasts they will turn. It seems to me that instead of ill-treating them we ought, with such a march as this before us, to have done everything in our power to show them that, although we were going to fight any armies that opposed us, we had no ill-feeling against the people at large. If they had found us ready to pay for everything we wanted, and to treat them as well as if they had been our own country people, there would have been no running away from us. Then, as we advanced we could have purchased an abundant supply of food everywhere. We should have had no fear as to our communications, and might have wandered a hundred yards outside our sentries without the risk of having our throats cut. However, it is of no use going over these arguments again. The thing has been done and cannot be undone, and we have but to accept the consequences, and make the best of them. A man who burns a wood mustn't complain a month afterwards because he has no fuel. However, I hope that in another day or two we shall be moving on. As long as we are going there is no time to feel it dull; it is the halt, after being so long in motion, that gives us time to talk, and puts fancies into our heads. We did not expect a pleasure excursion when we started."

CHAPTER XI.

WITH THE RUSSIAN ARMY.

WHEN Frank arrrived at Canterbury he found things in confusion, and received the news that two troops had orders to march the next morning for Portsmouth, where they were to embark for Spain.

"Why, the major said he would write!" he exclaimed. "His letter must have missed me somehow. I shall have enough to do to get ready to-night."

"You are not going, Wyatt," Wilmington, who was his informant, said. "The order expressly stated that Cornet Wyatt was not to accompany his troop, as his services were required in another direction, and that another officer was to take his place, and I am going with your troop. Lister has been grumbling desperately. What on earth can they want you for? However, there is a batch of letters for you in the ante-room, and I daresay you will learn something about it from them."

Frank ran in. There were two letters. One was an official document; the direction of the other was in Sir Robert Wilson's handwriting. He opened this first.

"My dear Wyatt, your letter inclosing Strelinski's certificate came in the nick of time. I had already made an application that you should be attached to me for service, on the ground that you belonged to my old regiment, and knew something of Russian; but your age and short service were against you, and I doubt whether I should have succeeded, as the post is considered an important one. However, when I went and showed them the Pole's report as to your knowledge of Russian, and pointed out that this was a far more important matter in the present case than any question of age or service, the commander-in-chief at once agreed, and you will no doubt receive an intimation that you are appointed my aide-de-camp. I have been made a brigadier-general. It is not as yet settled when we shall start. I have only just received my official appointment, and there is no saying when I may get my final instructions; for it is to a certain extent a political affair, and this sort of thing always drags on for a long time before it comes to a head. It is lucky that your matter is arranged now, for I hear at the Horse-guards that your troop is ordered out to Spain. No doubt, just at the moment, you will be sorry that you are not going with it, but I can assure you that this business will be vastly more useful to you in your profession, than anything you would be likely to meet with as a cavalry subaltern in Spain."

For a moment, indeed, Frank did regret that he was not going to accompany his troop. He was so sure, however, that Sir Robert Wilson was acting for the best that he put aside this feeling. The official letter was a simple notification that he was appointed aide-de-camp to General Sir Robert Wilson, but that he was to remain at the depôt and continue his ordinary duties until a further intimation reached him. The excitement of departure had, Frank was glad to find, quite thrown that caused by his duel into the background. All the officers who were to go were busy with their preparations, and Frank was occupied until a late hour that night in assisting them in packing not only the baggage that was to be taken, but the heavy cases that were to be stored away until their return. Many were the regrets expressed by the officers who were going out that Frank was not to accompany them, and much curiosity expressed as to the reason for which he was kept behind. He felt that, although Sir Robert Wilson had not specially enjoined silence, it would be undesirable that any information as to the probability of his proceeding to Russia should be given. He therefore said:

"I only know that Sir Robert Wilson, who was a great friend of my father's, and who obtained my commission for me, is going to have a command somewhere, and has asked for me as one of his aides-de-camp on the ground of his friendship for my father, and his former connection with our regiment."

"Well, then, very likely we shall see you out there before long, Wyatt," Captain Lister said. "Of course, it is a compliment to the regiment, but I daresay you feel it as a nuisance at present."

"I should like to be going with you all, Lister; but I suppose this is best for me in the long run."

"Of course it is. It is always a good thing for a fellow to serve on the staff. You have ten times as good a chance of getting mentioned in the despatches, as have the men who do all the fighting. Still, I have no doubt you will deserve any credit you may get, which is more than is the case nine times out of ten."

"How is Marshall getting on?"

"He is going on all right. He has sent in his papers, and I suppose he will be gazetted out by the time he is able to travel. I can assure you that there was quite as much satisfaction in the Lancers at the turn the affair took as there was with us."

"Does the major go with you, Lister?"

"No; he remains in command of the depôt for the present. Of course, he will go out if a vacancy occurs above him; but in any case he will go with the next draft, and the next two troops will be wound up to service pitch in another couple of months, so I expect by the spring he will be out there. I should not have minded if we too had waited until then, for of course the army have gone into its winter quarters, and there will be nothing doing for the next three or four months; and I take it we should be a good deal more comfortable here, than posted in some wretched little Spanish town till operations commence again. No doubt you will be out there long before the first shot is fired."

Another three months passed, and on the 28th of March, 1812, Frank received an official order to join Sir Robert Wilson at once, and a letter from the general, informing him that they were to sail on the 8th of April. The letter was written in haste, and gave no intimation whatever as to their destination. During this three months Frank had worked almost incessantly at Russian. He had informed the major in confidence that he believed Sir Robert Wilson was going as British Commissioner to the Russian army when the war broke out with France.

"Ah! that accounts for your working so hard at Russian, Wyatt," the major said in reply. "I suppose you had received a hint from Sir Robert."

"Yes, Major. He told me that as he had been commissioner with the Russians in their last war, it was probable that, if the rumours that Napoleon intended to invade Russia proved correct, he might be appointed again, and said that if I could get up enough of the language to speak it pretty fluently, he would apply for me."

"Well, you deserve it, Wyatt; for there is no doubt that you have worked hard indeed; and it will be a capital thing for you. Is there anything I can do?"

"Yes, sir. I thought, perhaps, that when you knew what I am going to do, you would relieve me of some of the ordinary drills, as I should like to spend as much time as possible before I go, in getting up Russian."

"Certainly," the major said. "After the official information that you were not to proceed with the draft, as you would be required for special service, I have a right to consider you as a supernumerary here, and will relieve you of all ordinary drills and parades. You must, of course, take your turn as officer of the day, and if there are any special parades ordered, or any field days with the Lancers, you will attend, but otherwise you will be free of all duty. The two next troops to go have their full complement of officers, so that really you are not wanted."

As soon as Frank received Sir Robert Wilson's letter he went to Strelinski.

"It has come," he said. "I have to go up to town tomorrow, as I embark on the 8th. I am awfully sorry that our lessons have come to an end. However, they have lasted over the year that we talked of at first."

"I am sorry too, Mr. Wyatt; though really I feel that in no case need you have continued your studies any longer. The last three months has made a great difference, for you have been talking Russian some eight or ten hours a day, and are now sufficiently acquainted with the language for any purpose whatever, except perhaps writing a book in it. If I had not known that you might leave at any time, I should myself have told you that I considered there was no advantage to be gained by your going on with me any longer. I shall, of course, go up to London with you tomorrow."

"I am sorry for your sake, as well as my own, that our lessons are over, Strelinski."

"It cannot be helped," the Pole replied. "It has been a Godsend to me. When I first met you, I was well-nigh hopeless. Now I shall begin the battle again with fresh courage. I have saved enough money to keep me, with care, for many months, and doubtless your recommendation that you have learned Russian from me, will make matters more easy for me than they were before."

On arriving in town Frank went at once to Sir Robert Wilson's lodging. He found the general in, and after the first greetings, learned from him that they were to accompany the newly-appointed ambassador to Constantinople. "Our object there," Sir Robert said, "is to arrange, if possible, a peace between Russia and Turkey. There is no doubt whatever that Napoleon intends war. It is not declared yet, but it is absolutely certain, and it is of vital importance that Russia should have her hands free in other directions. As soon as this is arranged,—and I have no doubt that it will be managed, for it is so necessary to Russia that she will grant any terms, in reason, that Turkey can ask,—I am to journey north and join the headquarters of the Russian army."

This was delightful news to Frank. European travel in those days was rare, and to have the opportunity of visiting Constantinople, as well as being present at the tremendous encounter about to take place, was an unexpected pleasure indeed.

"There is one thing I want to speak to you about, Sir Robert," he said presently. "It is about Strelinski. I have been thinking that perhaps, as war is about to break out between Russia and France, you might be kind enough to get a post for him as interpreter at the War Office or Foreign Office."

"I have already thought of that," the general said. "You wrote so highly of him in your letters, that I felt I could thoroughly recommend him, and I spoke about it only the day before yesterday to the Marquis of Wellesley, and he said at once that they should be glad to have such a man, as it would enable me to send over official documents and other Russian statements without the trouble and loss of time in translating them, and as the man is from Russian Poland, he could give information concerning the country and the roads and other matters that would help them to understand what is going on, especially as, until my arrival there, they will have to depend upon Russian documents sent over by our ambassador at St. Petersburg. Tell him to be here at eleven o'clock tomorrow morning, and be here yourself in uniform. I have an appointment with Lord Wellesley at half-past."

Frank had put up at the hotel where the coach stopped, and had invited Strelinski to stay there with him until he started; and on his return he delighted the Pole by telling him that there was some chance of Sir Robert Wilson obtaining for him an appointment as interpreter. The next day Frank and Strelinski accompanied Sir Robert Wilson to the War Office. They remained in the ante-chamber while the general went in to Lord Wellesley's apartments. In half an hour an officer came out and called Frank in.

"Sir Robert Wilson has spoken very warmly in your favour, Mr. Wyatt," Lord Wellesley said, holding out his hand, as Sir Robert introduced him, "and his report is confirmed by your commanding officer, Major Tritton, who gives an excellent account of you. But you must not deprive His Majesty's army of the services of any more of its officers, Mr. Wyatt. Of course I received full details of that affair, and I am bound to say that it seems you behaved admirably, and you must be a wonderful shot. You don't look like a fire-eater either. It is a bad practice, Mr. Wyatt, a very bad practice. Well, well," he broke off, seeing a slight smile on Sir Robert's lips, "I suppose I have no right to say anything about it, having been an offender myself. However, from what I have learned, if ever a duel was justified, yours was. Well, sir, I hope that your future career will correspond with the reports that I have received of your past conduct. You are very fortunate in having been chosen for so important a service as that upon which you are now embarking, and I need hardly say that it will be of great value to you in your profession."

Frank expressed his thanks, and then retired. Strelinski was then called in, and in a few minutes returned radiant.

"What do I not owe to you," he said, "to you and General Wilson? I have been appointed interpreter on a salary of two hundred a year. Think of it! my fortune is made."

"I congratulate you indeed," Frank replied warmly. "I did not like to raise your hopes too high, but I felt sure, by what Sir Robert said, that it was as good as settled. I am almost as pleased as you are, for I should have been awfully sorry to go away, without knowing that you were comfortably settled here."

"What are you going to do, Wyatt, till you start?" General Wilson asked, as they left the War Office.

"It depends whether I can be useful here; if so, I am of course ready to do anything; but if you will not in any way want me, I shall start this evening by the coach for Weymouth, and join you at Portsmouth. I will send my baggage off at once by waggon."

"Do so by all means, Wyatt. Direct it 'Care of General Wilson, His Majesty's ship *Argo*'. You had better be there on the afternoon of the 7th, and go on board at once. We shall be down that evening, and shall sleep at the *George*, and go on board the first thing in the morning."

Frank found his aunt in good health. He stayed there three days, and then posted to Portsmouth, getting there early on the morning of the 7th. The *Argo* was lying at Spithead. Taking a wherry he went out to her at once. He found that all was in readiness, and that a small cabin had been assigned to him next to that of Sir Robert Wilson. His trunk was already there, and leaving his small portmanteau in his cabin, he went ashore and took up his quarters at the *George.* The ambassador, his secretary, and General Wilson arrived together in a post-chaise in the evening, and at eight o'clock next morning they all went on board.

The voyage was long and tedious, but Frank was very glad of a stay for two or three days at Gibraltar, and as long at Malta.

The *Argo* arrived at Constantinople at the end of June, and they found that the treaty of peace between Turkey and Russia had been already arranged. A month was spent in vexatious delays, which were the more irritating as it was known that Napoleon had arrived at the frontier, and was on the point of crossing the Niemen, if he had not already done so. At last the British ambassador succeeded in overcoming the inertness of the Porte; on the 14th of July the treaty was finally ratified, and on the 27th Sir Robert Wilson was sent by our ambassador to Shumla to arrange details with the Grand Vizier. Thence he went to the Congress at Bucharest, which was the headquarters of the Russian Admiral, Tchichagow, who commanded their army of the Danube.

After having finally arranged these matters, he started north with Frank, furnished with an order to postmasters on the road to supply them instantly with relays of horses. Travelling night and day without a stop, they arrived at Smolensk on the day before the French attacked the place. Sir Robert had expected to find the Emperor here, but learnt that he was still at St. Petersburg. Being personally acquainted with all the Russian generals he was received with the greatest courtesy, and at once placed himself at the disposal of the commander-in-chief, while Frank was introduced to the members of the staff.

Sir Robert Wilson found that a very grave state of things was prevailing. The generals were in open dissension with Barclay for having suffered the enemy to overrun so many provinces, and for not making any dispositions to defend the line of the Dnieper.

Next morning the Englishmen were awakened by a roar of musketry. They had been furnished with horses, and, dressing hastily, mounted, and joined the commander-in-chief's staff, which was taking up its position on the hill, whence a general view could be obtained of what was passing on the other side of the river. An aide-de-camp was on the point of starting, as they rode up, to ascertain the exact position of things in the town, and Sir Robert ordered Frank to accompany him. Frank had been introduced to the aide-de-camp on the previous day, and as they dashed down towards the bridge, he said:

"The fighting seems very heavy."

"It will be heavier before they take Smolensk," the Russian said. "There are 20,000 men in the town, and reinforcements can be sent across as required. At present the fighting is in the suburbs, but they won't drive us out of them as quickly as they expect."

After crossing the bridge they made their way to the headquarters of General Doctorow, and were at once shown in. The Russian saluted: "The commander-in-chief sends his compliments to you, general, and wishes to know how things are going on, and whether you need reinforcements. He desires that you should send messengers every ten minutes acquainting him with the progress of affairs."

"All goes well at present. The troops are everywhere doing their duty. As yet we need no reinforcements. They are making but little way in any of the suburbs, but of course their attack is not yet fully developed."

"Allow me to introduce to your Excellency this British

officer, Mr. Wyatt, aide-de-camp to General Wilson, who arrived in our camp yesterday afternoon as British commissioner."

"You have come at an opportune moment, sir, to see fighting. If you had come sooner you would have seen nothing but running away. If you would like to make a tour of the walls to see what is going on, an officer shall accompany you."

Frank accepted the invitation with thanks. He had nothing at present to report more than the aide-de-camp would take back, and he knew that Sir Robert would be glad of further particulars. He therefore asked him to tell Sir Robert why he had stayed, and at once proceeded to the walls, accompanied by an officer of Doctorow's staff. From there, little could be seen of the fighting. The musketry fire, indeed, had almost ceased, and the French could be seen retiring up the hill, where dense masses of troops were drawn up. Returning to the general's quarters he mounted and rode back to the commander-in-chief's staff.

"The affair has scarcely begun yet," he said to Sir Robert, "but the whole of the French army is drawn up in line of battle, and, I should say, is about to assault the town in full force."

For some hours there was a lull, but about mid-day heavy masses of troops were seen descending from the French positions, and as they approached the suburbs a roar of musketry broke out. Twice in the course of the next two hours Frank was sent down into the town. He reported that, although resisting with the greatest obstinacy, the Russians were being driven out of the suburbs. Just as he returned the second time, Sir Robert Wilson, who was examining the enemy's position with a telescope, observed that ten batteries of artillery were making their way up the steep hill on the other side of the river. He at once reported this to the general, adding: "They will very speedily knock the bridges into pieces and isolate the garrison altogether. But I think, sir," he added, "if you place some batteries on the hill on this side, you will take them in flank. The two hills are both about the same height, and they will be completely exposed to your fire."

"Very well," General Barclay replied, "I will order eight batteries up there at once, and you will oblige me if you will accompany them and indicate the best position for them to take up. Colonel Stellitz, you will at once carry the order to the artillery, and request the officer in command of the batteries to post them as General Wilson may advise."

Sir Robert and the colonel, followed by Frank, at once rode off. Just as they reached the artillery, the French battery opened fire. Exclamations of rage burst from the soldiers as the shot splashed into the water round the bridges and the shell burst over them. The general in command of the artillery, on receiving the order, directed eight batteries to follow General Wilson. At a gallop they dashed up the hill, and in ten minutes had unlimbered and opened fire upon the French. The effect was visible at once. Much confusion was observed among the artillerymen, and in a short time several of the guns were dismounted, and four or five powder waggons blown up. Then a loud cheer burst from the Russian artillerymen as they saw the French bring up the horses from behind the shelter of the crest, limber-up, and drive off with the guns. But from other points of vantage 150 guns were now pouring their fire into the town, and, as the flames broke out from several quarters, exclamations of grief and fury were heard from the Russian soldiers.

Smolensk was, like Moscow, considered a sacred city, and the soldiers were affected rather by the impiety of the act than by the actual destruction that was being wrought. As General Wilson and Frank rode back to the spot where General Barclay was stationed, a mass of Russian infantry moved down the hill towards the bridges, and at once began to cross.

"Whose division is that?" Sir Robert asked an officer as they joined the staff.

"It is Prince Eugene's," he replied. "They are pressing us hard now, having driven Doctorow's men out of the covered way, and are massing for an assault on one of the gates."

The fire continued unabated until seven o'clock. Then a messenger came across with the news that the French were drawing off, and that the covered way was being reoccupied General Wilson was warmly thanked by the Russian commander-in-chief for having silenced the batteries that had threatened the bridges. That evening, when he issued the order for the evacuation of Smolensk, the disaffection with Barclay de Tolly broke out with renewed force, and during the night a body of generals came to Sir Robert Wilson's tent. He was at the time occupied in dictating a despatch to Frank, whom he requested to retire directly he saw the rank of his visitors. As soon as they were alone they said that it had been resolved to send to the Emperor not only the request of the army for a new chief, but a declaration in their own name and that of the troops "that if any order came from St. Petersburg, to suspend hostilities and greet the invaders as friends"—for it had all along been believed that the retrograde movements were the result of the advice of the minister, Count Romanzow —such an order would be regarded as one that did not express his Imperial Majesty's real sentiments and wishes, but had been extracted from his Majesty under false representations or external control, and that the army would continue to maintain its pledge and to pursue the contest till the invader was driven beyond the frontier."

"We are here, General Wilson," one of the generals said, "to beg you to undertake the delivery of this message to the Emperor. It would mean death to any Russian officer who undertook the commission, but, knowing your attachment to the Emperor, and his equally well-known feelings towards yourself, no person is so well qualified to lay the expression of our sentiments before him. Your motives in doing so cannot be suspected; coming from you, the Emperor's self-respect would not suffer in the same way as it would do, were the message conveyed to him by one of his own subjects."

One after another the generals urged the request.

Sir Robert listened to their arguments, and then said: "This is altogether too grave a matter for me to decide upon hastily. I know thoroughly well that there is no thought of disloyalty in the mind of any of you towards the will of the Emperor, but the act is one of the gravest insubordination, and it is, indeed, a threat that you will disobey His Majesty's commands in the event of his ordering a suspension of hostilities. As to the conduct of the commander-in-chief, I am not competent to express any opinion whatever, but as a soldier I can understand that this long-continued retreat and the abandonment of so many provinces to the enemy, without striking a single blow in their defence, is trying in the extreme, both to yourselves and your brave soldiers. I shall not leave the army until I see it fairly on the march again, but before I start I will give you my reply."

The generals thanked Sir Robert warmly, and then withdrew.

"I shall write no more to-night, Wyatt," the general said when Frank entered the tent. "I have other grave matters to think about. You had best lie down at once, and get a few hours' sleep. To-morrow is likely to be an eventful day, for the operation of withdrawing the army from this position and getting on to the main road again will be full of peril, and may indeed end in a terrible disaster."

As soon as the Russian army had repulsed the attacks of the French and resumed its march towards Moscow, Sir Robert Wilson left it and proceeded to St. Petersburg, where he had promised the Russian generals to inform the Czar of the opinion and disposition of the army, their dissatisfaction with the general, and their determination to continue the combat and to refuse to recognize any negotiations or armistice that might be made with the enemy.

"I shall leave you here, Wyatt," the General said, on the morning after the desperate defence of Loubino had saved the army. "There is little chance of the French pressing the Russians any further. I think it probable that they may go into winter quarters where they now are; but in any case they cannot hope to outmarch us, and, if they follow, the battle will be in the position the Russians may choose. Even were there more fighting imminent, I should still start to-day for St. Petersburg; I only came round by Smolensk, as you know, because I thought that the Emperor would be found there. My first duty is to see him, and to report to him the arrangements that have been made on the Danube with the Grand Vizier and his people, by which the whole of the Russian army there will be able to join in the defence against the French. As soon as I have done so, and explained to his Majesty the position here, I shall rejoin; and I hope the Czar will also be coming down here, for his presence would be most useful—not in the military way, for no men in the world could fight better than the Russians are doing,—but the army fears, above all things, that peace will be made before it has an opportunity of wiping out, what it considers its disgrace, in allowing the French to overrun so many rich provinces without striking a blow.

"In point of fact, the defence of Smolensk, and the way in which some 20,000 men yesterday withstood for hours the assault of three or four times their number, would be sufficient to prove to the world their fighting qualities. In my own mind, I consider that Barclay has acted wisely in declining to hazard the whole fortune of the war upon a single battle against an enemy which, from the first, has outnumbered him nearly threefold; but he should never have taken up his position on the frontier if he did not mean to defend it. Any other army than this would have become a disorganized rabble long ago. There is nothing so trying to troops as to march for weeks hotly chased by an enemy. Three times in the Peninsula we have seen what a British army becomes under far less trying circumstances. If the Russians did but know it, this retreat of theirs, and the admirable manner in which they have maintained their discipline, is as creditable as winning a great victory would be; still, one can understand that the sight of this flying population, the deserted fields, this surrender of provinces to an enemy, is mortifying in the highest degree to their pride.

"Nevertheless, Barclay's policy, though I think it has been carried a great deal too far—for with troops who will fight as ours did yesterday he might have fought a dozen battles like that of Loubino, and would have compelled the French to advance slowly instead of in hot pursuit—has been justified to a great extent. From all I hear, the invading army has already suffered very great losses from fever and hardship, the effect of the weather, and from the number of stragglers who have been cut off and killed by the peasantry. Their transport has especially suffered, vast numbers of their horses having died; and in a campaign like this, transport is everything. In the various fights that have taken place since they entered Russia, they have probably suffered a heavier loss than the Russians, as the latter have always fought on the defensive; and the French loss has fallen on Napoleon's best troops, while the Russian army is all equally good.

"Lastly, although the Russians are discontented at their continued retreat, their *morale* does not seem to have suffered in any way, and it is probable that the long marches, the inability to bring on a general engagement, the distance from home, and the uncertainty about the future has told heavily upon that of the French, who are vastly more susceptible to matters of this kind than are the Russians. You will remain with the headquarter staff, and I wish you, while I am away, to obtain accurate details of the movements of the various columns, and to write a full report every evening of the march and of all matters of interest. I do not want you to forward these to me, but to keep them for future reference. I hope to rejoin before any further fighting takes place."

Sir Robert reached St. Petersburg on the 24th of August, but it was not until ten days later that he saw the Emperor, who had gone with Lord Cathcart, the British Ambassador, to meet the King of Sweden, and to conclude the negotiations that secured his co-operation. The information that General Wilson had brought of the admirable behaviour of the army did much to allay the alarm that prevailed in St. Petersburg, and, after dining with the Emperor on the evening of the arrival of the latter at his capital, he had a long private interview with him. The Emperor had already been made acquainted with the dissatisfaction in the army, and Marshal Kutusow had been sent to replace General Barclay, and he asked Sir Robert whether he thought the new commander would be able to restore subordination and confidence in the army. Sir Robert replied that he had met the marshal, and had informed him of the exact state of things there: that the latter had conjured him to acquaint the Emperor with the fullest details, and in accordance with that request, and in order to prevent his Majesty having the pain of hearing it from the lips of one of his own subjects—who perhaps would be less able to convince him of the intense feeling of loyalty to himself that still prevailed—he had consented to be the mouthpiece of the generals of the army. He then reported to him the interviews that he had had with the general officers, suppressing the names of those present, and the message they had desired him to deliver.

The Emperor was greatly moved. However, the manner in which the general fulfilled the mission with which he was charged, and his assurances that the act of seeming insubordination and defiance of the imperial authority was in no way directed against him, but against his advisers, whom they believed to be acting in the interests of Napoleon, had their effect, and the Emperor promised to give the matter every consideration, and to answer him definitely on the following day. At the next meeting he gave Sir Robert his authority to assure the army of his determination to continue the war against Napoleon while a Frenchman remained in arms on Russian soil, and that, if the worst came to the worst, he would remove his family far into the interior, and make any sacrifice rather than break that engagement. At the same time, while he could not submit to dictation in the matter of his ministers, he could assure them that these should in no way influence him to break this promise.

During Sir Robert's stay in St. Petersburg the Emperor took every occasion to show him marked favour, as if anxious to assure those whose views Sir Robert had represented, that he was in no way displeased with them for the attitude they had assumed; and upon his leaving to rejoin the army the Emperor directed him to repeat in the most formal manner his declaration that he would not enter into or permit any negotiations with Napoleon; and added that he would sooner let his beard grow to his waist, and eat potatoes in Siberia.

Frank had been active during the battle of Loubino. Sir Robert Wilson had taken up his post with Touchkoff during the action which was so desperately fought to cover the retreat of the main army, and Frank had acted as aide-de-camp, and, having carried orders to various parts of the field, had excellent opportunities of seeing the whole of the battle; and the Russian general in making his report of the engagement had mentioned his name among those who had rendered distinguished services. His horse had been shot under him, his cap had been carried away by a bullet, and he had received a slight flesh wound in his leg. Although this was of small consequence, it had caused the insertion of his name among those of the officers wounded in the battle. He was to see no more fighting for a time; for, although the army of Wittgenstein fought two or three severe actions with the divisions of St. Cyr and Oudinot, the main army fell back without again fighting until it took up the position that Marshal Kutusow had selected for giving battle.

CHAPTER XII.

BORODINO.

BARBAROUSLY as the French army behaved on its advance to Smolensk, things were even worse as they left the ruined town behind them and resumed their journey towards Moscow. It seemed that the hatred with which they were regarded by the Russian peasantry was now even more than reciprocated. The destruction they committed was wanton and wholesale; the villages, and even the towns, were burnt down, and the whole country made desolate. It was nothing to them that by so doing they added enormously to the difficulties of their own commissariat; nothing that they were destroying the places where they might otherwise have found shelter on their return. They seemed to destroy simply for the sake of destruction, and to be animated by a burning feeling of hatred for the country they had invaded.

Since the days of the thirty years' war in Germany, never had war been carried on in Europe so mercilessly and so destructively. As he saw the ruined homes or passed the bodies of peasants wantonly shot down, Julian Wyatt regretted bitterly that he had not been content to remain a prisoner at Verdun. Battles he had expected; but this destruction of property, this warring upon peaceful inhabitants, filled him with horror; his high spirits left him, and he no longer laughed and jested on the march, but kept on the way in the same gloomy silence that reigned among the greater part of his companions. When half-way to Moscow a fresh cause of uneasiness manifested itself. The Russians no longer left their towns and villages for the French to plunder and burn, but, as they retreated, themselves applied fire to all the houses, with a thoroughness and method which showed that this was not the work of stragglers or camp-followers, but that it was the result of a settled plan. At last news came that the Russians had resolved to fight a pitched battle at Borodino, and the spirits of the army at once rose.

Napoleon halted them for two days, in order that they might rest and receive provisions from the baggage trains following. On the 4th of September they marched forward as before, in three columns, preceded by Murat's cavalry, which brushed aside the hordes of Cossack horse. Halfway to Gratz, a Russian division stoutly held for some time a height up which the road wound, but after some sharp fighting was forced to retreat.

The Russian position at Borodino was a strong one. The right was covered by the rivulet of Kolocza, which was everywhere fordable, but ran through a deep ravine. Borodino, a village on the banks of this rivulet, formed their centre, and their left was posted upon steeply rising ground, almost at right angles with their right. Borodino itself—which lay on the northern side of the Kolocza—was not intended to be held in force. The rivulet fell into the river Moskwa half a mile beyond Borodino. Fieldworks had been thrown up at several points, and near the centre were two strong redoubts commanding Borodino and the high-road. Other strong works had been erected at important points.

Considerably in advance of the general line of the position a strong work had been erected; this it was necessary to take before the main position could be attacked, and at two in the afternoon of the 5th, Napoleon directed an assault to be made upon this redoubt. It was obstinately held by the Russians. They were several times driven out, but, as often, reinforcements came up, and it was captured by them; and finally, after holding it until nightfall, they fell back to their main position, the loss having been heavy on both sides. The next day was spent by Napoleon in reconnoitring the Russian position and deciding the plan of attack. Finally he determined to make a strong demonstration against the village of Borodino, and, under cover of this, to launch his whole army upon the Russian left wing. On the morning of the 7th, Napoleon posted himself on an eminence near the village of Chewardino. Near the spot, earthworks were thrown up during the night for the protection of three batteries, each of twenty-four guns. Davoust and Ney were to make a direct attack on the enemy's left. Poniatowski was to endeavour to march through the woods and gain the rear of the Russian position. The rest of the force were to keep the Russian centre and right in check. The Imperial Guard formed the reserve.

On the Russian side Bagration's army formed the left, Beningsen's the centre, and Barclay's the right. The French force numbered about 150,000, the Russian from 80,000 to 90,000. The French had a thousand guns, the Russians 640. At six in the morning of the 7th of September the French batteries opened fire along the whole line, and the Russians at once replied. The roar of artillery was incessant, and ere long the rattle of musketry swelled the din, as Davoust launched the division of Desaix, and Ney that of Campans, against three small redoubts in front of the Russian position. Impetuous as was the assault, the Russians received it with unflinching courage; two of the Russian generals were wounded, but the assault was repulsed. Ney moved up another division, and after severe fighting the redoubts were carried. They were held, however, but a short time, for Woronzow led forward his grenadiers in solid squares, and, supporting the advance by a charge of cavalry, recaptured them, and drove the French back across the ravine in front of them.

There was now a short pause in the attack, but the roar of artillery and musketry continued unbroken. Poniatowski now emerged from the wood, and fell upon the Russian left rear, capturing the village of Outitska. Touchkoff, a brother of the general who had been captured at Loubino, who commanded here, fell back to a height that dominated the village and the ground beyond it, and maintained himself until midday. On the French left, where the Viceroy Beauharnois commanded, the advance was stubbornly opposed, and the French artillery was several times silenced by the guns on the eminence. At last, however, the Russians were driven across the rivulet, and the French occupied Borodino. Leaving a division of infantry to protect his rear, the Viceroy crossed the stream and advanced against a great battery in front of the village of Gorki. Davoust and Ney remained motionless until nine o'clock, as Napoleon would not forward the reinforcements they had asked for until he learned that Poniatowski had come into action, and that the Viceroy had crossed the stream and was moving to the attack of the Russian centre. Now, reinforced by the division of Friant, they moved forward.

For an hour the Russians held their advanced works, and then were forced to fall back; and the French, following up their advantage, crossed a ravine and occupied the village of Semianotsky, which had been partially destroyed on the previous day by the Russians, so that if captured it would afford no cover to the French. It was but for a short time that the latter held it. Coming up at the head of his grenadiers, Touchkoff drove them out, recrossed the ravine, and recaptured the advanced works they had before so obstinately contested. In turn the French retook the three redoubts; but, again, a Russian division coming up wrested the position from them, and replanted their flag there. Napoleon, seeing that no impression could be made on the Russian left, now sent orders to the Viceroy to carry the great redoubt before Gorki. In spite of the difficulties presented by the broken ground, the three French divisions pressed forward with the greatest gallantry, and, heedless of the storm of grape poured upon them, stormed the redoubt. But its late defenders, reinforced by some battalions from Doctorow's corps, dashed forward to recover the position, and fell with such fury upon the French that the regiment that had entered the redoubt was all but annihilated, and the position regained, while at the same moment two regiments of Russian cavalry fell upon reinforcements pressing forward to aid the defenders, and threw them into disorder.

The Viceroy now opened fire on the redoubt with all his artillery, inflicting such loss upon the defenders that it was soon necessary to relieve them with a fresh division. Ney, finding it impossible to carry and hold the three redoubts in front of him, directed Junot to endeavour to force his way between the main Russian left and Touchkoff's division; but he was met by Prince Eugene's Russian corps, which brought his advance to a standstill. Junot's presence there, however, acted as a support to Poniatowski, who, covered by the fire of forty pieces of cannon, advanced against Touchkoff's division. For a time he gained ground, but the Russian general, bringing up all his troops, assumed the offensive, and, driving Poniatowski back, recovered the lost ground. The brave Russian leader, however, was mortally wounded in the fight. It was now twelve o'clock, and so far the French had gained no advantage. Napoleon felt the necessity for a decisive effort, and concentrating his whole force, and posting 400 guns to cover the advance, sent it forward against the Russian left.

The Russians, perceiving the magnitude of the movement, despatched large reinforcements to the defenders, and at the same time, to effect a diversion, sent the greater portion of their cavalry round to menace the French rear at Borodino. Three hundred Russian guns opposed the four hundred of the French, and amidst the tremendous roar of the guns, the great mass of French infantry hurled themselves upon the Russians. For a time no impression could be made, so sternly and fiercely did the Russians fight, but Bagration, their commander, with several other generals, were badly wounded and forced to retire. Konownitsyn assumed the command, but the loss of the general, in whom they placed implicit confidence, told upon the spirits of his troops, and Konownitsyn was forced to abandon the three redoubts, and to take up a new position behind Semianotsky, where he re-established his batteries and checked the progress of the enemy.

A portion of the French cavalry now made a desperate attempt to break through the Russian left, but two regiments of the Imperial Guard, throwing themselves into squares, maintained their position until five regiments of Russian cuirassiers came up and forced their assailants back. At this critical moment the great mass of Russian cavalry that had been sent round to attack the Viceroy fell upon his rear, drove his cavalry into the village with great loss, and pressed the infantry so hard that the Viceroy himself had to take refuge in one of his squares. Having thus succeeded in distracting the enemy's attention, arresting his tide of battle, and giving time to the Russians to reform and plant their batteries afresh, the Russian cavalry withdrew. The Viceroy recrossed the stream again, and prepared to make another attack upon the great bastion he had before captured, and the whole line again advanced. While the Viceroy attacked the great redoubt in front, Murat sent a division of his cavalry round to fall upon its rear, and, although swept by artillery and infantry fire, the brave horsemen carried out their object, although almost annihilated by the fire of the defenders of the redoubt.

The French infantry took advantage of the attention of the defenders being diverted by this attack, and with a rush stormed the work; the four Russian regiments who held it fought to the last, refusing all offers of quarter, and maintaining a hand-to-hand conflict until annihilated. The Russian artillery, in the works round Gorki, swept the redoubt with their fire, and under its cover the infantry made repeated but vain attacks to recapture it, for their desperate bravery was unavailing against the tremendous artillery fire concentrated upon them, while the French on their part were unable to take advantage of the position they had gained. Napoleon, indeed, would have launched his troops against the works round Gorki, but his generals represented to him that the losses had already been so enormous, that it was doubtful whether he could possibly succeed, and if he did so, it could only be with such further loss as would cripple the army altogether.

At three o'clock Napoleon, whose whole army, with the exception of the Imperial Guard, had been engaged, felt that nothing further could be done that day, and ordered the battle to cease. He had gained the three redoubts on the Russians' left and the great redoubt captured by the Viceroy, but these were really only advanced works, and the main position of the Russians still remained entirely intact. At night the French retired from the positions they had won, to those they had occupied before the battle begun, retaining possession only of the village of Borodino. The loss of the combatants during the two days' fighting had been nearly equal, no less than 40,000 men having been killed on each side, a number exceeding that of any other battle in modern times. Napoleon expected that the Russians would again give battle next morning, but Kutusow, contrary to the opinion of most of his generals, decided on falling back. Beningsen, one of his best officers, strongly urged him to take up a position at Kalouga, some seventy miles to the south of Moscow. The position was a very strong one. Napoleon could not advance against Moscow, which was in a position to offer a long and determined resistance, until he had driven off the Russian army. At Kalouga they could at any moment advance on to his line of communication, cut off all his supplies, and isolate him from France.

The advice was excellent, but Kutusow, who was even more unfitted than Barclay for the post of commander-in-chief, refused to adopt this course, and fell back towards Moscow, followed by the French. The sufferings of the latter had already become severe—the nights were getting very cold, the scarcity of food was considerable, the greater part of the army was already subsisting on horse-flesh, the warm clothing, which was becoming more and more necessary, was far in the rear, their shoes were worn out, and it was only the thought that they would have a long period of rest and comfort in Moscow, that animated them to press forward along the fifty miles of road between Borodino and that city.

Julian had passed through the terrible battle unscathed. It seemed to him, when fighting had ceased for the day, that it was almost miraculous a single man should have survived that storm of fire. While the fight had actually been going on, the excitement and the ardour of battle had rendered him almost insensible to the danger. With the soldiers, as with their generals, the capture of the three small redoubts became, as the day went on, a matter on which every thought was bent, every energy concentrated; it was no longer a battle between French and Russians but a struggle in which each man felt that his personal honour was concerned. Each time that, with loud cheering, they stormed the blood-stained works, they felt the pride of victory; each time that, foot by foot, they were again forced backwards, there was rage in every heart and a fierce determination to return and conquer.

In such a struggle as this, when men's passions are once involved, death loses its terror; thickly as comrades may fall around, those who are still erect heed not the gaps, but with eyes fixed on the enemy in front of him, with lips set tightly together, with head bent somewhat down as men who struggle through a storm of rain, each man presses on until a shot strikes him, or he reaches the goal he aims at. At such a time the fire slackens, for each man strives to decide the struggle, with bayonet or clubbed musket. Four times did Julian's regiment climb the side of the ravine in front of the redoubts, four times were they hurled back again with ever-decreasing numbers, and when at last they found themselves, as the fire slackened, masters of the position, the men looked at each other as if waking from some terrible dream, filled with surprise that they were still alive and breathing, and faint and trembling, now that the exertion was over and the tremendous strain relaxed. When they had time to look round, they saw that but one-fourth of those who had, some hours before, advanced to the attack of the redoubt of Chewardino remained. The ground around the little earthworks was piled thickly with dead Frenchmen and Russians, and ploughed up by the iron storm that had for eight hours swept across it. Dismounted guns, ammunition-boxes, muskets, and accoutrements were scattered everywhere. Even the veterans of a hundred battles had never witnessed such a scene, had never gone through so prolonged and terrible a struggle. Men were differently affected, some shook a comrade's hand with silent pressure, some stood gazing sternly and fixedly at the lines where the enemy still stood unconquered, and tears fell down many a bronzed and battle-worn face; some sobbed like children, exhausted by their emotions rather than their labours.

The loss of the officers had been prodigious. Eight generals were killed and thirty wounded, and nearly two thousand officers. The colonel and majors of Julian's regiment had fallen, and a captain, who was but sixth on the list when the battle began, now commanded. Between three o'clock and dusk the men were engaged in binding up each other's wounds, eating what food they carried in their haversacks, and searching for more in those of the fallen. Few words were spoken, and even when the order came to evacuate the position and retire to the ground they had left that morning, there was not a murmur; for the time no one seemed to care what happened, or what became of him. Once on the ground where they were to bivouac fresh life was infused into their veins. The chill evening air braced up their nerves; great fires were lighted with brushwood, broken cartridge-boxes, and the fragments of gun-carriages and waggons; and water was brought up from the stream. Horse-flesh was soon being roasted, and as hunger and thirst were appeased, the buzz of conversation rose round the fires, and the minds as well as the tongues of men seemed to thaw from their torpor.

"Well, comrade, so you too have gone through it without a scratch," Julian's friend, the sergeant, said to him. "Well, you will never see such a fight again if you grow gray in the service. Where are those who scoffed at the Russians now? They can fight, these men. It was a battle of giants. No one could have done more than we did, and yet they did as much; but to-morrow we shall win."

"What! do you think we shall fight again to-morrow?"

"That is for the Russians to say, not for us. If they stand we must fight them again. It is a matter of life and death for us to get to Moscow. We shall win to-morrow, for Napoleon will have to bring up the Imperial Guard, 20,000 of his best troops, and the Russians put their last man into the line of battle to-day, and, never fear, we shall win. But I own I have had enough of it. Never before have I hoped that the enemy in front of us would go off without a battle, but I do so now. We want rest and quiet. When spring comes we will fight them again as often as they like, but until then I for one do not wish to hear a gun fired."

"I am sure I do not, sergeant," Julian agreed; "and I only hope that we shall get peace and quiet when we reach Moscow."

"Oh, the Russians will be sure to send in to ask for terms of peace as soon as we get there!" the sergeant said confidently.

"I hope so, but I have great doubts, sergeant. When people are ready to burn their homes rather than that we should occupy them, to desert all that they have and to wander away they know not where, when they will fight as they fought to-day, I have great doubts whether they will talk of surrender. They can bring up fresh troops long before we can. They will have no lack of provisions. Their country is so vast that they know that at most we can hold but a small portion of it. It seems to me that it is not of surrender they will be thinking, but of bringing up fresh troops from every part of their empire, of drilling and organizing and preparing for the next campaign. I cannot help thinking of what would happen to us if they burnt Moscow, as they have burned half a dozen towns already."

"No people ever made such a sacrifice. What, burn the city they consider sacred!—the old capital every Russian thinks of with pride! It never can be; but if they should do so, all I can say is, God help us all! Few of us would ever go back to France."

"So it seems to me, sergeant. I have been thinking of it lately, and after the way in which the Russians came on, careless of life, under the fire of our cannon to-day, I can believe them to be capable of anything."

The next morning it was found that the Russian lines were deserted. So the French army set forward again on its march, and on the morning of the 14th arrived within sight of Moscow. Kutusow had at one time seemed disposed to fight another battle in front of the city, and had given a solemn promise to its governor that he should have three days' notice of any change in his determination, and so allow time for him to carry out his intention to evacuate the town, when the municipal authorities were, methodically and officially, to proceed to destroy the whole city by fire. This promise Kutusow broke without giving any notice whatever. On the 13th, at a council of war, he overruled the objections of his generals, and determined to retreat, his arguments being that the ground was unsuited for defensive operations; that the defeat of the one disciplined army would endanger the final success of the war; and that it was for Russia, not for any one city, they were fighting.

The argument was not without reason; but, if he had resolved not to fight again, he should have accepted the advice to take up a position on Napoleon's flank. Had he done this, the French could have made no advance, and Moscow would have been saved from destruction.

As the army began its passage through the capital the exodus of the inhabitants commenced. Already the wealthier classes had removed their effects, and the merchants the greater part of their goods. Now the whole population poured out into the streets, and thousands of carts and vehicles of all descriptions, packed closely with household furniture, goods, and effects of all kinds, moved towards the gates. Out of 200,000 inhabitants 180,000 left the city, with 65,000 vehicles of every kind. In addition to these were enormous quantities of fugitives from every town and village west of Smolensk, who had hitherto accompanied the army, moving through the fields and lanes, so as to leave the roads unencumbered for the passage of the guns and trains.

Every Russian peasant possesses a roughly-made cart on two or four wheels, and as their belongings were very scanty, these, as a rule, sufficed to hold all their property. The greater portion of the fugitives had passed out of the city at two o'clock in the afternoon, and shortly afterwards Murat with his cavalry passed across the river by a ford and entered the town. A few desperate men left behind opened fire, but were speedily overpowered and killed, but a number of citizens, mad with fury, rushed so furiously upon Murat and his staff, that he was obliged to open fire upon them with a couple of light guns.

At three o'clock Napoleon arrived with his guards, expecting to be met on his arrival by the authorities of the city with assurances of their submission and prayers for clemency for the population. He was astounded with the silence that reigned everywhere, and at hearing that Moscow had been evacuated by the population. Full of gloomy anticipations he proceeded to the house Murat had selected for him. Strict orders were issued against pillage, and the army bivouacked outside the city. The troops, however, were not to be restrained, and as soon as it was dark stole away and entered the town in large numbers and began the work of pillage. Scarcely had they entered when in various quarters fires broke out suddenly. The bazaar, with its ten thousand shops, the crown magazines of forage, wines, brandy, military stores, and gunpowder were speedily wrapped in flames. There were no means of combating the fire, for every bucket in the town had been removed by the orders of the governor.

Many a tale of strange experience in all parts of Europe was told round the camp-fires of the grenadiers of the Rhone that evening. Several of the younger men had been among those who had gone into Moscow in search of plunder. They had returned laden with goods of all sorts, and but few without a keg of spirits. The colonel had foreseen this, and had called the sergeants together.

"My braves," he said, "I am not going to punish anyone for breaking orders to-night. If I had been carrying a musket myself I have no doubt that I should have been one of those to have gone into the town. After such a march as we have had here, it is only natural that men should think that they are entitled to some fun; but there must be no drunkenness. I myself shall be at the quarter-guard, and six of you will be there with me. Every bottle of spirits brought in is to be confiscated. You will take it in your charge and serve out a good ration to every man in the regiment, so that those who have done their duty and remained in camp shall fare as well as those who have broken out. I have no doubt there will be sufficient brought in for all. What remains over, you can serve out as a ration to-morrow. It is good to be merry, but it is not good to be drunk. The grenadiers have done their share of fighting and deserve their share of plunder, but do not let pleasure go beyond the line of duty. Give a good ration to each man, enough to enjoy the evening, and to celebrate our capture of Moscow, but not enough to make them noisy. It is like enough that the general will be round to-night to see how things are going on, and I should wish him to see us enjoying ourselves reasonably. Anything else that is brought in, with the exception of spirits, can be kept by the men, unless of course there is a general order issued that all plunder is to be given up."

As fully half the regiment were away, and as every man brought back one or more bottles or kegs of spirits, the amount collected at the quarter-guard was very considerable. Those of the men who, on coming back, showed any signs of intoxication were not allowed a share, but half a litre of spirits was served out to every other man in the regiment; and although a few of those who had brought it in grumbled, the colonel's decision gave general satisfaction, and there were merry groups round the bivouac fires.

"I have marched into a good many capitals," the old sergeant said. "I was with the first company that entered Madrid. I could never make out the Spaniards. At one time they are ready to wave their hats and shout 'Viva!' till they are hoarse. At another, cutting your throat is too good for you. One town will open its gates and treat you as their dearest friends, the next will fight like fiends and not give in till you have carried the last house at the point of the bayonet. I was fond of a glass in those days; I am fond of it now, but I have gained wit enough to know when it is good to drink. I had a sharp lesson, and I took it to heart."

"Tell us about it, comrade," Julian said.

"Well, it was after Talavera. We had fought a hard battle there with the English, and found them rough customers. The Spaniards bolted like sheep. As soldiers, they are the most contemptible curs in the world. They fought well enough in the mountains under their own leaders, but as soldiers, why, our regiment would thrash an army of 15,000 of them. The English were on the top of the hill—at least at the beginning there were a few of them up there, and we thought that it would be an easy job to drive them off, but more came up, and do what we would, we could not manage it; so it ended with something like a drawn battle. We claimed the victory, because they fell back the next morning, and they claimed it because they had repulsed all our attacks. However, we reaped the benefit; they really fell back, because those rascally Spaniards they were fighting for, starved them; and, besides that, we had two other divisions marching to interpose between them and Portugal, and that old fox Wellington saw that unless he went off as fast as he could, he would be caught in a trap.

"They got a good start of us, but we followed, and three nights after Talavera two companies of us were quartered for the night in the village right out on the flank of the line we were following. Well, I got hold of a skin of as good wine as ever I drank. Two or three of us stole out to enjoy it quietly and comfortably, and so thoroughly did we do it, that I suppose I somehow mistook my way back to my quarters, wandered aside, and then lay down to sleep. I must have slept soundly, for I heard neither bugle nor drum. When I awoke the sun was high, and there was a group of ugly-looking Spaniards standing near me. I tried to jump up on to my feet, but found that my arms and legs were both tied. However, I managed to sit up, and looked round. Not a sign of our uniform was there to be seen; but a cloud of dust rising from the plain, maybe ten miles away, showed where the army had gone.

"Well, I gave it up at once. A single French soldier had never found mercy at the hands of the Spaniards, and I only wondered that they had not cut my throat at once, instead of taking the trouble to fasten me up. I knew enough of their language to get along with, and, putting as bold a face as I could on it, I asked them what they had tied me up for. They laughed in an unpleasant sort of way, and then went away. 'Let me have a drink of water,' I said, for my throat was nearly as dry as a furnace. They paid no attention, and till sunset left me there in the full heat of the sun. By the time they came back again I was half mad with thirst. I supposed then, as I have supposed ever since, that they did not cut my throat at once, because they were afraid that some other detachment might come along, and that if they found my body or a pool of blood, they would, as like as not, burn the village over their heads. Anyhow at sunset four men came, cut the ropes from my feet, and told me to follow them. I said that I would follow willingly enough if they would give me a drink of water first, but that if they didn't they might shoot me if they liked, but not a step would I walk.

"They tried kicking and punching me with their guns, but finding that I was obstinate, one of them called to a woman down by the village to bring some water. I drank pretty near a bucketful, and then said I was ready to go on. We went up the hill, and then on some ten miles to a village standing in the heart of a wild country. Here I was tied to a post. Two of them went away and returned in a few minutes with a man they called El Chico. I felt before that I had not much chance, but I knew now that I had none at all, for the name was well enough known to us as that of one of the most savage of the guerrilla leaders. He abused me for ten minutes, and told me that I should be burnt alive next morning, in revenge for some misconduct or other of a scouting party of ours. I pointed out that as I was not one of that scouting party it was unfair that I should be punished for their misdeeds; but, of course, it was of no use arguing with a ruffian like that, so he went away, leaving me to my reflections.

"I stood all night with my back to that post. Two fellows with muskets kept guard over me, but even if they hadn't done so I could not have got away, for I was so tightly bound that my limbs were numbed, and the cords felt as if they were red hot. In the morning a number of women brought up faggots. El Chico himself superintended their arrangement, taking care that they were placed in a large enough circle round me that the flames would not touch me; so that, in fact, I should be slowly roasted instead of burned. I looked about in the vague hope one always has that something might occur to save me, and my heart gave a jump when I saw a large body of men coming rapidly down a slope on the other side of the village. They were not our men, I was sure, but I could not see who they were; anyhow there might be someone among them who would interpose to save me from this villain.

"Everyone round me was too interested in what was going on to notice anything else; and you may be sure that I did not look that way again, for I knew well enough that if the guerrilla had noticed them he would shoot me at once rather than run any risk of being baulked of his vengeance. So it was not until they began to enter the village that anyone noticed the new arrivals. A mounted officer, followed by four troopers, dashed down ahead and rode up to us, scattering the crowd right and left. I saw at once by his uniform that he was an English officer, and knew that I was saved. I fancy I must have been weak, for I had had nothing to eat the day before, and had been tied up all night. For a time I think I really fainted. When I recovered, some soldiers had cut my bonds, and one was pouring some spirits down my throat. The English officer was giving it hot to El Chico.

"'You dog!' he said, 'it is you, and the fellows like you, who bring discredit on your country. You run like sheep when you see a French force under arms. You behave like inhuman monsters when, by chance, a single man falls into your power. I have half a mind to put you against that wall there and have you shot; or, what would meet your deserts better, hang you to yonder tree. Don't finger that pistol, you scoundrel, or I will blow your brains out. Be off with you, and thank your stars I did not arrive ten minutes later; for if I had come too late to save this poor fellow's life, I swear to you that I would have hung you like a dog. Who is the head man of the village?'

"A man stepped forward.

"'What do you mean, sir,' said the officer sternly, 'by permitting this villain to use your village for his atrocities? As far as I can see you are all as bad as he is, and I have a good mind to burn the whole place over your ears. As it is, I fine the village 800 gallons of wine, and 4000 pounds of flour, and 10 bullocks. See that it is all forthcoming in a quarter of an hour, or I shall set my men to help themselves. Not a word! Do as you are ordered!'

"Then he dismounted, and was coming to me, when his eye fell on El Chico. 'Sergeant,' he said to a non-commissioned officer, 'take four men and march that fellow well outside the village, and then stand and watch him; and see that he goes on, and if he doesn't, shoot him.' Then he came over to me. 'It is well that I arrived in time, my lad,' he said in French. 'How did you get into this scrape?'

"'It was wine did it, sir. I drank too much at our bivouac in a village down the plain, and did not hear the bugles in the morning, and got left behind. When I awoke they had tied me up, and they kept me lying in the sun all day, not giving me as much as a drop of water. At sunset they marched me up here and tied me to that post, and El Chico told me that I should be roasted in the morning; and so it certainly would have been if you had not come up.

"I learned that he was a Colonel Trant. He commanded a force of Portuguese, and was a daring partisan leader, and gave us a great deal of trouble. I was never more pleased than I was at seeing the disgust of those villagers as they paid the fine imposed on them, and I should imagine that when El Chico paid his next visit there, his reception would not be a cordial one. The brigade had been marching all night, and halted for six hours, and the bullocks, flour, and wine furnished them with a good meal all round. It was an hour or two before I was able to stand, but after a while the circulation got right, and I was able to accompany them when they marched. They did not know until I told them that our force had passed on ahead of them in pursuit of Wellington. I made no secret of that, for they would have heard it from the first peasant they met. When we started, the colonel asked me what I meant to do.

"'I don't want to keep you prisoner, my man,' he said. 'In the first place, I don't wish to be troubled with looking after you; and in the second, you cannot be considered as a prisoner of war, for you were unarmed and helpless when we found you. Now, we are going to march all night. I am not going to tell where we are going; but I think it likely that we shall pass within sight of your camp-fires, and in that case I will leave you to make your way down to them, and will hand you back your musket and pouch, which you may want if you happen to fall in with a stray peasant or two.'

"I had noticed that they had taken along my musket and pouch, which had been brought up by the fellows that guarded me. They were strapped on to a mule's pack, of which they had about a couple of dozen with them, but I little thought the gun was going to be given me again.

"'Monsieur le Colonel,' I said, 'I thank you from my heart. I should have felt disgraced for ever if I were to go into the camp unarmed. Now, I shall be able to go in with my head erect, and take my punishment for having got drunk, and failing to fall in at the assembly, like a man. On the honour of a French soldier, I swear that I shall for ever regard the English as the most generous of foes.'

"It was noon when we started, and at nine o'clock at night, as we were keeping along high up on the hills, I saw our bivouac fires. A minute or two later, the colonel rode up.

"'There are your fires, lad,' he said. 'I don't fancy there is any village between us and the spot where your people are encamped. However, as there is a moon, you will be able to avoid one if you come upon it; and seeing you are armed, any peasants you may meet will scarcely venture to attack you within musket-shot of your own lines. Here is a note I have written to the colonel of your regiment telling him of the plight I found you in, and expressing a hope that what you have gone through may be considered a sufficient punishment for your indulgence in too much wine. Good-night!'

"Well, I got down safely enough. Of course, when I got to our line of pickets, I was challenged, and sent in a prisoner. In the morning I was taken before the colonel. He rated me soundly, I can tell you. When he had finished, I saluted and handed him the note. He read it through, and handed it to the major.

"'A letter from the enemy,' he said. 'It is from Trant, who must be a good fellow as well as a brave soldier, as we know to our cost. Tell me more about this, Rignold.'

"I told him.

"'I agree with the Englishman,' he said. 'You have had a lesson that will last you all your life. I wish I had means of sending an answer back to this English colonel, thanking him for his generous treatment. If he ever falls into our hands, I will take care that this action of his shall be brought to the general's notice. You can go.'

"Well, you see, that lesson has lasted all my life; and I am certainly not likely to forget it here, where the peasants are every bit as savage as the Spaniards. But as for the English, though I have fought with them half a dozen times since, and have been beaten by them too, I have always had a liking for them. That was one reason why I took to you, youngster, from the first."

"They fight well, do they?" one of the other sergeants asked. "I never was in Spain, but I thought from the bulletins that we generally beat them."

"Bulletins!" growled Rignold, "who can believe bulletins? We have got so accustomed to writing bulletins of victory that when we do get thrashed we can't write in any other strain. Why, I tell you that we who have fought and conquered in Italy and Austria, in Prussia and on the Rhine, have learned to acknowledge among ourselves, that even our best troops were none too good when it came to fighting the English. I fought a dozen battles against them, and in not one of them could I honestly say that we got the best of it. Talavera was the nearest thing. But we were fairly thrashed at Busaco and Salamanca. Albuera we claimed as a drawn fight, but such a drawn fight I never wish to share in again. The day had been going well. The Spaniards of course bolted, horse and foot. But at last matters cleared up, and we advanced against them in heavy columns. Soult called up all the reserves. We had captured six of their guns. Our columns had crowned the hill they held, and we cheered loudly, believing that the battle was won, when an English brigade in line fell upon us. Our guns swept them with grape, and that so terribly that for a time they fell into confusion. But to our astonishment they rallied, and came down on us. We were four to one, but we were in columns, and strove in vain to form into line to meet them. Volley after volley swept away the head of our formation. Soult exposed himself recklessly.

Officers and men ran forward, and we kept up a fire that seemed as if it must destroy them, and yet on they came, cheering incessantly. Never did I see such a thing. Never did any other man there see such a thing. They came down upon us with the bayonet. We strove, we fought like madmen; but it was in vain, and we were hurled down that hill in utter confusion.

"We heard afterwards that of the 6000 British soldiers who began the day, but 1800 stood unwounded at the end. They had with them 24,000 Spaniards, but, of course, we never counted them as anything, and they did their allies more harm than good by throwing them into confusion in their flight. We had 19,000 infantry, all veteran troops, mind you, and yet we could not storm that hill, and drive those 6000 Englishmen off it. We lost over 8000 men, and that in a battle that lasted only four hours. Our regiment suffered so that it was reduced to a third of its number. We fought them again at Salamanca, and got thrashed there; soon after that we were sent back to France to fill up our ranks again, and I for one was glad indeed when we were sent to the Rhine and not back to Spain; for I tell you I never want to meet the English again in battle. Borodino was bad enough, and for stubborn, hard fighting, the Russians have proved themselves as tough customers as one can want to meet; but the English have more dash and quickness. They manœuvre much more rapidly than do the Russians, and when they charge, you have either got to destroy them or to go."

"You are right there, comrade," another said. "I was with my regiment, the 5th, at Badajoz. It was a strong place. Phillipson, who was in command, was a thoroughly good officer. He had strengthened the defences in every way, and the garrison was 5000 strong. We reckoned we could hold out for three months anyhow. 15,000 men sat down before us on the 17th of March, and began to open trenches against a strong outlying fort. We made several sorties, and did all we could to hinder them, but on the 25th they stormed the fort. It was defended desperately, but in an hour it was all over. Still, that was only an outlying work. Soult was known to be advancing to our relief; but he waited to gather as large a force as possible, believing, reasonably enough, that we could hold out a month, while we still calculated on holding out for three. The English worked like demons, and on the 6th of April they had made two breaches. We had prepared everything for them. We had planted mines all over the breaches. We had scores of powder barrels, and hundreds of shells ready to roll down. We had guns placed to sweep them on both flanks and along the top. We had a stockade of massive beams in which were fixed sword blades, while in front of this the breach was covered with loose planks studded with sharp iron points.

"Every man behind the stockade had half a dozen spare muskets. A legion of devils could not have taken the place. They did not take it, but never did mortal men try harder. Even when they felt that it was absolutely impossible, they stood there amid that storm of shot and shell, exploding powder barrels, and bursting mines. Two thousand men were killed in that breach, and yet they still stood there. Our own triumph was but a short one, for another British division had carried the castle. While we were exulting in victory, the town was lost. Thus, you see, they had in twenty days captured the fortress that we and everyone else made sure we could defend for at least three months. Fortunately we were exchanged a short time afterwards, and so I escaped being sent to an English prison. I agree with you, Rignold. I am ready to do my share of fighting, but I would rather do it against any one, even against these

Russians, than against the English; and I think you will find that every man who has served in Spain would say the same."

"After all, comrades," another veteran said, "it seems to me that it does not make much difference who you have got to fight against, for you see the generals make things about even. If one of our generals finds that there are say 50,000 Spaniards marching against him, while his force is only 10,000, he gives battle. Well, he won't give battle to 50,000 Austrians unless he has got something like 35,000. I should say that after Borodino he would like to have 40,000, at least, against 50,000 Russians. No doubt the English calculate the same way, and, in Spain, we must admit that we always found them ready to fight when, as far as numbers went, we outmatched them. So I take it that the difference between the fighting powers of armies is not felt so much as you would think by each soldier, because allowance for that is made by the generals on both sides, and the soldiers find themselves always handicapped just in proportion to their fighting powers. So you see there is a big element of luck in it. The question of ground comes in, and climate, and so on. Now, taking Spain, though 10,000 against 50,000 would be fair enough odds in a fight in the open, if a hundred of us were attacked by 500 Spaniards among the mountains, it would go very hard with us. And, again, though 1000 Frenchmen might repulse 3000 of those Mamelukes if they attacked us in the cool of the morning or in the evening, yet if we were caught in the middle of the day, with the sun blazing down, and parched with thirst, we might succumb. Then, of course, the question of generals counts for a great deal. So you see that even supposing both sides agree, as it were, as to the fighting powers of their troops, the element of luck counts for a lot, and before you begin to fight you can never feel sure that you are going to win."

"Well, but we do win almost everywhere, Brison."

"Yes, yes; because we have Napoleon and Ney and Soult and the rest of them. We have had to fight hard many and many a time, and if the battle had been fought between the same armies with a change of generals, things would have gone quite differently to what they did."

"You were with Napoleon in Egypt, were you not?" Julian asked.

"Yes, I was there; and, bad as this desolate country is, I would anyhow rather campaign here than in Egypt. The sun seems to scorch into your very brain, and you are suffocated by dust. Drink as much as you will, you are always tormented by thirst. It is a level plain, for the most part treeless, and with nothing to break the view but the mud villages, which are the same colour as the soil. Bah! we loathed them. And yet I ought not to say anything against the villages, for, if it had not been for one of them, I should not be here now. I will tell you the tale. Two hundred of us had been despatched to seize some of the leading sheiks, who were said to be holding a meeting in some place fifteen miles away from where we were encamped. We had a squadron of horse and a hundred of our men. We afterwards found that the whole story was a lie, invented to get us into a trap. We were guided by a villainous-looking rogue on a camel, and beyond the fact that we were marching south-east, we had no idea where we were going. Half the cavalry kept ahead. We had marched four hours, when, on coming on to the crest of one of the sand-hills, we saw about half a mile away a little clump of mud huts. Near the foot of some high hills to the right were some tents.

"'There it is,' the guide said, pointing to the tents. And the cavalry set off at a gallop, followed by the guide, who soon fell far into their rear. Just as the cavalry reached the tents, we saw two great masses of horsemen appear from behind the sand-hills on either flank, and with loud yells ride down upon them. With a shout of fury we were about to break into a run, but the major who was in command said, 'It is useless, comrades. There is but one hope. Make for that village. We can hold that; and there, if any of our comrades escape, they will find shelter. Double— march.' Off we went, but it was against the grain. We could hear the cracking of pistols, the shouts of our brave fellows, the yells of the Arabs, and our hearts were there; but we felt that the major was right. There must have been fully a couple of thousand of the Arabs, and we should have but thrown away our lives. It was a terrible run. The heat was stifling; the dust rose in clouds under our feet. We could scarce breathe, but we knew that we were running for life. As we neared the village, we heard yells behind us.

"'A hundred yards further, lads,' the major shouted. We did it, and when we reached the first house we halted. Three hundred yards away were a dozen of our troopers, followed by a mob of Arabs. The Major faced twenty men about, and ordered the rest of us to divide ourselves among the huts. There were but nine of these. The villagers, who had seen us coming, had bolted, and we had just got into the houses when we heard the rear-guard open fire. There was a young lieutenant with the troopers, and, as they rode in, he ordered them to dismount, and to lead their horses into the huts. A moment later the rear-guard ran in. We felt for a moment like rats caught in a trap, for, in the hut I was in, there were but two rooms. One had no light but what came in at the door; the other had an opening of about nine inches square, and that not looking into the street. In a moment, however, we saw that there was a ladder leading up to the flat roof, and we swarmed up. These houses are all built with flat roofs made of clay like the walls. Some of them have a parapet about a foot high; some of them none at all. In better-class villages some of the parapets are a good deal higher; so that the women can sit there unobserved from the other roofs.

"The hut we were in had a low parapet, and we threw ourselves down behind it. The street was full of horsemen, yelling and discharging their guns at the doors; but when, almost at the same moment a rattling fire broke out from every roof, the scene in the street changed as if by magic. Men fell from their horses in all directions. The horses plunged and struggled, and so terrible was the *mêlée* that, had the houses stood touching each other, I doubt whether a man of those who entered would have got out alive. As it was, they rode out through the openings, leaving some sixty or seventy of their number dead in the street. We had breathing time now. The whole of the Arab horsemen presently surrounded us, but the lesson had been so severe that they hesitated to make another charge into the village. The major's orders, that we were not to throw away a shot, unless they charged down in force, were passed from roof to roof round the village. We were ordered to barricade the doors with anything we could find, and if there was nothing else, we were, with our bayonets, to bring down part of the partition walls and pile the earth against the door. Each hut was to report what supply of water there was in it. This was to be in charge of the non-commissioned officer, or the oldest soldier if there was not one, and he was to see that it was not touched at night. It was to be divided equally among all the huts.

"'You will understand, men,' he shouted from his roof, 'that our lives depend more upon the water than upon your arms. We could defend this place against that horde for a year; but if water fails altogether, there will be nothing to do but to sally out and sell our lives as dearly as we can.' Fortunately, we had still water with us, for it was not known whether we should find any on the march, and we had been ordered to leave our kits behind, and to carry, in addition to the water-bottles, a skin holding about a gallon. In our hut we found eight porous jars, each of which would hold about a couple of gallons. Six of them were full. The empty ones we filled up from our skins, for these jars keep the water wonderfully cool. In none of the other huts had they found so good a supply as ours, but all had more or less water; and, on totalling them up, it was found that there was an average of four jars in each hut, without, of course, counting that which we had brought. As there were a hundred and ten of us, this gave a total supply of a hundred and eighty-two gallons; rather better than a gallon and a half a man.

"The major ordered that the allowance was to be a pint night and morning for the first four days. If help did not come at the end of that time, it was to be reduced by half. We could see where the water came from. There was a well-worn path from the village to a hollow about three hundred yards away, and we could see that there was a great hole, and it was down this that the women went to fill their water-jars. It was a consolation to us that it was so close, for, if the worst came to the worst, half of us could go down at night and refill the jars. No doubt they would have to fight their way, but, as the rest could cover them by their fire, we felt that we should be able to manage it. For the next four days we held the place. We slept during the day. The Arabs did not come near us then; but as soon as it got dusk they began to crawl up, and flashes of fire would break out all round us.

"Unfortunately, there was no moon, and as they came up

pretty nearly naked, their bodies were so much the colour of the sand that they could not be made out twenty yards away. They were plucky enough, for they would come right in among the houses and fire through the doors, and sometimes a number of them would make a rush against one; but nothing short of bursting the doors into splinters would have given them an entry, so firmly did the piles of earth hold them in their places. In the middle of the fifth day a cloud of dust was seen across the plain from the direction in which we came. No one had a doubt that it was a party sent to our relief, and every man sprang to his feet and swarmed up on to the roof, as soon as the man on watch above told us the news; directly afterwards the major shouted, 'Each man can have a ration of water.'

"In a few minutes we saw the Arabs mount and ride off, and it was not long before five hundred of our cavalry rode into the village. We had only lost five men; all had been shot through the head as they were firing over the parapet. We had each night buried those who fell, and in five minutes after the arrival of the cavalry, were ready to start on our march back. If it had not been for that village, and for the quickness with which the major saw what was the only thing to be done, not a single man would ever have got back to camp to tell what had happened. They were brave fellows, those Arabs; and, if well drilled by our officers, would have been grand troops on such an expedition as this, and would have taught the Cossacks a good many things at their own game.

"The Egyptian infantry were contemptible, but the Arabs are grand horsemen. I don't say that in a charge, however well drilled, they could stand against one of our cuirassier regiments. Men and horses would be rolled over; but for skirmishing, vidette duty, and foraging, no European cavalry would be in it with them. They are tireless, both horses and men, and will go for days on a little water and a handful of dates; and if the horses can get nothing else, they will eat the dates just as contentedly as their masters."

Several times as these stories had been told, the group had risen to their feet to watch the fires that were burning in various parts of the town, and just as the sergeant brought his story to a close, the assembly sounded.

"I have been expecting that for some time," Brison said. "As our division is nearest to the city, I thought they would be sure to turn us out before long, to put out those fires. They must be the work of some of our rascally camp-followers, or of some of the ruffians of the town, who have been breaking into deserted houses and plundering them. Well, the liquor is finished, and there is always interest in fighting a fire."

Five minutes later, the Grenadiers of the Rhone and six other regiments of their division marched into Moscow to extinguish the flames.

CHAPTER XIII.

WITH THE REAR-GUARD.

NAPOLEON had as yet no idea that the fires were other than accidental, and the next morning removed his headquarters to the Imperial Palace, the Kremlin, from which he fondly hoped to dictate terms of peace to Russia. But it was not long before the truth became evident. Every hour fresh fires broke out, and, spreading rapidly, by nightfall the whole city was in flames. On the following day the Kremlin itself became so uninhabitable from the heat, that the Emperor was forced to withdraw from it, and could not return till the 20th, when heavy rain extinguished the flames, which had already consumed nine-tenths of the city. Of 48,000 houses only 700 escaped; of 1600 churches 800 were destroyed and 700 damaged; of 24,000 wounded French and Russians in the hospitals more than 20,000 perished in the flames. In the meantime Kutusow had tardily adopted the advice he had before rejected, had moved round with his army and taken up his position on the Oka river, near Kulouga, where he menaced the French line of communication. Already the Cossack cavalry were hovering round Moscow, intercepting convoys and cutting up small detachments, while the horses of the French cavalry were so worn out by fatigue and famine that in several affairs with the Russian cavalry the latter gained decisive advantages.

"You are right again, comrade," the old sergeant said to Julian, who had been promoted to the rank of sergeant after the battle of Borodino, as they stood together on the night of the 15th gazing at the terrible spectacle of the city enveloped in flames. "*Peste!* these Russians are terrible fellows. Who could have thought of such a thing? It is a bad look-out for us."

"A terrible look-out, there is no denying it," Julian agreed. "It is impossible for the army to stay here without food, without forage, without shelter, with our communications threatened, and the Russian army on our flank. I see nothing for it but to retreat, and the sooner we are out of it the better. Were I the Emperor I would issue orders for the march to begin at daylight. In another month winter will be on us, and none can say what disasters may befall the army."

Had the order been given that day the French army might have made its way back to the frontier, with heavy loss doubtless, but without disaster. But Napoleon could not bring himself to believe that the Russians would refuse to enter into negotiations. He tried through various sources to send proposals to Alexander, and even opened secret negotiations with Kutusow, and had arranged for a private meeting with him, when the matter was stopped by Sir Robert Wilson, who had received specific instructions from the Emperor Alexander to interpose in his name to prevent any negotiations whatever being carried on. Thus week after week of precious time passed, and then a portion of the army moved against the Russians. Several engagements took place, the advantage generally resting with the Russians, especially in an engagement with Murat, who suffered a decisive repulse.

Julian had, as soon as the fire in Moscow burnt itself out, employed himself in endeavouring to buy some warm garments. Money was plentiful, for there had been no means of spending it since they entered Russia, and he was fortunate in being able to buy some very warm under-garments that had been looted by the plunderers on the night of their first arrival before Moscow. He also purchased a peasant's sheep-skin caftan with a hood, and sewed this into his military cloak so as to form a lining, the hood being for the time turned inside. From another sheep-skin he manufactured a couple of bags to be used as mittens, without fingers or thumbs. Many of his comrades laughed at him as he did his work, but as the days grew colder most of them endeavoured to follow his example, and the skins of sheep brought in occasionally by the cavalry were eagerly bought up. Encouraged by his success, Julian next manufactured a pair of sheep-skin leggings, with the wool inside. They were sewn up at the bottom, so that they could be worn over his boots. The shape left much to be desired, but by cutting up a blanket he made two long bands, each three inches wide and some twenty feet long. These he intended to wrap tightly round the leggings when in use.

The leggings, gloves, and bands were stowed away in his knapsack, almost everything else being discarded to make room for them; for he felt sure that there would be no inspection of kits until the frontier had been crossed.

Still, Napoleon could not bring himself to issue a general order for a retreat, but corps after corps was moved along the western road. Mortier's division remained last in Moscow, and marched on the 23rd of October, after having, by Napoleon's orders, blown up the Kremlin, the Church of St. Nicholas, and the adjoining buildings. The safest line of retreat would have been through Witebsk, but Napoleon took the more southern road, and the army believed that it was intended to fight another great battle with the Russians.

The weather at first was fine. On the 24th the vanguard, under the Viceroy, came in contact with Doctorow's division, and a fierce fight took place near Malo Jaroslavets. The French were checked, and Kutusow, coming up with the main army, it was apparent to all, that the French vanguard could be overwhelmed and Napoleon's retreat brought to a standstill. But, just as the generals were all expecting the order to attack, Kutusow, whose previous conduct in entering into secret negotiations with Napoleon had excited strong suspicions of his good faith, announced that he had changed his mind, and ordered the Russian army to draw off, thus for a time saving the French from complete disaster.

The battle, however, had been a sanguinary one, no less than ten thousand being killed on each side. After the retirement of the Russians the retreat was continued. Davoust commanded the advance; Ney's division was to cover the rear. The French army at first moved very slowly, for it was not until the 29th that Napoleon reached Borodino. He himself had long been in ill-health; bodily pain had sapped his energy. He had for a long time been unable to sit on a horse, and had travelled in a close carriage. Consequently he seemed to have lost for a time all his energy and quickness of decision, and after five weeks thrown away at Moscow, another was wasted in slow movements when haste was of the greatest importance. The French suffered, too, from the disadvantage that, while their every movement was discovered and reported by the ubiquitous Cossacks, they themselves were in absolute ignorance of the strength and movements of the enemy.

On the 6th of November a bitter frost set in, and the soldiers awoke chilled to the bone, and with gloomy anticipations of what would happen when the full rigour of a Russian winter was upon them. In some respects the frost was an advantage, for it hardened the roads, that were before often almost impassable from the amount of heavy traffic that had passed over them. But, upon the other hand, floating masses of ice speedily covered the rivers, rendering the work of fording them painful and difficult in the extreme. A Russian division had, on the 3rd, pressed hotly on the retreating column just as they reached the Wiazma river. A sanguinary conflict took place, the corps of the Viceroy passed through the town on its banks, and crossed the river in fair order, but that of Davoust broke and crossed in great confusion, covered by Ney's division, which retreated steadily, facing about from time to time, and repulsing the infantry attacks, but suffering heavily from the artillery. Ney set the town on fire to cover his retreat, crossed the bridges, and there stemmed the further advance of the Russians.

The French loss in the engagement was 6000 killed and wounded, and 2000 prisoners. The Viceroy was directed to march on Witebsk, but he was overtaken by the enemy when endeavouring to throw a bridge over the half-frozen little river called the Vop. The bridge, hastily made, gave way. The banks were extremely steep. The Grenadiers waded through the river, though the water, full of floating ice, came up to their breasts; but the artillery following were unable to climb the bank, and the guns were soon frozen fast in the river, and they and the whole of the baggage had to be left behind. A similar misfortune befell another of the Viceroy's divisions, which had remained behind to cover the retreat, and of the 14,000 soldiers who commenced the march but 6000 remained with their colours, and but 12 of the 92 guns that had accompanied them.

The condition of the French army rapidly deteriorated. The cold had already become intense, and the soldiers being weak with hunger were the less able to support it. The horses died in great numbers, and their flesh was the principal food upon which the troops had to rely. No one dared straggle to forage, for the Cossacks were ever hovering round, and the peasants, emerging from their hiding-places in the forests, murdered, for the most part with atrocious tortures, everyone who fell out of the ranks from wounds, exhaustion, or frost-bite.

Julian had, since their retreat began, again recovered his spirits. He was now not fighting to conquer a country against which he had no animosity, but for his own life and that of the thousands of sick and wounded.

"I am glad that we are in the rear-guard," he said to a number of non-commissioned officers who were one evening, when they were fortunate enough to be camped in a wood, gathered round a huge fire.

"Why so, Jules? It seems to me that we have the hardest work, and, besides, there is not a day that we have not to fight."

"That is the thing that does us good," Julian replied. "The columns ahead have nothing to do but to think of the cold, and hunger, and misery. They straggle along; they no longer march. With us it is otherwise. We are still soldiers; we keep our order. We are proud to know that the safety of the army depends on us; and, if we do get knocked over with a bullet, surely that is a better fate than dropping from exhaustion, and falling into the hands of the peasants."

"You are right, Jules," several of them exclaimed. "It is better a thousand times."

"We have a bad prospect before us," Julian went on. "There is no denying that; but it will make all the difference how we face it. Above all things we have got to keep up our spirits. I have heard that the captains of the whalers in the northern seas do everything in their power to interest and amuse their crews. They sing, they dance, they tell stories of adventures, and the great thing is to keep from brooding over the present. I am but a young sergeant, and most of you here have gone through many a campaign, and it is not for me to give advice, but I should say that above all things we ought to try to keep up the spirits of our men. If we could but start the marching songs we used to sing as we tramped through Germany, it would set men's feet going in time, would make them forget the cold and hunger, and they would march along erect, instead of with their eyes fixed on the ground, and stumbling as if they could not drag their feet along. We should tell them why we sing, or they might think it was a mockery. Tell them that the Grenadiers of the Rhone mean to show that, come what may, they intend to be soldiers to the last, and to face death, whether from the Russians or from the winter, heads erect and courage high. Let us show them that, as we have ever done our duty, so we shall do it to the end, and that it will be a matter of pride that throughout the division it should be said, when they hear our songs,

'There go the Grenadiers of the Rhone, brave fellows and good comrades; see how they bear themselves.'"

"Bravo, bravo, Jules! bravo, Englishman!" the whole of the party shouted. "So it shall be, we swear it. The Grenadiers of the Rhone shall set an example."

Suddenly the voices hushed, and Julian was about to look round to see the cause of their silence, when a hand was laid on his shoulder, and, turning, he saw Ney standing beside him, with three or four of his staff. They had come up unobserved, and had stopped a few paces away just as Julian began to speak.

"Bravo, comrade!" the marshal said; "spoken in the true spirit of a soldier. Were there a dozen men like you in every regiment I should have no fear for the future. Did they call you Englishman?"

"Yes, General. I was a prisoner at Verdun, though neither an English soldier nor sailor, and when a call came for volunteers, and I was promised that I should not be called upon to fight against my own countrymen, I thought it better to carry a French musket than to rot in a French prison."

"And you have carried it well," the marshal said. "Had you not done so you would not have won your stripes among the men of the Grenadiers of the Rhone, where every man has again and again shown that he is a hero. Carry out your brave comrade's idea, lads. We all want comforting, and my own heart will beat quicker to-morrow as I ride along and hear your marching song, and I shall say to myself, 'God bless the brave Grenadiers of the Rhone!' I trust that others will follow your example. What is your name, sergeant?"

"Julian Wyatt, General."

"Put it down in my note-book," Ney said to one of his staff. "Good-night, comrades, you have done me good. By the way, a hundred yards to your left I marked a dead horse as I came along; it may help your suppers." Then, amid a cheer from the soldiers, Ney moved on with his staff.

It was not many minutes before portions of the horse were cooking over the fire.

"I feel another man already," one of the younger sergeants laughed, as they ate their meal. "Jules is right; good spirits are everything."

"Bear that in mind to-morrow, Antoine," another said. "It is easy enough to be cheerful when one is warm and has got some meat, even though it be only horse-flesh and mightily tough at that, between your teeth; but it is harder to be so after sixteen hours of marching and fighting."

"Well, we will try anyhow, Jacques."

Another quarter of an hour and the circle broke up, the non-commissioned officers going off to the companies to which they belonged.

Wood being plentiful, great fires were kept blazing all night, and round each was told what Julian had said, the commendation Ney had given the regiment, and his warm approval of the plan. As soon as the order was given to march in the morning, and Julian started one of their old marching songs, it was taken up from end to end of the column, to the astonishment of the officers and of the men of other regiments within hearing. The effect upon the men themselves was electrical. The dogged look of determination with which they had before plodded along was supplanted by an air of gaiety. They marched along in time to the music with a step that was almost elastic. Not since they had crossed the Niemen had the song been heard; occasionally a singer was silent for a minute or two, and passed his hand across his eyes as he thought of the many voices of comrades, now hushed for ever, that had then joined in the chorus. Half-an-hour later Ney, followed by his staff, rode along past the column. As he reached the head he spoke to the colonel, and the order was at once given for the regiment to form up in hollow square. When they had done so the colonel shouted, "Attention!" Ney took off his plumed hat and said, in a voice loud enough to be heard by all:

"Grenadiers of the Rhone, I salute you. All honour to the regiment that has set an example to the army of cheerfulness under hardships. You will be placed in the order of the day with the thanks of your marshal for the spirit you have shown. Maintain it, my friends; it will warm you more thoroughly than food or fire, and will carry you triumphantly through whatever fate may have in store for us."

A deep cheer burst from the regiment as the gallant soldier bowed to his horse's mane and then rode on with his staff, while the regiment, again breaking into a song, continued its march. Late in the afternoon they were again engaged. The long columns ahead were delayed by crossing a narrow bridge over a river, and for two hours the rear-guard had to stand firm against constant attacks by the Russians. At one time a heavy column of Russian infantry moved down upon them, but Ney, riding up to the grenadiers, said:

"I give you the post of honour, comrades. Drive back that column."

The colonel gave the order to charge, and the regiment rushed forward with such ardour to the attack, that the Russians were compelled to fall back with heavy loss, and shortly afterwards news came that the bridge was clear, and the rear-guard followed the rest of the army. Forty of the grenadiers had fallen, among them their colonel and two other officers. The next morning, before the regiment marched, the major as usual read out to it the order of the day. The marshal expressed his approbation of the spirit which the Grenadiers of the Rhone had manifested.

"This fine regiment," he said, "has ever merited eulogium for the manner in which it has sustained the honour of its flag in every engagement in which it has taken part. The marshal considers, however, that even higher praise is due to it for its bearing in the present stress of circumstances. Good spirits, and the resolution to look at things in a cheerful light, is the best method of encountering them, and it cheered the hearts of all near them to hear them singing their marching songs. The marshal in passing them was struck with the renewal of their martial appearance, as they marched, head erect, in time to their songs, and he hopes that their example will be followed by the other regiments of the corps, and is sure that not only will it be to the advantage of the discipline and efficiency of the troops, but it will greatly conduce to their own well-being, and the manner in which they will be able to support cold, hunger, and fatigue."

The marshal had brought the conduct and fine bearing of the Grenadiers of the Rhone under the attention of the Emperor. In spite of the fact that the soldiers of Ney's corps had to endure a larger amount of hardship than that of the rest of the army, from the necessity of constant vigilance, and from the long hours they were upon the road, their health suffered less than that of other troops. In the first place, they had an absolute faith in their commander; in the next, they were in the post of honour, and on them the safety of the whole army depended. Thus the constant skirmishing, and, occasionally, hard fighting that went on, braced them up, and saved them from the moody depression that weighed upon the rest of the army. They had, too, some material advantage from the broken-down waggons and vehicles of all sorts that fell behind. Every day they obtained a certain amount of stores, while from the bodies of those who had dropped from exhaustion, sickness, or cold they obtained a supply of extra clothing.

The morning after the reading of Ney's order of the day commending the regiment, an order from Napoleon himself was read at the head of the regiment, Ney taking his place by the side of the newly promoted colonel. The Emperor said that he had received the report of Marshal Ney of the conduct and bearing of the Grenadiers of the Rhone, together with a copy of his order of the day, and that this was fully endorsed by the Emperor, who felt that the spirit they were showing was even more creditable to them than the valour that they had so often exhibited in battle, and that he desired personally to thank them. The marshal had also brought before his notice the conduct of Sergeant Wyatt of that regiment, who had, he was informed, been the moving spirit in the change that he so much commended, and, as a mark of his approbation, he had requested the marshal himself, as his representative, to affix to his breast the ribbon of the cross of the Legion of Honour."

The colonel called upon Sergeant Wyatt to come forward. Julian did so, saluted, and stood to attention, while the marshal dismounted and pinned to his breast the insignia of the order, while the regiment saluted, and, as Julian returned to his place in the ranks, burst into a hearty cheer. As soon as the marshal had ridden off, and the regiment fell out, the officers gathered round Julian and congratulated him upon the honour he had received, and, at the same time, thanked him heartily for the credit that the regiment had gained, through his means, while the enthusiasm of the soldiers knew no bounds. A word of praise from the Emperor was the distinction that French soldiers and French regiments most coveted, and to have been named, not only by their marshal in his orders, but by the Emperor in a general order to the army, was an honour that filled every heart with pride.

    Julian had been a favourite before, but henceforth his popularity was unbounded. Many of the other regiments followed the example of the grenadiers, and, in spite of the ever-increasing cold and the constantly augmenting hardships, Ney's corps retained their discipline and efficiency. Their appearance, indeed, was no longer soldierly. Their garments were in rags. Many wore three or four coats. Their legs were encased in hay-bands, strips of blanket, or sheep-skins. Julian now took out for the first time from his knapsack the leggings that he had manufactured, and, with the strips of blanket that he wound round them, they differed in appearance in no degree from the leggings of some of his comrades, except that they enveloped the feet also. On the day following the reading of Napoleon's order, the grenadiers came upon an overturned caleche. It had been ransacked by a regiment that had preceded them. The driver and a woman lay dead beside it, and they would have passed on without paying any attention to it, had it not been for a faint cry that met the ears of Julian, as his company passed close by it. He dropped back a few paces to an officer, and asked leave to fall out for a minute. Going to the carriage he found lying there among the cushions a little girl some five or six years old. Her cloak had been stripped off her, and she was blue with cold. Julian hesitated.

    "I will try anyhow," he muttered to himself. He first ripped open one of the cushions, pulled out the woollen stuffing, and wrapped it round the child's arms and legs, binding it there with strips of the velvet covering the cushions. Then he took off his cloak, and raised her on to his back, having first cut off one of the reins. With this he strapped her securely in that position, put on his warm cloak again, and then, hurrying forward, soon overtook the rear of his regiment.

"Bravo, Jules!" many of his comrades said, as he passed along the column; while others asked, "Why do you encumber yourself with that child? It is enough now for every man to look to himself, and you cannot carry her far."

"I will do what I can," he replied. "She is not so heavy as my knapsack when it is full, and it is empty now; I am only keeping it because it is useful as a pillow. I can't say how far I can carry her, but as long as I can go she shall. We have taken lives enough, heaven knows. It is as well to save one if one gets the opportunity."

In half an hour Julian felt a movement on the part of his little burden, whose hands he had been chafing with his own unoccupied one. Presently something was said in Russian. He did not reply, and then there was a little struggle, and the voice said in French: "Nurse, where am I? Where are you taking me? Where is the carriage?"

"Do not fret, little one," Julian replied in the same language. "I am a friend, and will take care of you. Your carriage broke down, and so I am carrying you until we can get you another. Are you warm?"

"Yes," the child said. "I am quite warm, but I want my nurse?"

"Nurse can't come to you now, my dear; but I will try to be a good nurse to you."

"I want to see what you are like."

"You shall see presently," he said. "It would be very cold if you were to put your head outside. The best thing that you can do is to try to get to sleep."

The warmth doubtless did more than Julian's exhortation, for the child said no more, and Julian felt certain after a short time that she had gone off to sleep. He was now in his place with his company again, and joined in the song that they were singing, softly at first, but, as he felt no movement, louder and louder until, as usual, his voice rose high above the chorus. Nevertheless, his thoughts were with the child. What was he to do with her? how was she to be fed? He could only hope for the best. So far Providence had assuredly made him the means of preserving her life, and to Providence he must leave the rest. It might be all for the best. The weight was little to him, and there was a sense of warmth and comfort in the little body that lay so close to his back. What troubled him most was the thought of what he should do with her when he was engaged with the Russians. He decided that she must stay then in one of the carts that carried the spare ammunition of the regiment, and accompanied it everywhere. "At any rate, if I should fall," he said, "and she is left behind, she has only to speak in Russian when the enemy come up, and no doubt they will take care of her. Her father must be a man of some importance. The carriage was a very handsome one. If she can make them understand who she is, there is no doubt they will restore her to her parents."

There was but little fighting that day, and when the regiment fell out, fortunately halting again in a wood, Julian waited until the fires were lighted, and then unloosened the straps and shifted the child round in front of him. She opened her eyes as he did so.

"Well, little one, here we are at our journey's end," he said cheerfully. "You have had a nice sleep, and you look as warm as a toast."

She was indeed changed. A rosy flush had taken the place of the bluish-gray tint on her cheeks; her eyes were bright, and she looked round at the strange scene with a face devoid of all fear.

"Are you my new nurse?" she asked.

"Yes, dear."

"You look nice," she said calmly, "but I should like Claire, too."

"She can't come at present, little one, so you must put up with me."

"Are you one of those wicked Frenchmen?" she asked.

"I am an Englishman. Some of them are Frenchmen, but all Frenchmen are not wicked. You will see that all my friends here will be very kind to you, and will do everything they can to make you comfortable, till we can send you to your friends again."

The child was silent for some time.

"There was a great noise," she said gravely, "and guns fired, and the coachman fell off the box, and then nurse called out and opened the door and jumped out, and then the horses plunged and the carriage fell over, and I don't know any more."

"There was an accident," Julian said. "Don't think about that now. I will tell you about it some day."

"I am hungry," the child said imperiously. "Get me something to eat."

"We are going to cook our suppers directly, dear. Now let us go and sit by that fire. I am afraid you won't find the supper very nice, but it is the best we have got. What is your name?"

"I am the Countess Stephanie Woronski," the little maid said; "and what is your name?"

"My name is Julian Wyatt."

"It is a funny name," the child said; "but I think I like it."

Julian carried her to the fire, and seated her with her feet before it.

"Where is my cloak," she asked, as on setting her down

she perceived the deficiency; "and what are those ugly things?" and she looked at the swathing round her arms and legs.

"Some bad men took your cloak," he said; "none of these men here did it; and you were very cold when I found you, so I put some of the stuffing from the cushions round you to keep you warm, and you must wear them till I can get you another cloak. Comrades," he went on, to the soldiers who had gathered round to look at the little figure, "this is the Countess Stephanie Woronski, and I have told her that you will all be very kind to her and make her as comfortable as you can as long as she is with us."

There was a general hum of assent, and when the child went gravely among them, shaking hands with each, many an eye was moistened, as the men's thoughts went back to their own homes, and to little sisters or nieces whom they had played with there. Soon afterwards the colonel came by, and Julian, stepping forward, saluted him and said:

"I have picked up a little girl to-day, Colonel."

"So I have been told, Sergeant. I think it was a mistake, but that is your business. Everyone is getting weaker, and you are not likely to be able to carry her for long. However, of course, you can take her if you like, and as long as there are horses to drag the ammunition carts you can put her in them when you choose."

"It is only when we are fighting that I should want to stow her away. She does not weigh more than a knapsack, Colonel."

"Well; just as you like, Sergeant. If you wanted to take along ten children I could not say no to you. She is a pretty little thing," he added, as he went nearer to her.

"Yes, Colonel. She says that she is a countess."

"Poor little countess!" the colonel said tenderly. "She will want something warmer than she has got on now."

"We will manage that, Colonel. She will be warm enough as long as she is on the march with me; but as, even before that fire, she has not enough on her, we will contrive something. In the first broken-down baggage-waggon that we come across, we are pretty sure to find something that we can fit her out in."

As yet the pressure of hunger had not come severely upon the grenadiers. In the fights with the Russians some of the horses of their own cavalry and artillery, and those of the enemy, were daily killed, besides the animals which dropped from fatigue were at once shot and cut up. Moreover, a small ration of flour was still served out, and the supper that night, if rough, was ample. Julian sat facing the fire with his cloak open and the child nestling up close to him. As soon as supper was over half a dozen of the soldiers started off.

"We will bring back a fit-out, Jules, never fear. It will be strange if there is not something to be picked up in the snow between us and the next corps."

In half an hour they came in again, one of them carrying a bundle. By this time the child was fast asleep, and, taking off his cloak and wrapping it round her, Julian went across to them on the other side of the fire.

"What have you got?"

"A good find, Jules. It was a young officer. He was evidently coming back with an order, but his horse fell dead under him. The lad had lost an arm, at Borodino I expect, and was only just strong enough to sit his horse. We think that the fall on the hard snow stunned him, and the frost soon finished the work. He had been well fitted out, and some of his things will do for the little one. He had a fur-lined jacket which will wrap her up grandly from head to foot. Here are a pair of thick flannel drawers. If we cut them off at the knee you can tuck all her little clothes inside it, and they will button up under her arms and come down over her feet. She will look queer, but it will keep her warm. This pair of stockings will pull up her arms to her shoulders, and here is another pair that was in his valise. They are knitted, and one will pull down over her ears. You see they are blue, and if you cut the foot off and tie up the hole it will look like a fisherman's cap, and the other will go over her head and tie up under her chin."

"Splendid, comrade! That is a first-rate fit-out. I am obliged to you indeed."

"You need not talk of a little thing like that, Sergeant. There is not a man in the regiment who would not do a good deal more than that for you; besides, we have all taken to the child. She will be quite the pet of the regiment. Moreover, the lad's valise was well filled. We have tossed up for choice, and each of us has got something. Henri got the cloak, and a good one it is. I had the next choice, and I took his blanket, which is a double one. Jacques had the horse-rug, Ferron had another pair of drawers and his gloves, and Pierre, who has got a small foot, took his boots. So we have all done well."

As Julian lay down with his hood over his head and the child held closely in his arms under his cloak, he felt strangely warm and comfortable, and breathed a prayer that he might be spared to carry the little waif he had rescued, in safety across the frontier.

"I will keep her with me," he said, "until she gets a bit bigger. By that time the war may be all over, and I will send her to my aunt, if I dare not go home myself. She will take care of her, and if she should have gone, I know Frank will do the best he can for the child, and may be able, through the Russian embassy, to send her back to her friends."

The cold was so intense in the morning that the child

offered no objection to her novel habiliments. Some inches had to be cut from the bottom of the jacket to keep it off the ground, and the strip served as a band to keep it close round her waist.

"It is too big," she said a little fretfully.

"It is large, Stephanie," Julian said, "but then, you see, there is the advantage that when you like you can slip your arms altogether out of the sleeves, and keep them as warm as a toast inside. Now you get on my back, and we will fasten you more comfortably than I could do yesterday."

This, with the assistance of a couple of soldiers, was done. Then, putting on his cloak again, Julian fell in with his comrades, and, as usual, striking up a merry song, in which the rest at once joined, continued his march.

Day passed after day. The Russians pressed hotly on the rear, and many times Ney's corps had to face about and repel their attacks. Sometimes when the fighting was likely to be serious Julian handed his charge over to the care of the driver of one of the ammunition carts, but as a rule he carried her with him, for she objected strongly to leave him. On the march she often chose to be carried on his shoulder—a strange little figure, with the high fur collar of the jacket standing up level with the top of her head, and a yellow curl or two making its way through the opening in front. She soon picked up the songs that were most often sung, and her shrill little voice joined in. She was now a prime favourite with all the men.

Food became scarcer every day. The cavalry were now almost wholly dismounted, the horses still available being taken for the guns. Among the divisions in front the disorganization was great indeed. It was a mob rather than an army, and only when attacked did they form up and with sullen fury drive off the foe. At other times they tramped along silently, ragged, and often shoeless, their feet wrapped in rough bandages. Whenever one fell from weakness, he lay there unnoticed, save that sometimes a comrade would, in answer to his entreaties to kill him rather than to leave him to the mercy of the peasants, put his musket to his head and finish him at once. No one straggled, except to search a deserted cottage on the line, for all who fell into the hands of the peasants—who followed the army like wolves after a wounded stag—were either put to death by atrocious tortures, or stripped and left to perish by cold. All the sufferings inflicted by the army in its advance upon the peasantry were now repaid an hundredfold, and the atrocities perpetrated upon all who fell into their hands were so terrible that Sir Robert Wilson wrote to the Czar, imploring him for the honour of the country to put a stop to them. Alexander at once issued a proclamation offering the reward of a gold piece for every French prisoner brought in, and so saved the lives of many hundreds of these unfortunates. In the French army itself all feelings of humanity were also obliterated. The men fought furiously among themselves for any scrap of food, and a dead horse was often the centre of a desperate struggle. Those who fell were at once stripped of their garments, and death came all the sooner to put an end to their sufferings. The authority of the officers was altogether unheeded.

Day by day the numbers dwindled away. The safety of the French army thus far was chiefly due to the vacillation, if not the absolute treachery, of Kutusow. Moving on by roads well supplied with provisions, and perfectly acquainted with the movements of the enemy, he was able to outmarch them, and several times had it absolutely in his power to completely overwhelm the broken remains of Napoleon's army. But, in spite of the entreaties of the generals and the indignation of the army, he obstinately refused to give the order. The French army no longer travelled by a single road; sometimes the corps were separated from each other by great masses of Russian troops. Numerous detached battles were fought; but in each of these the French troops, although suffering heavily, displayed their old courage, and either by hard fighting cut their way through obstacles, or managed by long and circuitous marches to evade them.

Napoleon's plans, which, if carried out, would have saved the army, were brought to nought by the incapacity of the generals charged with the duty. The vast depôts and stores that had been formed at various points fell successively into the hands of the various Russian armies now operating against the French. Bridges of vital importance on the line of retreat were captured and destroyed, and repeated defeats inflicted upon the armies that should have joined Napoleon as he fell back. Everywhere fatal blunders were made by the French commanders, and it seemed as if Heaven had determined to overthrow every combination formed by Napoleon's sagacity, in order that the destruction of his army should be complete. The army of Macdonald that should have joined him was itself warmly pressed by the forces of Wittgenstein and the garrison of Riga, which had been greatly reinforced. Schwarzenberg, with the Austrian army, fell back without striking a blow; for the Austrians, in view of the misfortunes that had befallen Napoleon, were preparing to cast off their alliance with him; and to aid in his discomfiture, Wittgenstein was ordered by Alexander to withdraw at once from his operations against Macdonald and to march upon Borizow on the Berezina, the point towards which Napoleon was making; while Admiral Tchichagow, with the army of the Danube, that had been engaged in watching the Austrians, was to march in the same direction, and also interpose to cut off the French retreat.

CHAPTER XIV.

NEY'S RETREAT.

NEY'S corps, as usual, had remained at Smolensk as the rearguard of the army. The rest and abundance of food did much to restore their *morale*. Ney had utilized the time they remained there to see that the arms were examined, and new ones served out from the magazines in place of those found to be defective. A certain amount of clothing was also served out to the troops, and discipline restored. The numerous stragglers belonging to the divisions that had gone on were incorporated with his regiments, and all prepared for the toilsome and dangerous march before them. They believed that at Krasnoi they should come up with the main body of the army. But Krasnoi had already fallen, and the enemy were mustering thickly along the road.

"We have a rough time before us, Jules," one of the veterans said. "I should not say as much to any of the youngsters, but your spirits seem proof against troubles. You see, in the first place, we know really nothing of what is going on. For the last four days we have heard the sound of cannon in the air. It is a long way off, and one feels it rather than hears it; but there has certainly been heavy and almost constant fighting. Well, that shows that there are Russians ahead of us. Never was I in a country before where we could get no news. It is all guess-work. There may be 50,000 Russians already between us and Davoust's division, and there may be only a handful of Cossacks. It is a toss-up. Nothing seems to go as one would expect in this country. We are at a big disadvantage; for

ON THE MARCH LITTLE STEPHANIE OFTEN CHOSE TO BE
CARRIED ON JULIAN'S SHOULDER

the skill of our generals is thrown away when they are working altogether in the dark.

"Do you know, this reminds me a good deal of our pursuit of your army to Corunna; only there I was one of the hunters, while here we are the hunted. When we entered the towns they had quitted we heard that they were altogether disorganized—a mere rabble of fugitives. But whenever we came up to them they turned round and fought like their own bull-dogs; and never did they make a stronger stand than they did when we came up at last and caught them at Corunna. There was the army we had been told was a disorganized mass standing in as good order, and with as firm a front, as if they had but just landed from their ships. And it was not in appearance only. They had 16,000 men; we had 20,000. They had only six or eight cannon, having embarked the remainder on board their ships; we had over fifty guns; and with Soult in command of us, there was not a man but regarded the affair as being as good as over, and considered that the whole of them would fall into our hands. Well, it wasn't so. We were on higher ground than they were, and soon silenced their little guns; and the village of Elvira, in front of their position, was carried without difficulty.

"Suddenly their reserve marched round, fell on our flank, and threatened our great battery that was in position there. They drove us out of Elvira, and for a time held us in check altogether. The fight round there became very hot; but they pushed forward and continued to attack us so desperately that they partly rolled our left up, and if it had not been that night set in—the fight had not begun until two o'clock—things would have gone very badly with us, for we were falling back in a great deal of confusion. There was a river behind us with but a single bridge by which we could retreat, and I can tell you we were glad indeed when the English ceased to press us and the firing stopped. All night their picket-fires burned, and we were expecting to renew the battle in the morning, when we found that their position was deserted, and that they were embarking on board their ships. That shows that although troops may be greatly disorganized in a retreat they do not fight any the worse when you come up to them.

"The English had practically no guns, they had no cavalry, they were inferior in numbers, and yet they beat us off. Their back was against a wall. You see, they knew that if they didn't do it there was nothing but a French prison before them. It is the same thing with us, lad; we don't want to fight—we want to get away if we can. But if we have got to fight we shall do it better than ever, for defeat would mean death; and if a soldier has got to die, he would a thousand times rather die by a musket-ball or a bayonet-thrust than by cold and hunger. There is one thing in our favour, the country we have to cross now is for the most part forest; so we shall have wood for our bivouacs, and if we have to leave the road it will cover our movements and give us a chance of making our way round the enemy. You will find that child a heavy burden, Jules. I do not blame you for bringing her along with you, but when things come to such a pass as this a man needs every ounce of his strength."

"I am aware of that," Jules said, looking at Stephanie as she stood laughing and talking with some of the soldiers at a fire close by; "but I believe that I shall save her. I cannot help thinking she would never have given that little cry which met my ears as I passed by the broken carriage, if it had not been meant that she should be saved. To all appearance she was well-nigh insensible, and she would have suffered no more pain. It would have been a cruel instead of a kind action to save her, when she was already well-nigh dead. I firmly believe that, whoever falls during the struggle that may be before us, that child will get through safely and be restored to her parents. I don't say that I think that I myself shall go through it, but my death does not necessarily mean hers. If she falls into the hands of the peasants, and tells them who she is, they may take care of her for the sake of getting a reward, and she may in time be restored to her friends. At any rate, as long as I have strength to carry her I shall assuredly do so; when I cannot, I shall wrap her in my cloak and shall lie down to die, bidding her sit wrapped up in it till she sees some Russians approaching. She will then speak to them in their own language and tell them who she is, and that they will get a great reward from her parents if they take care of her and send her to them."

"You are a good fellow, comrade—a man with a heart. I trust that, whoever get out of this alive, you may be one of them. To most of us it matters little one way or the other. We have had our share of good luck, and cannot expect that the bullets will always avoid us. Now let us turn in, for we march at daybreak. At any rate, we may think ourselves lucky to have had five days' rest here, with no more trouble than was needed to keep the Russians from occupying that place across the river."

Julian called Stephanie to him, lay down by the side of his comrade near the fire, and was soon fast asleep. They were under arms before daylight broke, and in a few minutes were on the way. They had marched but half a mile when a series of tremendous explosions were heard— the magazines left behind at Smolensk had been blown up, together with such buildings as the fire had before spared. 112 guns had been left behind, there being only sufficient horses remaining to draw twelve. The fighting force was reduced to 7000 combatants, but there were almost as many stragglers, more or less armed, with them. The march led by the side of the Dnieper, and they bivouacked that night at Korodnia. The next day they arrived at a point within four miles of Krasnoi, where, on a hill, fronted by a deep ravine, 12,000 Russians, with forty guns, had taken up their position.

A thick mist covered the lower ground, and the advance of the French was not perceived by the enemy until they were within a short distance of its crest. Then the forty guns poured a storm of grape into the leading regiment. The survivors, cheering loudly, rushed forward at the batteries, and had almost reached them, when a heavy mass of Russian infantry flung themselves upon them with the bayonet, and after a short but desperate struggle hurled them down the hill again. The Russian cavalry charged them on the slope, and swept through their shattered ranks. Ney, ignorant that Napoleon had already left Krasnoi, and that the whole Russian army barred his way, made another effort to force a passage. He planted his twelve guns on a height above the ravines, and sent forward several companies of sappers and miners to endeavour to carry the battery again. Gallantly they made their way up the hill through a storm of fire. But the Russians again fell upon them in great force, and few indeed were enabled to make the descent of the hill and rejoin their comrades.

Darkness had set in now, and Ney, finding it impossible to make his way further, and feeling sure that had the Emperor been still at Krasnoi he would have sent a force to his assistance, fell back into the forest. His position was a desperate one; the scanty supply of provisions with which they had started was exhausted, and they were in an unknown country, surrounded by foes, without a guide, without carriage for the wounded, without an idea of the direction in which to march. The Russian general sent in two flags of truce, offering him terms of capitulation which would save the life of himself and of his brave soldiers. Ney, however, was not yet conquered. He detained the messengers with the flags of truce, lest they might take news to their general of the position of his force, and then, with all capable of the exertion, continued his march. They passed in silence within half a mile of the Cossack fires, and reaching a village on the Dnieper, attempted the passage; but the ice broke under the first gun, and it was necessary to abandon the whole of the artillery and every vehicle.

Before the entire body had passed, the Cossacks, attracted by the sound made by the troops marching across the ice, arrived and captured several hundred prisoners, for the most part stragglers. In a village further on they found temporary rest, surprising a few Cossacks and capturing their horses, which afforded a ration to the troops; but on the next morning a great swarm of Cossacks appeared on the plain and opened a heavy artillery fire. Unable to advance in that direction the column turned towards a wood on its left, but as it was about to enter the refuge, a battery concealed there poured a volley of grape into them. The column hesitated, but Ney dashed to the front, and they rushed forward and drove the battery from the wood. All day they continued their march through the forest, until, coming upon a village, they obtained a few hours' rest and shelter and some food.

It had been a terribly heavy day, for the snow here was not, as on the road, trampled down, and the marching was very heavy. Julian had carried the child the greater part of the day. The grenadiers had not been actively engaged, as they formed the rear-guard, and several times his friend the sergeant relieved him of Stephanie's weight.

"This is better luck than I looked for, comrade," he said as they cooked the food they had found in the village, filled their pipes, and sat down by a blazing fire. "*Peste!* I was frightened as we crossed the river last night. We knew the ice was not strong, and if it had given way as we crossed, not a man upon it would have reached the other side. However, it turned out for the best, and here we are again, and I believe that we shall somehow get through after all. Ney always has good luck. There is never any hesitation about him. He sees what has to be done, and does it. That is the sort of man for a leader. I would rather serve under a man who does what he thinks best at once, even if it turns out wrong, than one who hesitates and wants time to consider. Ney has been called 'the child of victory', and I believe in his star. Anyone else would have surrendered after that fight yesterday, and yet you see how he has got out of the scrape so far. I believe that Ney will cross the frontier safe, even if he carries with him only a corporal's guard."

Julian was too exhausted to talk, and every moment of rest was precious. Therefore, after smoking for a short time, he lay down to sleep. At daybreak the next morning the march through the forest continued. When from time to time they approached its edge, the Cossacks could be seen hovering thickly on the plain; but they dared not venture into the wood, which was so close that their horses would be worse than useless to them. At three o'clock, when within twenty miles of Orsza, two Polish officers volunteered to push ahead to that town on some peasants' horses that had been brought from the village where they had slept, to acquaint the commander of any French force that might be there with their situation, and to pray for assistance. After a halt of an hour the column pushed on again. When they had marched another twelve miles the forest ceased. Night had long since fallen, and a thick fog hung over the ground. This served to hide their movements, but rendered it difficult in the extreme for them to maintain the right direction.

Their way led over a steep hill, which was climbed with great difficulty by the exhausted troops; but on reaching the summit they saw to their horror a long line of bivouac fires illuminating the plain in front of them. Even the most sanguine felt despair for a moment. Ney himself stood for a few minutes speechless, then he turned to his men.

"There is but one thing to do, comrades," he said. "It is death to stay here. Better a thousand times meet it as soldiers. Let us advance in absolute silence, and then rush upon our enemies and strive to burst our way through. They cannot know that we are so near, and, aided by the surprise, we may force a passage. If we fail, we will, before we die, sell our lives so dearly that our enemies will long bear us in remembrance."

In silence the column marched down the hill. No sound proclaimed that the enemy had taken the alarm. When within charging distance, the line levelled its bayonets and rushed forward to the fires. To their stupefaction and relief, they found no foe to oppose them. The fires had been lighted by order of the Cossack general to make them believe that an army lay between them and Orsza, and so cause them to arrest their march. Half an hour was given to the men to warm themselves by the fires, then the march was resumed. Three miles further the sound of a large body of men was heard, then came a challenge in French, '*Qui vive!*' A hoarse shout of delight burst from the weary force, and a minute later they were shaking hands with their comrades of Davoust's division. The Polish messengers had, in spite of the numerous Cossacks on the plains, succeeded in reaching Orsza safely. The most poignant anxiety reigned there as to the safety of Ney's command; and Davoust, on hearing the welcome news, instantly called his men under arms and advanced to meet them.

The delight on both sides was extreme, and Ney's soldiers were supplied with food that Davoust had ordered his men to put in their haversacks. A halt of three or four hours was ordered, for the column had been marching for eighteen hours, and could go no further. At daybreak they completed the remaining eight miles into Orsza. Napoleon himself was there. Here they rested for five days. Food was abundant, and arms were distributed to those who needed them. Ammunition was served out, and Napoleon employed himself with great energy in reorganizing his forces and in distributing the stragglers,—who were almost as numerous as those with the standards,—among them. Ney's corps was now too small for separate service, and henceforth was united to that of Davoust. The halt did wonders for the men. They were billeted among the houses of the town, and warmth and abundant food revived their strength. They looked forward with some confidence to reaching the spot where great magazines had been prepared, and where they would take up their quarters until the campaign recommenced in the spring.

Napoleon's plans, however, were all frustrated by the inconceivable blunders and follies of the generals, to whom were entrusted the task of carrying them out. Everywhere, in turn, they suffered themselves to be deceived and caught napping. The important positions entrusted to them were wrested from their hands. Minsk, where there were supplies for the whole army for months, had been captured, and now Borizow, where the passage of the Berezina was to be made, was captured almost without resistance. Well might Napoleon when he heard the news exclaim in despair: "Will there never be an end to this blundering?"

Great as the cold had been before, it increased day by

day in severity. Happily for the French, Kutusow, with the main Russian army, was far in their rear, and they might well hope, when joined by Victor, who was to meet them near the Berezina with his division, to be able to defeat the two Russian armies that barred their way, either force being inferior to their own.

Stephanie had borne the march wonderfully well. Since leaving Smolensk, she had had no walking to do. The cold was so great that she was glad to remain during the day snuggled up beneath Julian's cloak. The marching songs had ceased. Hunted as they were, silence was imperative, and indeed the distances traversed and the hardships endured were so great that even Julian felt that he had no longer strength to raise his voice. Few words indeed were spoken on the march, for the bitter cold seemed to render talking almost impossible.

Being in ignorance of the forces concentrating to cut him off, Napoleon ordered Oudinot's corps to march forward to secure the passage at Borizow, and Victor that at Studenski, but Tchichagow arrived at Borizow before Oudinot, and began to cross the bridge there. Oudinot, however, fell upon him fiercely before his whole army had passed over, and the Russians drew back across the bridge, destroying it behind them. Napoleon on his arrival found the Russian army of the Danube drawn up on the opposite bank ready to dispute his passage. He at once sent bodies of troops up and down the river to deceive the Russian admiral as to the point at which he intended to force a passage. Victor had already come in contact with Wittgenstein and had fought a drawn battle with him, and now moved to join Napoleon at the spot decided upon for the passage of the Berezina, near Studenski.

On the evening of the 25th of November Napoleon arrived there with Oudinot's corps. The engineers immediately commenced the construction of two bridges, and the cavalry and light infantry crossed the river to reconnoitre the enemy, and some batteries were established to cover the work. Materials were very scarce, and it was not until noon on the following day that the bridges were reported practicable. Oudinot's corps crossed at once, but the rest of the troops passed over in great confusion, which was increased by the frequent breaking down of the bridges. Victor took up a position to cover the rear, but one of his divisions was cut off by Wittgenstein, and eight thousand men forced to surrender. The main body of the French army, completely panic-stricken by the thunder of guns in their rear, crowded down in a confused mass. The passage was frequently arrested by fresh breakages in the bridges; hundreds were pushed off into the river by the pressure from behind; others attempted to swim across, but few of these succeeded in gaining the opposite bank, the rest being overpowered by the cold or overwhelmed by the floating masses of ice. Thousands perished by drowning. By the 28th the greater part of the French army had crossed, Victor's corps covering the passage and repulsing the efforts of Wittgenstein up to that time; then being unable to hold the Russians at bay any longer he marched down to the bridge, forcing a way through the helpless crowd that still blocked the approaches.

Altogether the loss of the French amounted to 28,000 men, of whom 16,000 were taken prisoners.

On the same day Tchichagow attacked in front with his army, but, animated by Napoleon's presence, and by despair, the French fought so fiercely that he was repulsed with much loss, and the way lay open to Wilna. The intensity of the cold increased daily, and the sufferings of the army were proportionately great. On the 5th of December Napoleon handed over the wreck of the army, now reduced to 45,000 men, to Murat; while the Viceroy was to have the chief command of the infantry.

By the time they reached the Berezina, Davoust's corps had been diminished to a few thousand men, and on Victor taking the post of rear-guard, they were relieved from that arduous task, and were among the first who crossed the fatal bridge. From there to Wilna there was comparatively little fighting. Kutusow's army was still far behind, and although Wittgenstein and the Admiral hung on their rear, the French army still inspired sufficient respect to deter them from attacking it in force.

As the army approached the Berezina, scarce a hundred men of the Grenadiers of the Rhone still hung together, and these were so feeble that they staggered rather than marched along. Rations had ceased to be issued, and the troops depended solely upon the flesh of the horses of the waggons conveying the military chests, treasure, and artillery, and from what they could gather in the deserted villages. So desperate were they now that even the fear of falling into the hands of the peasants was insufficient to deter them from turning off, whenever a village appeared in sight, in the hope of finding food, or, if that failed, at least a few hours' shelter. Not one of them was in such good condition as Julian, who had been sustained not only by his naturally high spirits, but by the prattle of the child, and by the added warmth of her sleeping close to him at night.

She now, for the most part, trotted beside him, and it was only when very tired that the child would allow him to take her up. She herself had never been short of food, for however small the portion obtained, enough for her was always set aside before it was touched. One day Julian had, with some of his comrades, entered a village. The others had insisted on lying down for a sleep, after devouring a little food they were fortunate enough to find in one of the houses. Julian's efforts to induce them to continue the march were in vain. They lighted a huge fire on a hearth with wood obtained by breaking up some of the doors, and declared that they would be warm for once, whatever came of it. The column was already some distance off, and night was closing in. Julian therefore started alone. He was carrying the child now, and for an hour he kept on his way. Still there were no signs of a road, and he at last became convinced that he must have gone in the wrong direction. He walked for half an hour longer, and then, coming upon a small hut, he at once determined to pass the night there.

Laying the sleeping child down, he covered her over with his cloak. Then he broke up some woodwork, cut a portion of it into small pieces, mixed the contents of a cartridge with a little snow and placed it among them, and then drew the charge from his musket, put a little powder into it, and discharged it into the heap. In a few minutes a bright fire was blazing, and, taking the child in his arms, he lay down before it, and was soon asleep. He was awakened some time afterwards by a strange noise. He sprang up at once, threw some fresh wood on the embers, and, grasping his musket, stood listening. In a minute the noise was renewed; something was scratching at the door, and a moment later he heard a pattering of feet overhead. Then came a low whimper and a snarl, and the truth at once rushed upon him. He was surrounded by wolves.

For a long time the march of the army had been accompanied by these creatures. Driven from the forests by cold and hunger, and scenting blood from afar, they had hung upon the skirts of the army, feasting on the bones of the horses and the bodies of the dead. Julian examined the door. It was a strong one, and there was no fear of their making an entry there. The roof, too, seemed solid; and the window, which was without glass, had a heavy wooden shutter.

Hoping that by morning the wolves, finding that they could not enter, would make off, Julian lay down by the fire again, and slept for some hours. When he woke daylight was streaming in through a crack in the shutter. On looking through this and through the chinks of the door, he saw, to his dismay, that the wolves were still there. Some were sitting watching the house; others were prowling about. It was clear that they had no intention whatever of leaving. The child had been roused by his movements.

"Stephanie wants breakfast," she said decidedly, as he broke up some more wood and rekindled the fire.

"I am afraid, dear, you will have to wait," he said. "I have not got any to give you."

"Let us go and get some," she said, standing up.

"I would, Stephanie; but there are some wolves outside, and we can't go until they move."

"Wolves are bad beasts. Stephanie was out riding in the sleigh with papa, when they came out from a wood and ran after us, and they would have killed us if the horses had not been very fast. Papa shot some of them, but the others did not seem to mind, and were close behind when we got home, where the men came out with forks and axes, and then they ran away. Stephanie will wait for her breakfast."

Julian thought for some time, and then, going to the window, opened the shutters and began to fire at the wolves. Several were killed. They were at once torn to pieces by their companions, who then withdrew to a safe distance, and sat down to watch. Julian had not even hoped that it would be otherwise. Had he waited, it was possible that they would at last leave the hut and go off in the track of the army; but even in that case, he would not, he felt, be able to overtake it alone, for, weak as he was, he felt unequal to any great exertion, and he and his charge might be devoured by these or other wolves long before he came up with the column, or they might be killed by Cossacks or by peasants. The last were the most merciless enemies, for death at their hands would be slower and more painful than at the hands of the wolves, but at least the child might be saved, and it was in hopes of attracting attention that he opened fire. He continued therefore to discharge his gun at intervals, and to his great satisfaction saw in the afternoon a number of peasants approaching. The wolves at once made off.

"Stephanie," he said, "there are some of your people coming. They will soon be here, and you must tell them who you are, and ask them to send you to your father, and tell them that he will give them lots of money for bringing you back to him."

"Yes," the child said, "and he will thank you very, very much for having been so good to me."

"I am afraid, Stephanie, that I shall not go back with you. The people kill the French whenever they take them."

"But you are not French; you are English," she said, indignantly. "Besides, the French are not all bad; they were very good to me."

"I am afraid, dear, that it will make very little difference to them my being an Englishman. They will see that I am in French uniform, and will regard me as an enemy just as if I were French."

"I will not let them hurt you," she said sturdily. "They are serfs, and when I tell them who I am they will obey me, for if they don't I will tell them that my father will have them all flogged to death."

"Don't do that, dear. You are a long way from your father's house, and they may not know his name; so do not talk about flogging, but only about the money they will get if they take you back. They are poor men, they have had a great deal to suffer, and have been made very savage; so it is best for you to speak kindly and softly to them. Now, dear, let us turn down that collar, so that they can see your face, and take your things off your head, and then go out and speak to them. They are close here."

The child did as he told her, and as he opened the door she stepped out. The peasants, who were only some twenty yards away, stopped in surprise at the appearance of the strange little figure before them. Her golden hair fell over her shoulders, and the long loose jacket concealed the rest of her person. She spoke to them in Russian, in a high, clear voice:

"I am the Countess Stephanie Woronski. I am glad to see you. I was travelling to go to my father, when there was an accident, and my nurse and the coachman were both killed; and I should have died too, but a good man—an Englishman—took me up, and he has carried me many days, and has fed me and kept me warm and been my nurse. He must go with me back to my father; and my father will give you lots of money for taking us both to him, and you must remember that he is an Englishman and not a Frenchman, although somehow he has been obliged to go with their army; and he is very, very good."

All this time Julian was standing behind her, musket in hand, determined to sell his life dearly. The peasants stood irresolute; they conferred together; then one of them advanced, and took off his fur cap and bowed to the child.

"Little mistress," he said, "we are but peasants, and do not know the name of your honoured father; but assuredly we will take you to our village, and our priest will find out where he lives, and will take you home to him; but this man with you is a Frenchman, and an enemy."

The child stamped her foot angrily. "Pig of a man!" she exclaimed passionately, "Do I, then, lie? I tell you he is English. I have a French coat on, just as he has. Will you say next that I am a French girl? I tell you that my friend must come with me, and that when I come to my father he will give you much money. He is a friend of the Czar, and if I tell him that you have hurt my friend, he and the Czar will both be angry."

A murmur broke from the group of peasants. The anger of the Czar was, of all things, the most terrible. Doubtless this imperious little countess was a great lady, and their habitual habit of subservience to the nobles at once asserted itself, and, while they had hesitated before, the threat of the Czar's anger completed their subjugation.

"It shall be as the little mistress wills it," the peasant said humbly. "No harm shall be done to your friend. We cannot promise that the troops will not take him away from us, but if they do not he shall go with you when we find where your father lives. If he has saved your life, he must be, as you say, a good man, and we will take care of him."

"They will take care of you," the child said in French, turning to Julian. "I told them that my father would reward them, and that the Czar would be very angry with them if they hurt you; and so they have promised to take you with me to him."

Julian at once placed his gun against the wall, and, taking her hand, walked forward to the peasants.

"Tell them," he said, "that the English are the friends of Russia, and that there are some English officers now with their army, for I have several times seen scarlet uniforms among the Russian staff."

The child repeated this to the peasants. One of them went into the hut, and looked round; and then securing

"I AM THE COUNTESS STEPHANIE WORONSKI. I AM GLAD TO SEE YOU."

Julian's musket, rejoined the others, who at once started across the snow, one of the party carrying Stephanie. On her telling them that she was hungry, some black bread was produced. She gave the first piece handed her to Julian, and then sat contentedly munching another. The peasants had now come to the conclusion that the capture would bring good fortune to them, and one of them took from the pocket of his sheep-skin caftan a bottle, which he handed to Julian. The latter took a drink that caused him to cough violently, to the amusement of the peasants, for it was *vodka*, and the strong spirit took his breath away after his long abstinence from anything but water. It did him good, however, and seemed to send a glow through every limb, enabling him to keep pace with the peasants. Their course lay north, and after four hours' walking they arrived at a good-sized village at the edge of a forest.

Their arrival created much excitement. There was a hubbub of talk, and then they were taken into the largest house in the village. Stephanie, who had been asleep for some time, woke up; and Julian threw aside his cloak, for the close heat of the interior was almost overpowering. A very old man, the father of the families that occupied the house,—for in Russia married sons all share the houses of their parents,—made a deep bow to Stephanie, and placed a low seat for her before the stove. Julian helped her off with her jacket and her other encumbrances, and her appearance in a pretty dress evidently increased the respect in which she was held by the peasants. In a short time bowls of hot broth were placed before them, and, weak as was the liquor, both enjoyed it immensely after their monotonous diet of horse-flesh. Then Stephanie was given a corner on the cushion placed on a wide shelf running round the apartment. The place next to her was assigned to Julian, who, after swallowing another glass of vodka, was in a few minutes sound asleep, with a sweet consciousness of rest and security to which he had long been a stranger.

In the morning there was a gathering composed of the papa or priest of the village and the principal men. When it was concluded, Stephanie was informed that none of them knew the place of residence of her father, but that a messenger had been sent off to the nearest town with a letter from the priest to the bishop there, asking him to inform them of it. She was asked how many days had passed since she had fallen in with the French, and how long she had been travelling before she did so. Julian was able to say exactly where he had fallen in with her—about thirty miles from Smolensk. Stephanie herself was vague as to the time she had travelled before the accident to the carriage, "days and days" being the only account that she could give of the matter. The priest then spoke to her for some time in Russian.

"They want you," she said to Julian, "to take off your uniform and to put on clothes like theirs. They say that though they wish to take you with me to my father, they might on the way fall in with other people or with soldiers, who would not know how good you are, and might take you away from them and kill you, so that it would be safer for you to travel in Russian dress. You won't mind that, will you?"

"Not at all, Stephanie; I think that it is a very good plan indeed."

A quarter of an hour later Julian was equipped in the attire of a well-to-do peasant, with caftan lined with sheepskin, a round fur cap, a thick pair of trousers of a dark rough cloth, bandages of the same material round the leg from the knee to the ankle, and high loose boots of untanned leather with the hair inside. The transformation greatly pleased the peasants, whose hatred of the French uniform had hitherto caused them to stand aloof from him, and they now patted him on the shoulder, shook his hand, and drank glasses of *vodka*, evidently to his health, with great heartiness. Julian could, as yet, scarcely believe that all this was not a dream. From the day that he had crossed the Niemen he had been filled with gloomy forebodings of disaster, and sickened by the barbarities of the soldiers upon the people, while, during the retreat, he had been exposed to constant hardship, engaged in innumerable fights and skirmishes, and impressed with the firm belief that not a Frenchman would ever cross the frontier save as a prisoner. After this the sense of warmth, the abundance of food, and the absence of any necessity for exertion seemed almost overpowering, and for the next three or four days he passed no small proportion of his time in sleep.

Stephanie was quite in her element. She was treated like a little queen by the villagers, who considered her presence among them a high honour as well as a source of future reward. They were never weary of listening to the details of her stay among the French, and accorded to Julian a good deal of deference both for the kindness he had shown the little countess and for the service that he had thereby rendered to themselves. It was ten days before an answer was received as to the count's estates. They lay, it said, far to the south, but the bishop was of opinion that the little countess had better be sent to St. Petersburg, as the count had a palace there, and would be certain to be at the capital at the present juncture of affairs. He offered that, if they would bring her to him, he would see that she was sent on thither by a post-carriage, but that in view of the extreme cold it would be better that she should not be forwarded until the spring.

A village council was held on the receipt of this letter,

and the proposal that she should be sent by the bishop was unanimously negatived. It seemed to the villagers that in such a case the glory of restoring Stephanie to her parents, and the reward that would naturally accrue from it, would not fall to them; but, at the same time, no alternative method occurred to them. Finally, after much consultation, Stephanie was asked to interpret the bishop's letter to Julian, and when she had done so she was told to add: "They think, Julian, that if they send us to the bishop papa will not know that it was they who found me and took care of me."

Julian understood the difficulty. He first inquired how much the village could raise to pay for the expenses of a post-carriage to St. Petersburg. He said that it would, of course, be only a loan, and would be repaid by the count. This led to a considerable amount of discussion, but the difficulty was much diminished when Julian said that he could himself supply five napoleons towards the fund. It had been decided that three times that amount would be required to pay all expenses of travel, and the priest agreeing to contribute an equal amount to Julian's, the remaining sum was speedily made up. It was then arranged that the priest would himself go to Borizow and obtain the *podorojna* or order for the supply of post-horses at the various stations. He would have to name those who would accompany him. The head man of the village was unanimously elected to go with him, and after some talk it was settled that Julian should be put down as Ivan Meriloff, as a foreign name would excite suspicion and cause much trouble, and possibly he might be detained as a prisoner, in which case the peasants saw that there would be considerable difficulty in inducing the little countess to go with them. The priest was absent three days, and then returned with the necessary document authorizing him to start from Borizow in four days' time. Julian was sorry when the time came for his departure. After four months of incessant hardship and fatigue, the feeling of rest and comfort was delightful. He had been more weakened than he was aware of by want of food, and, as his strength came back to him, he felt like one recovering from a long illness, ready to enjoy the good things of life fully, to bask in the heat of the stove, and to eat his meals with a sense of real enjoyment.

Rumours had come in every day of the terrible sufferings of the French as they were hotly pressed by the triumphant Russians, and of the general belief that but few would survive to cross the Niemen. Still, while the French were thus suffering, the Russians were in but little better plight, following, as they did, through a country that had been swept bare of everything that could be burned by the retreating French. Their sufferings from cold were terrible, 90,000 perished, and out of 10,000 recruits, who afterwards marched for Wilna, as a reinforcement, only 1500 reached that city, and the greater portion of these had at once to be taken to the hospital mutilated from frost-bite. Thus, then, the number of Russians that perished was at least as great as that of their harrassed foes, and this in their own climate, and without the necessity for the constant vigilance that had assisted to break down the retreating army.

Julian was instructed in the Russian words to reply if asked by any of the postmasters whether he was the Ivan Meriloff mentioned in the passport, and, on the day after the return of the priest, they started in a sledge filled with hay and covered with sheep-skins.

Julian with Stephanie were nestled up in the hay at one end of the sledge, the two Russians at the other. On reaching Borizow they stopped at the post-house, and on producing the *podorojna* were told that the carriage and horses would be ready in half an hour. They had brought a considerable amount of provisions with them, and now laid in a stock of such articles as could not be procured in the villages. When the post-carriage came round, a large proportion of the hay in the sledge was transferred to it, together with the sheep-skins. There was no luggage, and four horses were deemed sufficient. The wheels had, of course, been taken off the vehicle, and it was placed on runners. The driver climbed up to his seat, cracked his whip furiously, and the horses started at a gallop. The motion was swift and pleasant, indeed travelling in Russia is much more agreeable in winter than in summer, for the roads, which in summer are often detestable, are in winter as smooth as glass, over which the sledge glides with a scarce perceptible movement, and the journeys are performed much more rapidly than in summer.

The distance between the post-houses varied considerably, being sometimes only nine miles apart, sometimes as many as twenty, but they were generally performed at a gallop, the priest, at Julian's suggestion, always giving somewhat more than the usual drink-money to the driver, and in five days from the time of their leaving Borizow they arrived at St. Petersburg, halting only for a few hours each night at post-houses. They had no difficulty in ascertaining where the Woronski palace was situated, and, taking a *droski*, drove there at once. Stephanie clapped her hands as she saw it.

"You ought to have put on your cloak, Julian, and to have packed me up under it as you used to carry me, and to take me in like that."

"I am afraid that grand-looking personage at the door would not have let me in. As it is, he is looking at us with the greatest contempt."

"That is Peter," the child said. "Peter, Peter, what are you standing staring for? Why don't you come and help me down as usual?"

The porter, a huge man with a great beard, and wearing a fur cap and a long fur-trimmed pelisse, almost staggered back as the child spoke. He had, as Julian said, been regarding the *droski* and its load with an air of supreme contempt, and had been about to demand angrily why it ventured to drive up into the court-yard of the palace. He stood immovable until Stephanie threw back her sheep-skin hood, then, with a loud cry, he sprang down the steps, dashed his fur cap to the ground, threw himself on his knees, and taking the child's hand in his, pressed it to his forehead. The tears streamed down his cheeks, as he sobbed out, " My little mistress, my little mistress! and you have come back again to be the light of our hearts—oh, what a joyful day is this!"

"Thank you, Peter. Now, please lift me down. I am quite well. Are papa and mamma well?"

"The gracious countess is not well, little mistress, but when she knows that you are back, she will soon regain her health. His excellency, your father, is not ill, but he is sorely troubled. He has been away for a fortnight searching for news of you, and returned but last week. I don't know what his news was, but it was bad, for the countess has been worse since he returned."

"This gentleman has told me, Peter, that I must not run in to see them without their being told first that I am safe, and that you had better fetch Papa Serge. This is the English gentleman, Peter, who saved my life when I was almost dead with cold, and carried me for days and days under his cloak, and kept me warm close to him when we lay down in the snow at night."

Again the Russian fell on his knees, and, seizing Julian's hand, put it to his forehead. Then he jumped up, "Why am I keeping you out in the cold?" he said. "Come in, little mistress, and I will send to fetch the papa."

"Cover up your head, Stephanie," Julian said as, holding his hand tightly, they entered the hall together. "If others were to see you the news would run through the house like wildfire, and it would come to your mother's ears before it had been broken to her. Tell Peter to take us into a quiet room, and not to inform the man he sends to the priest that you are here."

Followed by the village priest and the peasant they entered a room fitted as a library.

"It is here papa writes his letters," Stephanie said, throwing back her hood again and taking off her cloak; "isn't it nice and warm?"

Coming in from the temperature of some forty degrees below freezing, it was to Julian most uncomfortably warm. It was some four or five minutes before the door opened, and Papa Serge, the family chaplain, entered with a somewhat bewildered face, for he had been almost forcibly dragged down by Peter, who had refused to give any explanation for the urgency of his demand that he should accompany him instantly to the count's study. When his eyes fell on Stephanie, who had started up as he entered, he gave a cry of joy. A moment later she sprang into his arms.

"Dear, dear, Papa Serge!" she said, as she kissed his withered cheeks warmly. "Oh I do love to be home again, though I have been very happy, and everyone has been very kind to me! Now, you musn't stay here, because I want to see papa and mamma; and this gentleman says—he is my great friend, you know, and I call him Nurse Julian—that you must go and tell them first that I have come, and that you must tell them very gently, so that it won't upset poor mamma."

"Tell him, Stephanie, that he had better say at first only that someone has just come with the news that you are quite safe, and that you will be here soon, and then, after a little while, he had better call your father out and tell him the truth. By the way, ask if they are together now "

The child put the question.

"No, the countess is in bed and the count is walking up and down the great drawing-room. He does it for hours at a time."

"In that case, Stephanie, tell Serge to speak first to your father, and to bring him down here to you. He will break it to your mother better than anyone else would do."

The priest was too deeply moved to speak, but upon Stephanie translating what Julian had said, put her down and left the room. As soon as he had done so the priest who had travelled with them, and who, with his companion, had been standing in an attitude of respect while Stephanie was speaking, said to her:

"Little countess, we will go out into the hall and wait there. It were better that his excellency, your father, should meet you here alone."

"He would not mind," Stephanie said; "but if you think that you had better go, please do."

The two peasants left the room somewhat hastily. They had been absolutely awed at the splendour of the house, which vastly surpassed anything they had ever imagined, and were glad to make an excuse to leave the room and so avoid seeing the count until his daughter had explained the reason of their presence there. Julian guessed their reason for leaving and was about to follow them when Stephanie took him by the hand.

"No," she said, "you are not to go, Julian. It is you who saved my life, and it is you who must give me back to papa." A few minutes elapsed, then the door was suddenly thrown open and the count ran in.

"My Stephanie! my little Stephanie!" he cried, as he caught her up. "Oh, my little girl! we never thought to see you again—it seems a miracle from heaven. Do not cry, darling," he said presently, as she lay sobbing with her head on his shoulder. "It is all over now, and you will come to think of it in time as a bad dream."

"Not a *very* bad one, papa. It has been funny and strange, but not bad. Oh, and I meant this gentleman—he is an English gentleman, papa—to have put me into your arms, only somehow I forgot all about it when you came in. I call him Nurse Julian, papa, because he has been my nurse. He has carried me for days and days on his back under his warm cloak, and I have slept curled up in his arms; and sometimes there were battles. Oh, such a noise they made! When it was a big battle he stowed me away in a waggon, but sometimes when it was a small one, and he had not time to take me to the waggon, he carried me on his back, and I used to jump at first when he fired his gun, but I soon got accustomed to it, and he always got me plenty of food, though it was not very nice. But he didn't often get enough, and he became very thin and pale, and then I used sometimes to run along by his side for a bit, and I only let him carry me when I was very tired, and at last we were in a little hut by ourselves, and some peasants came. They looked very wicked at first, but I told them who I was, and that you would give them money if they brought me back to you, and so we went to their village and stayed there, and it was warm and nice, and there was plenty of food, and dear Julian got strong again, and then they brought us here in a post-carriage, and two of them came with me. They are out in the hall now."

The count set his little daughter down, and coming up to Julian threw his arms round his neck and kissed him in Russian fashion. "My benefactor!" he exclaimed, "I don't understand all that Stephanie has told me, but it is enough that you saved her life, and that you nursed her with the tenderness of a mother, and have restored her to us as one from the grave. Never can I fully express my thanks or prove my gratitude to you, but now you will, I trust, excuse me. I am burning to carry the news of our dear one's return to her mother, whose condition is giving us grave anxiety. She is far too weak to stand any sudden shock, and I will merely tell her now that news has come that a little girl whose description corresponds with that of Stephanie has been found and is on her way here, and may arrive very shortly. More than that I shall not venture upon to-day, unless, indeed, I find that the excitement and suspense is likely to be even more injurious to her than the state of dull despair in which she now lies. If I see that it is so I must go on, little by little, till she guesses the truth. Now, Stephanie, you had better come up to your own room. Of course, your friend will come with you," he added with a smile as Stephanie took Julian's hand. "But you had better wait three or four minutes so that I may give strict orders to the household that everything is to be kept perfectly quiet, and that not a sound is to be heard in the house. There will be time enough for rejoicings afterwards."

The count, who was a handsome man some thirty years old, now left the room. He paused in the hall for a minute, shook the priest and his companion warmly by the hand, and assured them that they should be handsomely rewarded for the kindness they had shown to his daughter, and then, after speaking to Peter, he ran lightly upstairs to his wife's room. Stephanie waited for about five minutes and then said:

"I should think that papa has had time to give the orders. Now, Julian, shall we go?"

"Yes, dear, I think we might do so."

On going out into the hall a singular spectacle presented

itself. The grand staircase was lined on each side with kneeling men and women. There was a sound of suppressed sobbing, and a low murmur was heard as Stephanie appeared.

"Go first, Stephanie dear," Julian said in a low voice; "they want to kiss your hands."

Stephanie showed no shyness, for, stopping on each step, she held out her hands to the kneeling figures, who murmured prayers and blessings. As they kissed them, she said softly to each, "Thank you very much, but I must not talk now. This gentleman is my friend. It is he who saved my life, and nursed me, and carried me. You must all love him for my sake;" whereupon, as Julian followed her, he met with a reception similar to that given to their young mistress. He was glad when at last they reached the top of the stairs and Stephanie led the way into her own room, which was a sort of glorified nursery. Here two or three maids were laying a table, and as the door closed behind him they crowded round her and by turns kissed and hugged her. Then an old woman, who had sat apart until the girls had had their turn, came forward. She placed her hands solemnly on the child's head:

"May the great Father bless you, my child! I have seen many glad days since I entered the service of your house sixty years ago. I was present at your grandfather's wedding, and your father's, but never was there so bright and happy a day as this, which but half an hour ago was so dark and sad. It was but three days ago that the whole household went into mourning for you, for the news your father brought home seemed to show that all hope was at an end. In five minutes all this has changed. You see the maids have got on their festive dresses, and I will warrant me they never changed their things so rapidly before. Now we have but to get your beloved mother strong again, which, please God, will not be long, and then this will be the happiest house in all Russia."

"This is my nurse, my new nurse, Elizabeth. His name is Julian, and he is an English gentleman, as you will see better when he gets some nice clothes on. He has carried me days and days across the snow, and kept me warm by night and day, and done everything for me. He doesn't speak Russian, but he can speak French, and so, of course, we got on very nicely; and I have been in battles, Elizabeth, think of that! and I was not afraid a bit, and I was quite happy all the time, only, of course, I am very, very glad to get home again."

The meal was now laid, and Julian and the child sat down to it with a vigorous appetite. Their food while in the village had been coarse though plentiful, and Julian especially appreciated the delicate flavour and perfect cooking of the many dishes of whose names and contents he was absolutely ignorant. An hour after they had finished, the count came in.

"Your mother has borne it better than I expected, Stephanie," he said. "I have been able to break the news to her sooner than I expected. Come with me; be very quiet and do not talk much. She will be well content to have you lying quietly in her arms." So saying, he lifted her and carried her off, saying to Julian, "I will return and have the pleasure of a talk with you after I have left Stephanie with her mother."

CHAPTER XV.

IN COMFORTABLE QUARTERS.

IT was an hour before the Count returned to the nursery. "Ah, my friend," he said, "what happiness have you brought to us! Already my wife is a new creature. I had begun to think that I should lose her too, for the doctors told me frankly that they feared she would fall into a decline. Now her joy is so great that it was with difficulty that I could tear myself away from contemplating her happiness, but the doctor came in and recommended that she should try and sleep for a time, or if she could not sleep that she should at least lie absolutely quiet, so Stephanie has nestled down by her side, and I was able to come to you." He now led the way to a luxuriously furnished smoking-room.

"This is my snuggery," he said. "The library below is where I go into matters with my stewards, receive persons who come on business, and so on. This is where I read and receive my friends. Now, will you help yourself to those cigars, and let us talk. At present I know nothing. Stephanie was left down at our estate, near Kieff, under the charge of her French nurse, who has been with her since she was born. She was rather governess than nurse of late. She was a French *émigré*, and of good French family, and we had implicit confidence in her. I wrote to her when the invasion first began, saying that as at present we could not tell whether St. Petersburg or Moscow would be Napoleon's object of attack, but as all the centre of Russia would be involved in the war, I wished that Stephanie should remain quietly with her. I said that, should any

French army approach Kieff, she was to take Stephanie at once to my estate near Odessa.

"After the invasion began I sent off several letters to the same effect, two by my own couriers, but owing to our army falling back so rapidly, I imagine that none of the letters ever reached the nurse. Of course, the whole postal communication of the country has been thrown into confusion. At last, two months ago, a messenger from Kieff brought me a letter from her making no allusion to those I had sent her, but saying that as she heard that the French army was at Moscow she felt sure I should wish her to bring Stephanie to us, and that, after a consultation with my steward, she would in three days start direct after sending off her letter. We were, of course, thunderstruck. She apparently had the idea that the whole of the French were at Moscow, and that it would, therefore, be perfectly safe to cross the roads between them and the frontier. The poor woman said that, should they by any chance come across any body of her countrymen, she was sure that they would not interfere with a woman and child. Her anxiety seemed to relate solely to the weather and food, but she assured me that she would bring an abundance of wraps of all sorts, and a supply of provisions in the *fourgon* sufficient for the journey.

"Half an hour after I received the letter I sent off two couriers. They were, of course, to go round east of Moscow and then to Kieff. They were to drive at the top of their speed the whole way, and I obtained a special order for them to be instantly furnished with post-horses everywhere. In the meantime there was nothing to do but to wait. My orders were that immediately they arrived they were to send off a fresh messenger by the way they had come, saying whether Stephanie had started, and they were bearers of letters of instruction to the steward that six mounted men were instantly to follow the road the carriage had taken, making inquiries at every post-house, and to endeavour to trace them, and if the clue was anywhere lost to bring word to me. I waited ten days, then I got news that Stephanie had left five weeks before my messengers arrived there. The nurse's letter had been a very long time in coming to me, and they had started, as she said, three days after it was written, therefore if they had got safely through the country occupied by the French they should have arrived here at least three weeks before.

"According to the dates there was little doubt that they must have crossed the main road from Moscow to the frontier at the very time when the French army on its retreat would be moving along. All that we had heard and knew of the terrible distress, both of their army and of our own, showed that at that time the intense suffering of the French and the savage reprisals of our peasantry had reduced them to a state when nothing was respected, and that a pair of valuable horses and a heap of costly furs, to say nothing of the food carried, would be prizes almost beyond value. Deprived of these, a nurse and child would, in a few hours, die of the cold. That some such fate must have befallen them seemed almost certain, for otherwise they must have joined us.

"I could tell pretty well the road that they would follow, and started along it. Half-way between here and Smolensk I met the six men. What they said confirmed my worst fears. They had learnt where the carriage had last halted for the night. The party had not travelled post, but had kept their own horses and had travelled only by day. Had they lingered only one day anywhere on the way they would have crossed the Moscow road on the day after the rearguard of the French had passed.

"But news travelled slowly, and no doubt, at the posthouse where they slept, no word that the French army was passing along had been received. Beyond that, the men had been able to gather no news whatever of the carriage. The country was a desert, tenanted only by dead; and the men's descriptions of what they saw were so horrible that my blood was frozen. However, I kept on my journey, taking them with me. We went to the post-house where the carriage had last stopped, and then took up the search. There were half a dozen roads by which they might have proceeded; however, we took the most easterly one, and then, when it crossed the main road, followed the latter. It was choked with deserted waggons and guns. Dead bodies lay everywhere; many partly devoured by wolves; all stripped of their clothing. After making our way through this terrible scene for a few miles, we saw, fifty yards from the road, the remains of a sleigh. Its bright yellow colour caught our eyes, and when we got to it there was no room for doubt. The body of the sleigh was gone—had been burnt for firewood; but the colour was that of my own carriage, and two of the men who belonged to the stables at Kieff said that they could swear to it, owing to a new iron that had been put on to one of the runners the day before it had started. But there were other signs. Portions of the harness lay about, and on one of these enough of the silver-work remained to show that it was ours.

"Then we searched farther. Turning over a mound of newly-fallen snow, we found the bodies of the coachman and the nurse. We searched for hours, but could not find that of the child; but as to her fate we had no doubt. She might have run away into the forest, or she might have been devoured by wolves. That she was dead was certain. I left four of the men there. They were to establish themselves in the nearest village, and to continue the search day by day, and to remain there, if necessary, till the spring came and the snow disappeared. I returned here ten days ago with the news that all hope was at an end, and that Stephanie was lost to us for ever. Now, sir, will you tell me how it was that you saved her? You were doubtless with the French army, though how you came to be there is almost as great a puzzle as how Stephanie was saved."

"I will tell you that afterwards, Count," Julian replied.

Then he related how, on marching past the overturned carriage, he heard what would doubtless have been Stephanie's last cry, and had found her lying half-frozen among the cushions. He stated the means he had taken to restore warmth to her, and how he had strapped her to his back under his warmly-lined cloak.

Then he gave, as well as he could remember, the details of each day's experience: how Stephanie had become a general pet of the soldiers; how they had manufactured a warm cloak and hood for her; how she had ridden on shoulders, and had joined in the marching songs of the regiment, and had really kept well and in good spirits on the march; how, as he got too weak to carry her, she had trotted by his side; and how his comrades, in spite of their exhaustion, had been willing to relieve him of her weight. Then he told how, at last, they had separated from the regiment when but a few hours' march from the Berezina; and how Stephanie in turn had saved his life from the peasants.

"So you see, Count," he concluded, "the kindness that I had shown your child has already been repaid to me many fold. Not only did she save my life from the peasants, but I have no doubt that her pretty talk, and the occupation she offered to my thoughts, and her warmth as she nestled close to me at night, were the means of my retaining my strength to a far greater degree than was the case with most of my comrades, and enabled me to survive when so many dropped dead from cold and exhaustion."

"That may be so, my friend," the count said. "God has doubtless rewarded you for your good action, but that in nowise lessens our obligations towards you. Now, will you tell me somewhat of your own history?"

"It is a long story, Count."

"All the better, my friend. I trust that my wife is asleep by this time, and the child with her, and nothing can be of greater interest to me than to hear it."

Julian therefore related his story in full, and produced the paper given him on his enlistment, guaranteeing that he should not be called upon to fight against his countrymen.

"Since we entered Russia, Count," he said, "and I have seen the savage manner in which the peasantry were treated, not so much by the French troops as by the allies, I bitterly regretted that I had enlisted; but, at the time, no notion of this had ever entered my mind. I have told you that the life at Verdun was intolerable. We died in hundreds, for a sort of dull despair seemed to settle on everyone; and, although for a long time I had borne up against it, I had come to the point when death would have been welcome. A return to my own country seemed closed to me, owing to the circumstances I have related to you; and I entered the French service, just as, in the wars a couple of hundred years ago, Englishmen and Scotchmen were to be found fighting as soldiers of fortune in the armies of well-nigh every power of Europe."

"I cannot blame you, Mr. Wyatt. Yours is a singular and most unfortunate story, and it seems to me that, had I been in your place, I should have acted precisely the same, and should have been glad to take service under any flag rather than have remained to rot in a prison. Certainly you had a thousand times better excuse than had the Austrians and Prussians, who, after having been our allies, entered upon this savage war of invasion without a shadow of excuse, save that it was the will of Napoleon. However, I think that it will be as well, in order to save any necessity for explanation, that I should introduce you to my friends as an English gentleman who has come to me with the warmest recommendations, and whom I am most anxious to serve in any way. This is not a time when men concern themselves in any way with the private affairs of others. There is not a family in Russia, high or low, who has not lost one or more members in this terrible struggle. Publicly, and as a nation, we rejoice at our deliverance, and at the destruction of our enemies. Privately, we mourn our losses.

"They have been terrible. As yet we scarcely know how great; but I imagine that they will be found to have been no less than that of the enemy. We hear that, in the pursuit, and without having taken any part in the actual fighting after Krasnoi, Kutusow's army alone has lost nearly 100,000 men from cold and fatigue; while, of the central army of Napoleon, but four hundred infantry and six hundred cavalry repassed the Niemen with their arms and standards. The other Russian divisions suffered as severely as those with Kutusow. The Emperor has himself gone to Wilna to endeavour to alleviate the sufferings of the sick and wounded, with which the city is crammed. Wide as will be the mourning in France, it will be no less so in Russia. Now, the first thing to do is to provide you with suitable garments. This I will put in hand immediately; but, until they can be procured, you must content yourself with some of mine, though, as you are some four inches taller than

I am, and far wider, they will suit you but poorly. However, I have an ample store of dressing-gowns and wraps, and you must remain indoors a prisoner until you are properly fitted out. By the way, I had an interview with the two honest men who came with you before I returned to you, and have arranged their business fully to their satisfaction. The Papa will be able to build himself a new church, and the villagers to repair all the losses they have suffered in the campaign.

"They were," he said, with a smile, "anxious to see you, as they said that they had an account to settle with you, as you had furnished one-third of the money required for the trip. However, I told them that they could set their minds at rest on that score, for that I would settle with you privately. I only mention it that you should not think they had gone off without any remembrance of your share in the business."

An hour later, a tailor with his assistant came to measure Julian. Three days later, the Count suggested that he should go for a drive with him in his sledge, and, wrapped up in furs, Julian took his place beside him in a splendidly-appointed open vehicle. Stephanie sat between them. The sledge was drawn by three horses—the centre one in shafts, while those on either side ran free. A purple net covered the three animals almost touching the ground, and so preventing the particles of snow being thrown up by their hoofs into the sledge. The driver, in fur cap and pelisse, and with an immense beard, sat on a seat in front. A number of bells were attached to the harness of the horses, and to a bow-shaped piece of wood that arched over the head of the central horse.

"This is an improvement on the post-waggons, Stephanie," Julian said.

The child nodded brightly. "You said it would all seem like a dream, Julian," she remarked presently, as they dashed swiftly down the broad street of the Nevsky, crowded with vehicles of all kinds, from the splendidly-appointed sledges, like their own, to the lumbering vehicles of the peasants piled up with firewood. "It almost seems like a dream already, and yet you know I was very comfortable with you."

"It will be something for you to look back upon all your life," her father said. "There will be many who will have strange and sad memories of the war, but not one who will have a stranger experience than you have to talk about. Happily, there was, as far as you are concerned, but little sadness in it."

Julian was delighted with the brightness and gaiety of St. Petersburg, with its broad streets, its stately palaces, its fine cathedrals, and its busy population. The universal use of furs prevented the symbols of mourning being apparent, and, as they drove along in the luxurious equipage, even he, like the child, could scarce believe that the desperate fight at Smolensk, the even longer and more obstinate contest at Borodino, and the terrible scenes on the retreat, were realities. On his return to the palace, Julian understood the object of the Count in having taken him for a drive, for he found the *armoires* and wardrobes of his room crammed with garments of all descriptions.

Here was underclothing of every kind, sufficient for a lifetime; morning suits, riding suits, dress suits, visiting suits, in bewildering variety. In one wardrobe were three superb overcoats, lined with the most costly furs, half a dozen fur caps of various patterns, four huge fur rugs, high boots lined with fur, a dozen pairs of fur gloves for walking and driving; and arranged along the wall were ten pairs of boots of different kinds, fur-lined slippers, and dress boots. He examined them all with something like consternation.

"What nonsense!" he exclaimed. "What am I to do with all these things? It is magnificent; but it is too much altogether. Why, these furs alone are worth hundreds of pounds! No doubt the count is extremely rich. I have already heard him speak of three or four estates in different parts of Russia, and this palace is fit for a prince. Of course, he can afford it well enough, but to me all this is quite overpowering. I should like to see Aunt's face if I were to turn up at Weymouth with all this kit."

There was a letter lying on the table. He opened it. It was, as he had expected, from the count.

"My dear Mr. Wyatt, you will, I am sure, accept the little outfit that I have provided, in the same spirit in which I have obtained it, and will oblige me by making no allusion to it whatever, or to the contents of the inclosed pocket-book, which will provide you with ready money while you are staying here. They are but poor tokens of the life-long obligations you have conferred upon the countess and myself."

The pocket-book contained a roll of Russian notes to the value of a thousand pounds. Julian felt that there was indeed nothing to do but, as the letter said, to accept the presents in the spirit in which they were made. Everything showed that thoughtful kindness had been exercised. On the dressing-table stood a superb travelling-case of Russian leather, fitted with all necessaries of the toilet in ivory, mounted with silver, and with his initials engraved upon the back of the various brushes. Hitherto he had made no attempt to remove the soft brown beard that had grown untouched from the day when the army had turned its back upon Moscow. He now set to and shaved himself, and then dressed for dinner. In glancing at one of the long cheval glasses in the room, he could not but feel a distinct satisfaction at his appearance. Except in shop windows in Germany, he had not, since he left home, had the opportunity of seeing more of himself than could be gathered from the tiny glass that formed part of his kit.

He now saw himself as he was, a tall figure of six feet two in height, with a broad pair of shoulders. The scenes of the last six months had given an expression of power and decision to his face that it had lacked before. The stern, set look of battle had left its mark upon it, and though a distinctly pleasant and kindly one, it was undoubtedly that of a soldier who had seen hard service and had looked death many times in the face. All question as to what he should say to the count was set at rest on his entry into the drawing-room, for the count took him by the hand, and, leading him across the room, presented him to the countess, who had for the first time made her appearance. She rose as they came across, and with trembling hands and eyes full of tears, came up to him.

"Ah, Mr. Wyatt," she said, "what can I say to the saviour of my child? I have had difficulty in restraining my patience so long; but it was only to-day that the doctor gave me permission to leave my room."

She held out both her hands to him. He bowed deeply over them and raised them to his lips. "My happiness is no less than your own, countess," he said, "that God has permitted me to be the means of bringing your child back again. It was no great thing to do on my part; and, as I have told the count, the little act of kindness was vastly more than repaid, for your daughter assuredly saved my life from the peasants, as I saved hers from the cold. Your little daughter is quite a heroine," he said more lightly. "I can assure you that even when the bullets were flying about thickly she evinced no signs of fear, and the way in which she stood before me facing those enraged peasants was splendid."

"It shows her perfect faith in you, Mr. Wyatt. A child who has absolute confidence in the person in whose charge she is, is almost without fear. Her idea of danger is derived almost entirely from the conduct of those around her. If they show fear, she is terrified; while if their manner convinces her that they have no fear, she does not understand that danger can exist. She is evidently deeply attached to you, as indeed she has reason to be, and when I get tired with talking to her, and say to her, 'Now you must go, dear,' she trots off as contentedly to you as if you were indeed what she calls you, her nurse, much more so than she used to do to Claire. The poor woman was a most careful nurse and an excellent instructress, although she did start so madly, as it would seem, on this journey. But the child never really took to her, as she had not the faculty of winning affection. She was thoroughly trustworthy, and would, I believe, have given her life for the child, but she was certainly rather precise in manner, and was perhaps a little too peremptory in giving her orders. That was, I admit, a fault on the right side, for Stephanie is so accustomed to adulation on the part of the servants, that she rather needs a firm hand over her. However, the child has scarcely mentioned Claire's name since her return, while yours is incessantly on her lips."

"She has not been in any way spoilt by adulation, countess, and has been as amenable to my slightest wish as the humblest peasant child could be; but she certainly has a pretty little air of dignity. It was funny to see how she queened it among the French soldiers, who always called her Mademoiselle la Comtesse, and always put aside the best piece of their scanty ration of meat for her."

"Yes, she has been telling me how good they were to her. What a war this has been, Mr. Wyatt!"

So they chatted until dinner was announced; then the countess lay down on the sofa, and Stephanie came in and sat on a low stool beside her, while her father and Julian went to the dining-room. After the meal was over, the count proposed that Julian should accompany him on a visit to the Nobles' Club. The sledge was already waiting at the door, and in a few minutes they arrived, not, as Julian had expected, at a stately building, but at a garden.

"This is our skating place," the count said as they entered. "We have guest-nights here once a week during the winter. As a rule, those present are simply the invited guests of members; but to-night the tickets are sold at twenty roubles each, and the proceeds go to the funds for the benefit of the wounded. It will furnish a handsome sum, for everyone is here, and there are few indeed who have paid as little as the twenty roubles. Some sent cheques for as much as five hundred roubles for their tickets, and a hundred may be taken as the average. This is the first time that we have had a military band, for music is naturally considered out of place when everyone is in mourning and such vast numbers of our soldiers are still suffering horribly; but as this is for their benefit it is considered as an exception. You will not see much skating; the ice will be far too crowded."

"It was indeed a brilliant scene. The gardens were lighted with myriads of lamps. The sheet of ice was of a very irregular shape and broken by several islets, upon which grew trees. From their branches hung numbers of lanterns, while the bank round the ice was studded with lamps. The crowds walking about by the edge of the lake were all wrapped up in furs. A large proportion of those on skates wore uniforms, while the ladies were in short, tightly-fitting jackets, trimmed with fur, and with coquettish little fur caps. The crowd was far too great for any attempt at figure-skating, but they moved swiftly round and round the lake in a sort of procession, each lady accompanied by a cavalier, who held her hand, and all skating with a grace and freedom that was to Julian surprising indeed. The scene, with its bright colours and rapid movement, was almost bewildering, and Julian was glad to turn away and go up to the pavilion, where hot coffee and liquors were handed to all comers.

The count spoke to many acquaintances, introducing Julian to each of them as his great friend, Monsieur Wyatt, an Englishman. After waiting an hour in the gardens they drove to the club itself. There were here a large number of gentlemen, all of whom had been for a few minutes at the garden. Here more introductions took place, and the count put down Julian's name as an honorary member. "You will have a long day's work to-morrow, Monsieur Wyatt."

"How is that, count?"

"It will be your duty to call upon every gentleman to whom I have introduced you; that is to say, to leave a card at the door, and every one of them will leave a card at my house for you. I will make out a list for you in the morning of the names and addresses. You will find a sledge at the door at three o'clock; it will be at your disposal while you remain with me. It is a small and light one, like this, with a pair of horses. It is seldom that three horses are used unless ladies are of the party. There is much for you to see, and it will be more pleasant for you to be your own master and go about as you please."

The following morning, after breakfast, the count said, as they lit their cigars, "Have you formed any plans yet, Mr. Wyatt? Of course I do not mean for the present. It is understood that this is your home as long as you will be good enough to make it so, and the longer you stay the greater pleasure it will give us; but I mean for the future. Are you thinking of returning to England?"

"I am intending to write at once to my brother. Whether he is at home or not, of course I cannot say. He was going into the army, but I greatly fear that the unfortunate affair in which I was engaged will have rendered that impossible. At any rate, I shall also write to my aunt; if alive, she is sure to be there. In the first place, I shall tell them what has become of me. There has been no possibility of my sending a letter from the time I left home, with the exception of one written while crossing the Channel, and which the smugglers promised to deliver on their return. They must think that I am dead by this time, and my letter will, at any rate, relieve their anxiety. In the next place, I am most anxious to know if anything has been heard further from the smuggler. He gave me his solemn promise that in the event of his death a letter acknowledging that he was the murderer should be sent to the magistrates of Weymouth. I have no reason in the world for supposing that he is dead, for he was not above middle age, and if, as is but too probable, no such letter had been received, I cannot return home. I might, however, return to London, and thence take ship to some foreign country—either to the United States or to South America, or perhaps to our own colony of Canada, and settle down there or enlist in the English army."

"Or you might stay here?"

"I might stay here, count, but as I am ignorant of Russian, and have no trade or profession, I do not well see what I could possibly do."

"You would not be long in picking up Russian," the count said, "and if you could make up your mind to settle down here until you learn that your innocence of this foul charge has been completely proved, there would be no necessity for any trade or profession. Why, Monsieur, you do not suppose that the countess and I are without heart, or would allow you, the preserver of our child, to struggle for an existence here or anywhere else! We have more money than we know what to do with. We have six estates in different parts of Russia. We have some ten thousand serfs. However, we can settle nothing until you receive an answer to your letter; after that we will talk matters over seriously. At any rate, do not trouble about your future. This is the reason that I have spoken to you to-day. Your future is our care, and you can leave it safely in our hands."

"You are too good altogether, Count," Julian said; but the Russian checked him with a peremptory gesture of his hand.

"Let us have no talk like that, Mr. Wyatt. You will only pain me deeply, and make me think less well of you than I do now. Stephanie is to us infinitely more than all our possessions, and did we assign to you all else that we have in the world we should feel that the balance of obligation was still against us. Now let us talk of other matters. In the first place, about sending your letter. Of course, at present the Baltic is frozen, and the ports beyond are all in the hands of the French. Sweden, however, is in alliance with us, and our despatches for England go up through

Finland, then across the ice to Sweden, and by land to Gothenburg, and thence by sea to England. It is a roundabout journey, but it is performed rapidly; and as there are English packets always ready to sail from Gothenburg, your letters should, under favourable circumstances, be in England in a fortnight.

"I should incline to advise you to write them in duplicate, for the packet might be captured by a French privateer on its way, and it would be safer therefore to despatch copies of your letters ten days after those you first send off. In five weeks, if all goes well, you may expect an answer. In the meantime, I hope you will find enough to amuse you here, although the opera is closed, and there will be nothing like gaieties this season; still, there will be dinner parties and the club; and when you feel that you want a change I have an estate some five hours' sledge drive from here. It consist largely of forest, but there is plenty of game, elk and bears. If you are fond of shooting I can promise you good sport."

"Thanks, indeed, Count. I am quite sure that I shall not be tired of St. Petersburg in five or six weeks' time; and as for shooting, I do not feel at present as if I should ever care to fire a gun again, certainly not to take life, unless to satisfy hunger. I have seen so many horses and dogs die, and have felt so much pity for them, that I do not think that I shall ever bring myself to take the life of a dumb beast again. I am afraid I became somewhat callous to human life. I have seen thousands of men die, and came somehow to regard it as their fate; and certainly, during the retreat it came in most cases as a happy release from suffering. But I could never, to the end, see a horse that had fallen never to rise again, or a starving dog lying by its master's body, without having intense pity for the poor creatures, who had, through no fault or will of their own, come to this grievous end. No doubt you, as a sportsman, Count, may consider this as overstrained feeling. I am quite willing to admit that it may be so. I can only say that at present I would not fire at an elk or a bear on any condition whatever."

"I can understand your feelings. I myself have had the cry of a horse, pulled down by wolves, in my ears for days, and I can well imagine how the sight of so much suffering day after day among thousands of animals would in time affect one."

The next three weeks passed most pleasantly for Julian. Every day there were calls to make, excursions to various points to be undertaken, and dinner parties nearly every evening, either at the count's, at the houses of his friends, or at the club. He found French almost universally spoken among the upper class, and was everywhere cordially welcomed as a friend of the count's. The latter was sometimes questioned by his intimate acquaintances as to his English friend, and to them he replied, "Monsieur Wyatt is the son of a colonel in the English army. He has rendered me a very great service, the nature of which I am not at liberty to disclose. Suffice that the obligation is a great one, and that I regard him as one of my dearest friends. Some day, possibly, my lips may be unsealed, but you must at present be content to take him on my sponsorship."

The countess had gained strength rapidly, and there were no grounds for any further uneasiness as to her health; she was now able to take daily drives with Stephanie.

"The child has become quite a military enthusiast," she said to Julian one day. "Nothing pleases her so much as to look on at the troops drilling."

St. Petersburg was indeed crowded with soldiers. Now

armies were rising in all parts of Russia, and great preparations were being made to recommence the campaign in the spring, this time upon foreign ground. No sacrifices were too great to demand from the people. Nobles and merchants vied with each other in the amount of their contributions, and as it was certain that Austria, and probably Prussia, would join the alliance, hopes were entertained that the power that had dominated Europe for so many years would be finally crushed. Already serious disasters had fallen upon France in Spain. It was probable that ere long the whole of the Peninsula would be wrested from her, and that she would be threatened with an invasion in the south, as well as in the east. In spite, therefore, of the terrible losses and calamities she had suffered, Russia looked forward with ardent hope and expectations to the future.

CHAPTER XVI.

AN UNEXPECTED MEETING.

FRANK WYATT'S work throughout the campaign had been arduous in the extreme. It is true that it was done on horseback instead of on foot, that he had not hunger to contend against, and that for the most part his nights were passed in a shelter of some kind. But from daybreak until sunset, and frequently till midnight, he was incessantly occupied, from the moment when Napoleon turned his back on Moscow, until the last remnant of his army crossed the frontier. Until after the battle at Malo-Jaroslavets, on the 24th of October, when the French army owed its safety solely to Kutusow's refusal to hurl all his

forces against it, he had remained at headquarters, where he was assisted in his work by the Earl of Tyrconnel, who was now also acting as aide-de-camp to Sir Robert Wilson. He was a delightful companion and a most gallant young officer, and a fast friendship became established between him and Frank, during the time the Russian army was remaining inactive, while Napoleon was wasting the precious time at Moscow, unable to bring himself to acknowledge the absolute failure of his plans caused by the refusal of the Russians to treat with him, after his occupation of their ancient capital. But after Kutusow had allowed the French to slip past they saw but little of each other, for one or other of them was always with the troops pressing hard on the French rear, it being their duty to keep Sir Robert, who was necessarily obliged to stay at headquarters, thoroughly informed of all that was going on in front, and of the movements both of the French and Russian divisions.

Sir Robert himself was so utterly disgusted with the obstinacy and, it almost seemed, deliberate treachery of Kutusow that, for the most part, he accompanied General Benningsen, who was a prompt and dashing soldier, and who, with the whole of the Russian generals, was as furious with the apathy and delays of the worn-out old man who was in command, as they had been with those of Barclay. The English general still acted as the Emperor's special representative, and kept him fully acquainted with all that was going on. Alexander was as much dissatisfied as were his generals and soldiers with Kutusow's refusal to put an end to the terrible struggle, by an action which must have ended in the destruction or capture of Napoleon and his army. He felt, however, that he could not at present remove him from his command. Kutusow was a member of the old nobility, who were straining every nerve for the national cause, were stripping their estates of their serfs, and emptying their coffers into the military chests, and who would have greatly resented his removal.

The people at large, too, overjoyed at the retreat of Napoleon and the success of their arms, and ignorant of all the real circumstances of the case, regarded Kutusow with enthusiastic admiration; and Alexander felt that, great as might be his faults, the injury that would be inflicted by his supercession would be greater than the benefits derived from it. An ample supply of horses had been placed at the disposal of the English general and his aides-de-camp, and Frank, having three always at his orders, was able to ride them by turns, and therefore got through an immense amount of work. The scenes that everywhere met his eyes were far more trying than the fatigues he had to undergo. The hideous barbarities that were perpetrated by the peasants upon the French who fell into their hands, filled him with burning indignation, and at times placed his life in serious danger when he endeavoured to interfere on their behalf. He always started on his rides in the morning with his saddle-bag stored with provisions, and a small keg of spirits fastened behind him, and these were divided during the day among the unfortunate men, Russians and French alike, who, wounded or exhausted, had sunk by the way.

Innumerable were the appeals made to him daily to end their sufferings with a pistol-ball; and, although he could not bring himself to give them the relief they craved, on several occasions, when he saw that the case was altogether beyond hope, and that but a few hours of mortal agony remained, he yielded to their entreaties, handed them one of his pistols, and walked a few paces away, until the sharp report told him that their sufferings were over.

AN UNEXPECTED MEETING.

The horrors of the hospitals at Wilna and other places affected him even more than the scenes of carnage that he had witnessed at Borodino. At Wilna the Earl of Tyrconnel was seized with a fever and died, and Frank lay for some time ill, and would probably have succumbed had not Sir Robert obtained a lodging for him at the house of a landed resident, three or four miles from the infected city. He was, in a sense, thankful for the illness, because it spared him the sight of the last agony of the broken remains of Napoleon's army. Quiet and rest soon did their work. The breakdown was the result more of over-fatigue, and of the horrors of which he was so continually a witness, than of actual fever. Frank, therefore, rapidly recovered, and declared after a fortnight that he could again sit on his horse.

The general, however, would not hear of this.

"I shall be leaving for St. Petersburg myself in a few days," he said, "and we will travel together by post. You will be sorry to hear that to-day Kutusow has been decorated with the great Order of St. George. The Emperor himself begged me not to be present. He called me into his cabinet and confessed to me that it would be too humiliating to him were I to be there. He acknowledged he felt that by decorating this man with the great Order he was committing a trespass upon the institution; but he had no choice. It was a cruel necessity to which he had to submit, although he well knew that the marshal had done few things he ought to have done, with nothing against the enemy that he could avoid, and that all his successes had been forced upon him."

Sir Robert himself had urgent need of change and rest. The responsibility upon his shoulders had been tremendous. The Emperor had relied upon him entirely for information as to the true state of things in the army, and the Russian generals, regarding him as specially the Emperor's representative, had poured their complaints into his ears.

Had they but received the slightest encouragement from him they would have led their divisions against the French in spite of the orders of the marshal, and it was with the greatest difficulty that he persuaded them to restrain their exasperated troops, and to submit to carry out the disastrous policy, which entailed as much loss and suffering upon the Russian soldiers as upon the French.

It was the end of January when Sir Robert Wilson and Frank reached St. Petersburg, and, putting up in apartments assigned to them in the palace, rested for a few days.

One bright morning Frank strolled down to the Nobles' Club, of which he and the general had been made honorary members. It was his first visit to St. Petersburg. His fur coat was partly open and showed his British uniform. He was looking about with interest at the scene in the Nevsky Prospect when he noticed a gentleman in a handsomely appointed sledge looking fixedly at him. As the uniform attracted general attention he thought little of this, but after going a short distance the sledge turned and passed him at a slow rate of speed. The gentleman again gazed fixedly at him, then stopped the coachman, and leaped from the sledge to the pavement.

"Frank!" he exclaimed, "is it you, or am I dreaming?"

Frank stepped back a pace in astonishment. It was the voice rather than the face that he recognized.

"Julian!" burst from his lips, "my brother, can it be really you?"

Julian held out both his hands, and they stood for a moment in silence, gazing into each other's face. Julian was the first to break the silence.

"Jump in here, Frank," he said, leading the way to the

sledge. "They must all think that we have gone mad, and we shall have a crowd round us in a minute."

Still completely bewildered, Frank followed his brother.

"Drive out into the country," Julian said to the coachman as he took his seat. "This is little short of a miracle, old fellow," he said, as they drove off. "I thought you were living quietly at Weymouth; you thought I was rotting in a French prison, and here we run against each other in the heart of Russia."

"I can hardly believe even yet that it is you, Julian, you have altered so tremendously. Thank God, old man, that I have found you!"

"Thank God, my dear Frank, that, as I see, that stupid business of mine has not prevented your entering the army, as I was afraid it would do; though how you come to be here is more than I can guess!"

"I am General Wilson's aide-de-camp, and have been with him all through the war; and you, Julian, what on earth are you doing here? But first of all, I suppose you have not heard that you have been cleared completely of that charge of murder."

Julian's face paled at the sudden news, and he sat for a minute or two in silence.

"Quite cleared, Frank?" he asked in a low tone; "cleared so that no doubt remains, and that I can go home without fear of having it thrown into my face?"

"Completely and entirely," Frank replied. "You were cleared before you had been gone a day. The coroner's jury brought in an open verdict, but a warrant was issued against that poacher Markham; and your letter first, and his confession a year later, completely bore out the evidence at the inquest, and established his guilt beyond question."

"To think that I should never have known it!" Julian

said. "If I had dreamt of it I would have attempted to break out from Verdun, and make my way home. I don't know that I should have succeeded, but at any rate I should have tried. But tell me all about it, Frank; my story will keep just at present."

"You seem to have fallen on your legs, anyhow," Frank remarked. "May I ask if this is your Imperial Highness's sledge. I have learned something of the value of furs since I came out here, and that coat of yours is certainly worth a hundred pounds, and this sable rug as much more."

"It is not my sledge, nor is it my rug, though I have two or three of them quite as handsome. The coat is my own, the sledge belongs to my intimate friend Count Woronski, with whom I am at present staying."

"You really must tell me your story first," Frank said, laughing. "Now that you know you are cleared, you can very well wait to hear all the details, and I refuse to say a word until you have told me what all this means."

"Well, Frank," Julian said seriously, "mine is not altogether a pleasant story to tell now; but I acted for the best, and under the belief that there was no chance of my being able to return for years to England. The story is too long for me to give you the details now, but I will give you the broad facts. I was sent prisoner to Verdun. I was there about ten months. There was fever in the place, and we died off like sheep. There seemed no possibility of escape, and if I could have got away I could not, as I thought, make for England. I was getting hopeless and desperate, and I don't think I could have held out much longer. Then there was an offer made to us that any of us who liked could obtain freedom by enlisting in the French army. It was expressly stated that it was going east, and that at the end of the campaign we should,—if our corps was ordered to a place where it was likely to come in contact with the English,—be allowed to exchange into a regiment with another destination.

"Well, it seemed to me that it mattered very little what became of me. Even should I be exchanged and sent to England I could not have stayed there, but must have gone abroad to make my living as best I could, and I thought I might as well go as a soldier to Russia as anywhere else; so I accepted the offer, little knowing what would come of it. I regretted it heartily when I saw the misery that was inflicted by the misconduct, partly of the French, but much more of the Poles and Germans, on the unfortunate inhabitants. However, there I was, and I did my duty to the best of my power. When I tell you that I was in Ney's division, you may imagine that I had my share of it all."

"Extraordinary!" Frank said. "To think that you and I should both have been through this campaign, and on opposite sides! Why, we must have been within musket shot of each other a score of times."

"I have no doubt I saw you," Julian said; "for I often made out a bit of scarlet among the dark masses of the Russians, and thought that there must be some English officers with them. The first time I noticed them was on the heights opposite to Smolensk. Two officers in scarlet were with the batteries they planted there and drove our own off the hill on our side of the river."

"Those were the general and myself, Julian. We had only joined two days before. But still, I am as much in the dark as ever. What you have said explains how you come to be in Russia, but it does not at all explain how you come to be here like this."

"It was on the day after we got past the Russians. It was a strong place with a hard name—Jaro something or other. The next day, as we were marching along, we came across an overturned carriage. A coachman and a woman were lying dead. On nearing it, I heard a little cry, and I stepped out from the side of my company—I was a sergeant and was marching on the flank—and I found among the cushions a little girl, about six years old, who was already almost frozen to death. I fastened her on to my back under my cloak, and carried her along with me. She came round, and was a dear little creature. Well, I carried her all through the retreat. Sometimes, when there was an alarm, I had time to stow her away in one of the waggons; when there was not, she went on my back into the middle of the fighting, and you know that was pretty rough occasionally. However, we both of us seemed to possess a charm against balls. We got on all right until the day before we were to arrive at the Berezina. Then I went out foraging with some companions; they got into a hut, lit a fire, and would not leave, so I started alone with her.

"I lost my way, and was found by a lot of peasants, who would have made very short work of me; but the child stepped forward like a little queen and told them that she was the Countess of Woronski, and that her father was a friend of the Czar's, and that if they sent us to him they would get a great reward. Thinking that it was good enough, they took us to their village and dressed me up in peasant's clothes, and kept us there a fortnight. Then the head man and the village Papa came with us here by post. The child's father and mother had given her up as dead, and their gratitude to me is boundless. It has been deemed unadvisable to say anything about my ever being with the French, and I am simply introduced by the count as an English gentleman whom he regards as his very dear friend. I sent letters home to you and Aunt a fortnight since, and if I had heard that the charge of murder was still hanging over me I should probably have remained here for good. The count has already hinted that there is an estate at my disposal. He is as rich as Crœsus, and he and the countess would be terribly hurt if I were to refuse to accept their tokens of gratitude. They have no other child but Stephanie, and she is, of course, the apple of their eye."

"Well, you have had luck, Julian. I did think that if you once got out of prison you would be likely to fall upon your feet, because you always had the knack of making yourself at home anywhere; but I had no idea of anything like this. Well, I don't think you are to blame for having entered the French service rather than remaining a prisoner, especially as you were, as far as you knew, cut off from returning home. Still, I agree with you that it is as well not to talk about it at present. It is marvellous to think that you were with Ney through all that fighting. The doings of the rear-guard were, I can assure you, the subject of the warmest admiration on the part of the Russians. Sir Robert Wilson considers that the retreat from Smolensk was one of the most extraordinary military exploits ever performed. And so you were made a sergeant after Borodino? Well, Julian, to win your stripes among such a body as Ney led is no slight honour."

"I received another, Frank; not so much for valour as for taking things easy." He took from his pocket the cross of the Legion of Honour. "This, Frank, is an honour Napoleon sent to me, and Ney pinned on my breast. I would rather that it had been Wellington who sent it, and say Picton who pinned it on; but it is a big honour none the less, and at any rate it was not won in fighting against my own countrymen. This document it is wrapped up in, is the official guarantee that I received on enlisting, that I should under no circumstances whatever be called upon to serve against the English."

"You have a right to be proud of the cross, Julian. I should be proud of it myself, British officer as I am. But how do you say that you got it for taking things easy?"

"It was not exactly for taking things easy, but for keeping up the men's spirits. Discipline was getting terribly relaxed, and they were losing their military bearing altogether. A lot of us non-commissioned officers were talking round a fire, and I suggested that we should start marching songs again as we used to do on our way through Germany. It would cheer the men up, get them to march in military order and time, and shorten the road. Ney and some of his staff happened to be within hearing, and he praised the idea much more than it deserved. However, the men took it up, and the effect was excellent. Other regiments followed our example, and there can be no doubt that, for a time, it did have a good effect. Ney reported the business to Napoleon, who issued an order praising the Grenadiers of the Rhone for the example they had set the army, bestowing the Legion of Honour on me, and ordering that henceforth marching songs should be sung throughout the army. However, singing was dropped at Smolensk. After leaving there we were reduced to such a handful that we had not the heart to sing, but it did its work, for I believe that the improvement effected by the singing in the *morale* of Ney's troops had at least something to do with our being able to keep together, and to lessen the fatigues of those terrible marches.

"Now tell me more about yourself. How was it that you had the wonderful luck to be chosen to accompany Sir Robert Wilson as his aide-de-camp?"

"It was to his suggestion when I first joined, Julian,

and to nearly a year's steady work on my part. He got me gazetted into his old regiment, the 15th Light Dragoons, and at the same time told me that if, as was already anticipated, Russia broke off her alliance with Napoleon, he was likely to be offered his former position of British commissioner at the Russian headquarters. He said that if by the time that came off I had got up Russian, he would apply for me to go with him, so I got hold of a Russian Pole in London, a political exile, a gentleman and an awfully good fellow. I took him with me down to Canterbury, where our depôt was, and worked five or six hours a day with him steadily, so that when, at the outbreak of war, Sir Robert got his appointment he was able to apply for me upon the ground that I had a thoroughly good colloquial knowledge of Russian."

"You always were a beggar to work, Frank," his brother said admiringly. "I worked for a bit myself pretty hard at Verdun, and got up French well enough to pass with, but then you see there was no other mortal thing to do, and I knew that it would be useful to me if ever I saw a chance of escape. Of course, at that time I had no idea of enlisting: but it must have been a different thing altogether for a young officer to give up every amusement, as you must have done, and to slave away at a crack-jaw language like Russian."

"It required a little self-denial I have no doubt, Julian, but the work itself soon became pleasant. You may remember in the old days you used to say that I could say 'No', while you could not."

"That is true enough, Frank. I was a great ass in those days, but I think that now I have learnt something."

"I should think you have, Julian," Frank said, looking closely at his brother. "The expression of your face has very much changed, and you certainly look as if you could say 'No' very decidedly now."

By this time they had, after a long drive, re-entered the city.

"You must come home with me first, Frank. I must introduce you to the count and countess, and to Stephanie. Then to-morrow morning you must come round early. I have heard nothing yet as to how the truth about that murder came out so rapidly. It seemed to me that the evidence was conclusive against me, and that even the letter that I wrote telling you about it, was so improbable that no one but you and Aunt would credit it in the slightest."

"It did look ugly at first, Julian. When I heard Faulkner's deposition I could see no way out of it whatever. I could not suppose that a dying man would lie, and, absolutely sure of your innocence as I was, could make neither head nor tail of the matter. Is this the mansion? You certainly have fallen on good quarters."

Leaving their fur coats in the hall they went upstairs. They found the countess seated in an arm-chair. The count was reading the last gazette from the army to her, and Stephanie was playing with a doll. The count and his wife looked surprised as Julian entered with a young English officer.

"I have the honour, countess," Julian said, "to present to you my brother, who is aide-de-camp to the English General, Sir Robert Wilson, whom he accompanied throughout the campaign. Count, you will, I am sure, rejoice with me in this unexpected meeting."

"We are glad, indeed, to make the acquaintance of the brother of our dear friend," the countess said, holding out her hand to Frank.

"I regret, countess, that I am not able to reply to you

in French," Frank said in Russian. "I had thought that Russian would be absolutely necessary here, but I find that almost everyone speaks French. Had I known that, I could have saved myself a good deal of labour, for to us your language is very difficult to acquire."

"You speak it extremely well, Mr Wyatt," the count said. "I can scarcely imagine how you have acquired such familiarity with it in your own country."

"I learned it from a Russian Pole, a political exile, with whom I worked for about six hours a day for nearly twelve months, in order that I might qualify myself to accompany Sir Robert Wilson."

"This is my little friend Stephanie, Frank," Julian said, lifting the child up on his shoulder, her favourite place.

"And this is my Nurse Julian," the child said with a laugh. "Isn't he a big nurse?"

"He is big," Frank agreed, looking up at him. "I feel quite small beside him. He was always a great deal taller than I was, and he has grown a good bit since I saw him last. But he looks rather big for a nurse."

"He is not too big at all," Stephanie said earnestly. "He could never have carried me so far if he had not been very big and strong. Could he, papa?"

"No, Stephanie; though I think goodness of heart had as much to do with it as strength of body. Your brother has, of course, told you, Mr. Wyatt, how deep an obligation he has laid us under."

"He said that he had had the good fortune to find your little girl, and that he took her along with him in the retreat; but he seemed to consider that the service she did him when they fell among the Russian peasants quite settled matters between them. Doubtless, they mutually saved each other's lives,"

"Mr. Wyatt," the count said gravely, "the one act was momentary and without risk. The other was done at the cost of labour and sacrifice daily and hourly for nearly a month. You have been through the campaign, and know how frightful were the sufferings, how overwhelming the exhaustion of the soldiers. You can judge, then, how terrible was the addition to a soldier's labours to have to carry a child like that for so long, when his own strength was hourly weakening, and when every additional pound of weight told heavily upon him. The tears come into the eyes of the countess and myself every time we think of it. It was an act of self-devotion beyond words; altogether beyond the understanding of those who know not how terrible were the sufferings endured on the march."

"They were indeed terrible, Count," Frank said gravely. "It was agony for me to witness them, and I cannot but share your wonder how my brother supported the extra weight, even of your little daughter, and came through it safely, while tens of thousands of men not so burdened fell and died along the road."

Julian did not understand what was being said, but he guessed by their faces what they were speaking of.

"I suppose you are saying that it was hard work carrying the child," he broke in in English; "but I can tell you that I believe it aided me to get through. It gave me something to think of besides the snow, the distance, and the Russians. She was always cheerful and bright, and her merry talk lightened the way, but in addition to that the warmth of her body against my back by day and curled up in my arms at night, greatly helped to keep life in me. I think that it was largely due to her that I got through safely where many men as strong as myself died."

The count looked inquiringly at Frank, who translated

what Julian had said. He smiled, " Your brother is determined to try to make out that the obligation is all on his side, but it will not do. There is the simple fact that we have our little daughter again, safe and sound. If it had not been for him she would have been lost to us for ever."

Julian went down to the door with Frank. "Of course you will tell the general all about it, Frank. I suppose he knows something of the circumstances under which I went away, as he was a friend of our father's, and got you your commission, and takes such an interest in you. I daresay he will be shocked to hear that I have been carrying a French musket, but I am not ashamed of it myself, and consider that under the circumstances I was perfectly justified in doing so. Come round in the morning the first thing after breakfast. I have yet to learn all about how you found out that Markham committed that murder, and then you can tell me, too, what the general says."

On going upstairs Julian told his hosts that he had been completely cleared of the charge that had hung over him and darkened his life, and that there was nothing to prevent him from returning to England. They expressed much gratification at the news, but at the same time said that for themselves they could not but regret that this would prevent their having the pleasure they had looked forward to of having him settled near them.

"This, however, we must talk about again," the count said. "At any rate, I hope that you will from time to time come over to stay for a while with us and Stephanie."

"That I will assuredly do, Count," Julian said warmly. "I do not quite know at present what I shall do. As I have told you, I shall, in addition to my share of my father's money, inherit some from my aunt, and shall be able, if I choose, to buy a small estate and settle down. I am too old to go into our army now, but, besides, I think that ere long this European struggle will be over, and in that case there will be nothing for a soldier to do. Still, in any case I shall be able occasionally to make a voyage here; and I can assure you that it will be one of my greatest pleasures to do so."

Sir Robert Wilson was greatly surprised when he heard from Frank of his meeting with his brother, and of the adventures through which he had passed.

"I do not blame him in any way," he said. "Had he been a king's soldier or sailor the matter would have been altogether different. To have entered a foreign army then would have been a breach of his oaths. But as a private individual he was free to take service abroad, as tens of thousands of English, Scotch, and Irish have done before him. It would, of course, have been much better had he entered the army of a power friendly to England, but the document that he received on enlisting goes far to absolve him from any responsibility in the matter. At any rate, he was not a deserter, and seeing that he could not go back to England even if he escaped, that he was practically friendless in the world, and that had he not acted as he did he might have died at Verdun, I do not think that even a severe moralist would be able to find any fault with his decision. So he was one of Ney's heroes! Well, Frank, when this war is over, and the bitterness between the two nations has passed away, he will have good cause to feel proud of having been one of that unconquerable band. No troops have ever gained greater glory by victory than they have by retreat; besides, to have won his stripes in such company, and to have received the Legion of Honour from Ney, is as high an honour as any soldier could wish for. At the same time, I think that he and his friends have done wisely in keeping silence as to the part he played—it might have led to all sorts of trouble. Had it been known, he might have been claimed as a prisoner of war; and even if this had not been done, he might have been embroiled in quarrels with hot-headed young Russians; and it is scarcely probable, Frank, that he is such a dead shot with the pistol as you are."

The next morning Julian heard from Frank full details of the manner in which the truth had been arrived at of the circumstances of Mr. Faulkner's murder.

"By Jove, Frank," he exclaimed, when his brother brought the story to a conclusion, "you ought to have been a Bow Street runner! I can't think how it all occurred to you. Thinking it over, as I have done hundreds of times, it never once occurred to me that the footprints in the snow might prove that I had set off in pursuit of Markham, and that they would have shown that he was standing behind that tree whence the shot was fired, while I went straight from the road to the place where Faulkner was lying. What a head you have, old fellow!"

"It was simple enough, Julian. I was certain that you had not committed the murder, and it was therefore clear that someone else must have done so. Then came the question, first, how Faulkner had come to charge you as he had done, and, second, how and why you had disappeared. The only conceivable explanation that I could find was that you must have run into the wood, caught sight of the murderer, and followed him up. Directly we found your footprints on the snow overlapping his it made that a certainty. We had only then to go into the wood and pick up the whole story bit by bit. For a time I certainly thought that you had been killed by the friends of the man that you had followed, and you may imagine what a relief it was to us when your letter came.

"And now, old fellow, I suppose you will be going home?

Sir Robert has told me that he will be willing to give me leave at once, and that he considers I ought to have a thorough rest, to get the seeds of that horrible hospital fever out of my blood. Therefore I am ready to start with you whenever you are ready to go. He does not know yet whether he will continue as commissioner here when the campaign recommences in the spring; but there is little doubt that he will do so, and in that case I shall rejoin as soon as the weather breaks sufficiently for operations to commence. I got my lieutenancy three months ago owing to the vacancies made in the regiment during the campaign in Spain; and Sir Robert has been good enough to speak so strongly of my services here that I have every chance of getting another step before I return."

"I see no reason why I should not start at the end of the week, Frank. Of course I am extremely comfortable here; but now that I know I can go back all right I am longing to be home again. Indeed I should soon get tired of having nothing to do but to drive about and eat dinners here; and besides, I cannot but feel that I am in a false position, and am very anxious to get out of it."

Frank nodded. "I quite understand that, old fellow, and I agree with you thoroughly. A question might be asked any day that you could not reply to without saying how you came to be here; and for the sake of the count as well as yourself, that should be avoided if possible."

The count was loud in his expressions of regret when he heard that Julian was about to leave with his brother at once; but when Julian urged that he was constantly in fear that some chance question might be asked, and that the falseness of his position weighed heavily upon him, the count could not but admit the justice of the view he took. Preparations were immediately begun for departure. They were to travel by sledge through Finland, passing through Vibourg to Abo, and there to cross the Gulf of Bothnia to the Swedish coast, a few miles north of Stockholm, and to travel across the country to Gothenburg. The count placed one of his travelling carriages on runners at their disposal as far as Abo, and insisted on sending one of his own servants with them to attend to their wants on the road.

Stephanie was inconsolable at the approaching departure of her friend, and even the promise that he would return and pay them another visit before very long, scarcely pacified her. In three days all was ready. The luggage, packed in a light waggon, had been sent off in charge of one of the count's servants forty-eight hours before; and the travelling carriage had but to take three or four great hampers stored with provisions and wines. The count and countess had had on the previous day a long talk with Frank, who at their request called at an hour when Julian would be out paying a long round of farewell visits. The conversation was a serious one, and had ended by the count saying:

"You see, Mr. Wyatt, nothing will alter the determination of the countess and myself in this matter; and if you had not consented to accept our commission and to carry out our wishes, we should have had no course open but to communicate with our embassy in London, and to request them to appoint someone to act as our agent in the matter. This would not have been so satisfactory, for the agent would of course have been ignorant of your brother's tastes and wishes; whereas you will be able to learn from him exactly the position that would be most agreeable. All we ask is that you will not go below the minimum we have named, and the more you exceed it the better we shall be pleased. You know well how we feel in the matter, and that anything that can be done in this way will still fall very far short of the measure of gratitude we feel towards your brother."

"I will carry out the commission that you have given me to the best of my abilities, Count; and will endeavour to act as if my brother was an entire stranger."

"Thank you greatly, Mr. Wyatt. I agree with you that if you dismiss altogether from your mind the fact that your brother is interested in the matter, and that you regard yourself as simply carrying out a business transaction as our agent, it will simplify matters greatly. I don't wish you to have the trouble of the actual details. I shall write myself to our ambassador, who is a personal friend of mine, and request him, as soon as he hears from you, to instruct an English lawyer to carry out all the business part of the arrangement."

The journey across Finland was a very pleasant one. Both were in high spirits. The cloud that had hung over Julian had been dispelled, and Frank's constant anxiety about him had been laid to rest. They had gone safely through the most wonderful campaign of modern times, and were now on their way home. Julian's supply of money was untouched save for the purchase of a variety of presents for his aunt. They travelled only by day. The carriage was constructed with all conveniences for sleeping in, and when, on their arrival at the end of their day's journey, they returned from a stroll down the town to an excellent dinner prepared by their servant, they had but to turn in for a comfortable night's rest in the vehicle. At Abo they found their baggage awaiting them.

"By Jove, Julian," Frank said laughing, as he looked at the great pile of trunks in the post-house, "one would think that you were carrying the whole contents of a household! Those modest tin cases comprise my share of that pile."

"It is tremendous!" Julian said almost ruefully. "I feel quite ashamed to turn up with such an amount of baggage. The first thing we must do, as soon as we get back, is to effect a division. I am afraid that my outside clothes will be of no use to you—they would require entire remaking; but all the other things will fit you as well as me. I do believe that there are enough to last me my lifetime; and it will be downright charity to relieve me of some of them. You may imagine my stupefaction when I came back one day to the count's and found my room literally filled with clothes."

"I will help you a bit," Frank laughed. "The campaign has pretty well destroyed all my kit, and I sha'n't be too proud to fill up from your abundance."

They found that the servant who had preceded them with the baggage had already made all the arrangements for their crossing the gulf. The extreme cold had everywhere so completely frozen the sea that there was no difficulty in crossing, which, they learned, was not often the case. Three sledges had been engaged for their transport. The distance was about 120 miles; but it was broken by the islands of the Aland Archipelago, and upon one or other of these they could take refuge in the event of any sudden change of weather. They were to start at midnight, and would reach Bomarsund, on the main island of Aland, on the following evening, wait there for twenty-four hours to rest the animals, and would reach the mainland the next day.

The frost continued unbroken, and they crossed the gulf without difficulty, travelled rapidly across Sweden, and reached England without adventure of any kind. They waited for a day in London. Frank carried despatches from Sir Robert Wilson, and was occupied at the War Office all day, having a very long interview with the minister, to whom he gave a much more detailed account of the campaign than had been given in the general's reports. The minister expressed much satisfaction at the information he afforded, and said at the conclusion of the interview:

"Sir Robert has spoken several times as to your services, and I am happy to inform you that your name will appear in the next gazette as promoted to the rank of captain. I consider that the manner in which you devoted yourself to the acquisition of the Russian language was most highly meritorious, and I wish that many young officers would similarly acquire foreign or oriental languages. I trust that you will thoroughly recover your health, so as to be able to rejoin Sir Robert Wilson by the time that the troops take the field again. The campaign is likely to be a most important, and—we have great grounds for hoping—a final one."

Before leaving the building Frank found out where Strelinski was at work. He was engaged in translating a mass of Russian documents. He rose from his seat with an exclamation of delight when he saw Frank, who, after a short chat, asked him to come that evening to his hotel. He there learned that the Pole was getting on very well. His knowledge of German as well as of Russian had been very valuable to him; his salary had already been raised, and he was now at the head of a small department, having two of his countrymen and three Germans under him, and his future in the office was quite assured.

"The work is somewhat hard," he said, "for when a ship comes in from Germany or Russia we are often at work all night, sometimes eight-and-forty hours at a stretch, but we are all paid overtime. The work is pleasant and interesting, and your officials are good enough to say that we get through a wonderful amount in the time, and the minister

AN UNEXPECTED MEETING.

has twice expressed his approbation to me. Ah! Mr. Wyatt, how much do I owe to you and the good general!"

"I owe fully as much to you as you owe to me, Strelinski," Frank said. "Putting aside the interest there has been in witnessing such mighty events, it has been a splendid thing for me in my profession. I shall be gazetted captain this week, while I am pretty sure of a brevet majority at the end of the next campaign, and of further employment in the same line afterwards."

Julian was not present at the interview. He had never been in London before, and after spending the day in strolling through the streets and visiting the principal sights, had gone to a theatre, leaving Frank to talk with the Pole. The latter had not left when Julian returned. He and Frank had found such an abundance of subjects to talk about that they were scarcely aware how the time had passed. The latter proposed that they should go to one of the fashionable taverns to supper. Julian would have excused himself, but Frank insisted on his accompanying him. As they were sitting there, two gentlemen passed by their table. One of them stared hard at Frank, and then with an angry exclamation turned away. Then Strelinski said:

"That is your old antagonist, unless I am mistaken, Mr. Wyatt. You pointed him out to me once when I was in barracks with you, and I thought I remembered his face; that empty sleeve assures me that it is him."

Frank nodded.

"What is that?" Julian asked.

"Oh, it is nothing!" his brother said hastily.

"No, no, Mr. Wyatt, it was a grand thing. Has not your brother told you of it, Mr. Julian?"

"No, he has told me nothing about an antagonist."

"You do not know, then, that Mr. Frank may claim to be the finest pistol shot in the British army."

Julian looked at his brother in astonishment. "I did not know that you had ever fired a pistol in your life, Frank."

"I practised pretty hard while I was at Canterbury," Frank answered. "I suppose that I had a good eye for it, and certainly came to be what you would call a good shot, though I dare say there are others just as good. I got involved in a quarrel with the man who has just passed me, who was a captain in the Lancers, and a notorious bully and duellist. We went out. I hit him in the hand, and he lost his arm above the elbow, and there was the end of it."

"Perhaps you will be kind enough to tell me a little more about it, Mr. Strelinski," Julian said, turning to the Pole, and in spite of a growl from Frank that there was nothing to tell, the Pole related the whole circumstances of the quarrel, the feeling that had been excited by it, Frank's expressed determination not to inflict serious injury upon the man but to carry away his trigger-finger only, and so put an end to his duels in the future, and the manner in which his intention was carried out.

"Well, I congratulate you, Frank, very heartily," Julian said, when Strelinski had finished. "Why on earth did you not tell me about this before?"

"Really, Julian, there was nothing to tell about. It was a disagreeable incident altogether, and I considered then, as I have considered since, that it was hardly fair of me to go out with him when I was so certain of my shooting, and it was a hundred to one in my favour. I should never have done it if he had not forced the quarrel upon young Wilmington; for the young fellow must either have gone out, which would have been throwing away his life, or left the service."

"Unfair, my dear Frank! why the man himself had always relied upon his superior skill, and you were able to beat him at his own game. Well, I wish I could shoot as well. However, as I am not going to do any more soldiering, I don't know that it would be of much use to me; still I should like to be able to do it."

The next morning they started by coach for Weymouth, leaving Julian's heavier luggage to follow by carrier wagon. Mrs. Troutbeck's joy, when her two nephews arrived together, for a time completely overpowered her, and smelling-salts and other restoratives had to be brought into play before she recovered. The event created quite an excitement in Weymouth. The appearance of Frank's name so frequently in Sir Robert Wilson's despatches had been a source of pride to the whole town, and especially to his old school-fellows, while the clearing up of the mystery that had so long hung over Julian's fate was no less interesting. The sympathy with him was so great and general that no one was surprised or shocked that, under the circumstances, he had been driven to enlist in the French army, and had taken part in the Russian campaign. Indeed, the fact that he had been one of Ney's celebrated division, whose bravery had excited general admiration, was considered a feather in his cap, especially when it became known that he had been awarded the Cross of the Legion of Honour by Napoleon himself. Had not the brothers received the proposal most unfavourably, a public dinner would have been got up to celebrate their return.

"Well, Julian, you will have to settle what you mean to do with yourself," Frank said one day. "You can never settle down here without any occupation whatever, after what you have gone through."

"No, I quite feel that, Frank. I have had enough of

soldiering; that one campaign is enough for a lifetime. I really can hardly make up my mind what to do. Aunt was speaking to me yesterday afternoon when you were out. The dear old soul said that it was nonsense for me to wait for her death, wasting my life here, and that she was anxious to hand me over at once half her money. She said that that would be £10,000, and with the £8000—my share of father's money—I could then buy an estate."

"It would be the best thing you could do, Julian, but, of course, there is no hurry about it. What part of the country would you prefer to settle in?"

"I don't know, Frank, I have never thought much about it. I don't think I should choose anywhere near Weymouth, and I would rather go to a flatter country, and a better wooded one. If I bought land, I should like to have land that I could cultivate myself, so as to give me an interest in it, and I should like, after a time, to be on the bench, which would give one a good deal of occupation. I suppose I shall marry some day, and so would prefer to be within reach of a town. I should think, from what you say, the country round Canterbury must be pretty. There is a garrison there, Dover is within reach, and it is a good deal more handy for getting up to town than it is from here. However, as you say, there is plenty of time for me to think about that."

Mrs. Troutbeck was, as Julian had predicted, astounded upon the arrival of his baggage. "I never saw such a thing!" she exclaimed, as trunk after trunk was carried into the house. "That Russian count of yours, Julian, must be a little cracked, I should think. Why, my dear boy, if you were to get stout what in the world would you do with all these things?"

"That is a contingency I have never thought of, Aunt.

AN UNEXPECTED MEETING.

You quite frighten me. I must go in for a course of severe exercise to prevent the chance of such a thing occurring."

"You might take to shooting," Mrs. Troutbeck said doubtfully; "and I am sure that at present there is not a gentleman round who would not be glad to give you a day's shooting."

"I have done enough shooting, Aunt," Julian said gravely. "It was the means of my getting into a bad scrape here. In Russia it was often part of my duty to shoot dying horses, to say nothing of shooting men, and I have no desire ever to take a gun in my hands again. I have looked up my old friend Bill, and shall take to sailing again, but I will promise you that I will keep clear of smugglers."

Two days later Frank announced his intention of going up to London for a few days, as he thought he had better offer to be of any assistance he could at the War Office. He was away for nearly three weeks, and on his return mentioned that he had run down to Canterbury, and had seen some of his old friends at the depôt. A fortnight later he received a bulky letter from town, and in the course of the day asked his aunt if she felt equal to taking a journey with him?

"A journey, my dear!" she repeated in surprise. "Where do you want to go to?"

"Well, Aunt, I want to go to London in the first place; we will travel by post-chaise, so that everything will be comfortable; afterwards we may go somewhere else. I can't tell you anything about it now; it is a little secret. But I do very much want you and Julian to go with me."

"Then, of course we will, my dear," the old lady said. "I should very much like to visit London again, and see the theatres and shows. What do you say, Julian?"

"Of course I will go, Aunt, though I can't think what Frank has got in his head. Still, I am very tired of Weymouth, and it will be a change. I was saying to Dick Halliburne yesterday that unless I could hit on something to do, I should have to ask them if they would let me go to school again."

Six days later they drove up in a post-chaise to a fine mansion some three miles from Canterbury. Julian's astonishment at Frank's mysterious proceedings had been growing ever since they left Weymouth.

"Who on earth are we going to see here?" he asked, as they approached the mansion.

"Restrain your impatience for a few minutes longer, Julian, then you shall know all about it. This mansion, I may tell you, belongs to a friend of mine. It is the centre of an estate of some 2000 acres, and its rent-roll is about £3000 a year."

"Very nice indeed!" Julian said. "Well, I won't ask any more questions till we get there."

A gentleman appeared at the door as the carriage drove up. He shook hands warmly with Frank, who introduced him to his companions as Mr. James Linton, solicitor to the Russian embassy. The gentleman led the way to a very handsome drawing-room, then he looked inquiringly at Frank, who nodded. From a mahogany box on the table Mr. Linton produced a large packet of papers.

"Mr. Wyatt," he said to Julian, "it is my pleasant duty to present you with these documents. They are the title-deeds of this mansion and the surrounding property. In purchasing them I have followed out the instructions of Count Woronski, and have had the benefit of the assistance of your brother in selecting an estate that would, he thought, from its situation, be agreeable to you."

Julian looked at the speaker as if unable to take in the sense of his words.

"I beg your pardon," he said hesitatingly. "I don't think I quite understand you."

"It is as I said, Mr. Wyatt. Count Woronski wrote to me expressing his desire to present you with an estate here as some slight token, as he expressed it, of the enormous obligation under which you have placed him and the countess, his wife. I may say that his instructions to me would have authorized the purchase of a much larger estate than this, but he begged me to be guided by the advice of your brother, Captain Wyatt, in the matter, and the latter obliged me by taking the responsibility of choosing an estate off my hands, and has selected this. My part in the business has therefore been confined to carrying out the legal part in the matter and completing the purchase."

"My dear Frank," Julian said, "this is monstrous."

"I have only carried out the wishes of the count, Julian. He and the countess had a long conversation with me, and it was with some reluctance that I accepted the mission to select an estate for you, and only because he said that if I refused, he should have to request the Russian ambassador to ask one of his secretaries to do so, and that it would be very much more satisfactory to him that the place chosen should be, in point of situation and other respects, just what you would yourself like."

"I am overpowered, Mr. Linton. It has all come upon me so much by surprise that I do not know what I ought to say or do."

"There can be no doubt what you ought to do," the solicitor replied. "Count Woronski is a very wealthy nobleman. You have rendered to him and his wife one of the greatest services one man can render to another. The count mentioned in his letter that had you remained in Russia it was his intention to transfer one of his estates to you, and the smallest of them is of much greater value than this. As to your refusing the gift, it is, if I may say so, impossible. Nothing could exceed the delicacy with which the count has arranged the business, and he would naturally feel deeply hurt were you to hesitate to accept this token of his gratitude. I am sure you must see that yourself."

"I do indeed see it," Julian said, "and I feel that it would be not only ungrateful but wrong for me to refuse this noble gift. But you will admit that it is natural that I should for a time be overwhelmed by it. I am not so ungracious as to refuse so magnificent a present, although I feel that it is altogether disproportionate, not to the service I was fortunate enough to render, but to my action in rendering it. Well, Mr. Linton, I can only thank you for the part you have taken in the matter. Of course, I shall write at once to the count and countess expressing my feelings as to this magnificent gift, and will send the letter to the embassy to be forwarded at the first possible opportunity. And now what is the next thing to be done, for I feel almost incapable of forming any plans at present?"

"I would suggest, Mr. Wyatt, that in the first place you should drive round your estate. There are horses and carriages in the stable. The estate had only been advertised a day or two before your brother came up to town, and the purchase included the furniture, horses and carriages, and the live stock on the home farm. I engaged the coachman, grooms, and gardeners to remain until, at least, you should decide whether to take them into your service. I should suggest also that, after driving round the place, you should return to Canterbury for the night. Beyond an old man and his wife, who are in charge of the house, I have not made any arrangements, thinking it better to leave that to you and Mrs. Troutbeck."

"You will have to move here, you know, Aunt," Frank said. "I gave orders, before we came away from Weymouth, to Mary to lock up the house, and to come up to town by the coach two days later, and then to come on to Canterbury. I have no doubt that we shall find her at the *Fountain* when we get there. I daresay you will be able to hear of some good servants at the Hotel."

"You have taken away my breath altogether, Frank," Mrs. Troutbeck said. "However, I am too bewildered to think for myself, and for the present must do whatever you tell me."

Before Frank started three weeks later to rejoin Sir Robert Wilson he had the satisfaction of seeing Julian comfortably established in his new position, and settling down to the life. He himself went through the tremendous campaign that brought about the conclusion of the war and the downfall of Napoleon, and was present at the great battles of Lutzen, Bautzen, Reichenbach, Dresden, Culm, and Leipsic. At the termination of the war he received the rank of brevet major, and the appointment of military attaché to the British embassy in Russia. He remained there for some years, and then retired from the army with the rank of colonel.

Mrs. Troutbeck had by this time passed away, having first had the pleasure of seeing a mistress installed at Julian's. The latter was now a justice of the peace, and one of the most popular land-owners in the county. Mrs. Troutbeck, at Julian's earnest request, left the whole of her property to Frank, nor could the latter persuade his brother to take any share of it. Frank had no inclination for a country life, and settled down near London, where, after a time, he too married. He then went in for politics, and was returned for a Kentish constituency. Although he took no very prominent part in party politics he became one of the recognized authorities in the house on all matters connected with the affairs of Eastern Europe, and took a lively interest in the movements set on foot for the benefit of the British soldier. Julian kept his promise to the count, and for many years went over occasionally to stay with him. His wife accompanied him until the cares of a rising family detained her at home. To the end of their lives neither Frank nor he ever regretted that they had taken part in the memorable campaign in Russia.

www.ingramcontent.com/pod-product-compliance
Lightning Source LLC
Chambersburg PA
CBHW020237240426

43672CB00006B/552